The Toy Chest

THE TOY CHEST

A COMPLETE SOURCEBOOK OF TOYS FOR CHILDREN

by

Stevanne Auerbach, Ph.D.

Lyle Stuart Inc.   Secaucus, New Jersey

Published by Lyle Stuart Inc.
120 Enterprise Ave., Secaucus, N.J. 07094
In Canada: Musson Book Company
A division of General Publishing Co. Limited.
Don Mills, Ontario

Queries regarding rights and permissions should be
addressed to: Lyle Stuart, 120 Enterprise Avenue,
Secaucus, N.J. 07094

Manufactured in the United States of America

Designed by CATHERINE GALLAGHER

Library of Congress Cataloging-in-Publication Data

Auerbach, Stevanne.
    The toy chest.

    Bibliography: p.
    1. Toys. 2. Toys—Catalogs. I. Title.
TS2301.T7A78   1986   688.7'2   86-4436
ISBN 0-8184-0410-8
ISBN 0-8184-0405-1 (pbk.)

**Dedicated
to
the children
who want to play in
a peaceful world**

ACKNOWLEDGMENTS

Many people contributed to the creation of THE TOY CHEST. First, thanks to my editors Carole Stuart, and David Goodnough, who cooperated fully in the support of the entire production. I am very grateful for the advice, support, and encouragement the following people gave me while this book was in development. Tom Arbuckle, Beth Blossom, Arnold Bolka, Brad Countryman, Bernie de Koven, Eugene de Christopher, Ted Erickson, Fred Ertl, Richard Fishbaine, Jack Fox, Fred Gates, Robert Gaynor, Sy Gelber, Bob Gold, Jonathon Gubin, Harry Guckert, Jack Guenthard, Steven Hassenfeld, Karen Hewitt, Astrid Kamar, Michael Katz, Harry Kislevitz, Julie Korver, Andras Kron, Irwin Kurns, Ray Larsen, Bernard Loomis, Manny Luhn, Jeff Malester, Frank Martin, George Merritt, Mark Michtom, Mark Mosco, Lane Nemeth, Harry Nizamian, Stan Pollock, Roy Raymond, Paul Roche, Lou Schwartz, James Skahill, Marvin Smollar, Harvey Stern, Maury Streicker, Michael Stramiello, Doug Thomson, Jim Tindall, Sandy Vinella, Alex Vinniski, Michael Weisman, Charles Zadeh, and Sy Ziv.

Thanks to all of the people interviewed for their contributions, who shared their time, experience, and insight. Not all of their interviews could be included due to space considerations. A complete list of those interviewed for THE TOY CHEST will be found in part three.

The involvement of Grace Kennan Warnecke was perfect as a superb photographer and a supportive co-seeker into the world of toys.

Special acknowledgments to Maja Evans Schile for the astute typing of the manuscript; Henry Dakin for his shared vision, support and technical help; Stephanie Willett-Shaw for manuscript typing; Janet Gordon for the bibliography resource preparation; and Kim Yee, who's attention to detail kept the whole production effectively "on-line." Appreciation to Barry Kaplan for his cover photograph and to the models Alexander Miller and Lauren Soloway. Special acknowledgment and thanks goes to those friends who have contributed support throughout the entire preparation of THE TOY CHEST.

Sam and Solange Abecassis, Jonathan Adler, Julius Blackman, Al Brod, Don Carlson, Hyla Cass, Harold R. Christensen, Margaret Elke, Wayne Everton, Stanley Finkelstein, David Finn, Charles Flewellen, Zvika Greensfield, Peter Hartman, Greg David Heuston, David Kaufman, Robert Kutler, Barbara Meislin, David Multack, Ruth Pantcost, Suzie Prudden, David Schonbrunn, Judith and Martin Schwartz, Paul Silbey, Marvin Silverman, Hal Slate, John Steiner, and Jean Stockheim.

Personal hugs to Amy, my daughter, who was a delight to watch and learn from while she was playing with her toys from infancy through all the stages of development discussed in this book. Now it is enjoyable to see her learning to play with toys all over again when she babysits with young children. I thank her for her fine assistance in the preparation of the bibliography.

Special thanks to all the children we observed and talked with and to their parents.

I thank all the toy stores I visited, all of the publishers who contributed their books, and all of the toy manufacturers of America and around the world who shared their creations, expertise, and vision. I commend all of you for your work on behalf of children.

Thank you to the many people who contributed ideas, sources, and experiences. I appreciate very much the contribution of everyone. I hope the result is a book that is a useful source of information, insight, and guidance to the wonderfully zany world of toys. Acknowledgments to the Consumer Product Safety Commission and the editors of the following major toy industry publications: *Playthings, Toy & Hobby World, American Baby, British Toys & Hobbies, Chain Store Age, Craft Digest, Doll Reader, Electronic Games, Family Computing, Game Merchandising, Games, Hobby Merchandiser, Home Video, Licensing Today, Marketing Times, Ms Magazine, Parents Magazine* and *Young Children.*

The books from all of the publishers who sent them now comprise the most complete library on play and toys. The library is available by appointment for research. An annotated list of holdings is available from the Institute for a small charge.

I am particularly indebted to Chilton Books, China Books, Dover Publications, Hawthorne, Hobby House, Putnam-Perigee-, B. Schackman, Price Stern & Sloan, Sterling, and Wallace-Homestead.

Thanks to all of the salespeople who took the time to present their products, share their experiences during the extensive research phase of this book, and who inspired me with their enthusiasm; to the many store owners who shared their experiences and insights; to the talented designers who express their creativity in the most amazing opportunities for enjoyment for children; to the toy distributors, and all the toy representatives; to the staffs of the Waldorf Schools, the Montessori Schools, and the child care centers I visited; and finally, to the friends who shared the memories of their childhood and parental experiences with toys and for their understanding of the fascination THE TOY CHEST held for me during the years of development.

Through it all, I have become an independent, objective and professional appraiser of the toy industry, its products, purpose, insights, and directions. My research findings will, as a result, benefit all toy consumers, and most of all, I hope THE TOY CHEST will assist children in having the best toys possible for their playtime.

PHOTO CREDITS

We thank all of the toy manufacturers who sent in photographs of products to be reviewed.

Illustrations
Lynn Johnston—cartoon
Steven Roberts—Teddy and Butterfly
Claus Sievert—Bear and Blocks, Toys in Basket
Antonio Torrice—Organizing Toys

Special Photographs
Stevanne Auerbach
William Lupardo
Barry Kaplan
David Touch
Grace Kennan Warnecke
AMC Testing
Bobbs-Merrill
FAO Schwarz
Miniatures by Joan
R. Dakin
Johnson and Johnson
Fisher-Price
Forbes Magazine
Marklin
Museum of the City of New York
Smithsonian Institution
Toy Manufacturers of America

Chapter One
Avalon
Connor Toy
Fisher America
Free Mountain
Froebel Blocks
Johnson and Johnson
Kadon
Kenner
Korver-Thorpe
Mattell
Milton Bradley

Chapter Two
Associated Merchandising Corporation (AMC)
Combi
Fisher-Price
R. Dakin

Chapter Three
Atari
Colorforms
Discovery World
Fischertechnik
Fisher-Price
Knickerbocker
Matchbox
Mattell
Milton Bradley

Chapter Four
Child Guidance (CBS)
Fisher-Price
Fisher America
Johnson and Johnson
Playskool
Mattel

Chapter Five
Child Guidance (CBS)
Combi
Connor
FAO Schwarz
Fisher America
Johnson and Johnson
Just Wood
Kransco
Little Tikes
Playskool
Small World
Tonka

Chapter Six—Preschoolers
Child Guidance (CBS)
Coleco
Connor
Country Wood Shop
FAO Schwarz
Frechettess Heirloom Toys
Horseman
Kenner
Kransco

Little Tikes
Mattell
MJO
Playskool
Quadro
South Bend
Tonka

Chapter Seven—School Age
Brimm-Shield
Country Wood Shop
Effanbee
Ertl
Fisher-Price
Ideal
Kadon
Kenner
Learning Materials Workshop
Mattell
Matchbox
Nomadic Tipi
Playskool
South Bend
Tonka
Viewmaster

Chapter Eight—Older Child
Atari
Brimm-Shield
Effanbee
FAO Schwarz
Fisher America
Huffy
Ideal
International Games
Kadon
Kamar Playjour
Seamer Products
Selchow & Righter
Tasco
Western Publishing

Table of Contents

PART THREE
HISTORY

PART FOUR
RESOURCES

A NOTE FROM THE AUTHOR

WARNING! *on toy chests*

The U.S. Consumer Product Safety Commission has warned potential users of the serious accidents possible due to careless use of toy chests. **Please use a toy chest with a safety hinge for the protection of the child.**

Please do *NOT* use any toy chest with heavy lids for daily toy storage by your children. If you do want a toy chest to keep certain kinds and quantities of toys in, use one, but then please lock it to prevent accidents. If it is kept locked it will not hurt your child with the lid possibly falling on fingers or the head. Open it only to take out certain toys kept inside for protection, surplus, or recycling and be sure a young child is not playing nearby.

I recommend toys be put away in a chest or closet for periods of time so that when they are taken out again they are "just like new" and are interesting to the child again.

Most of all, I want to assist you to protect children and guard against unnecessary accidents with any toy. Toys, if used properly at an age and level of development right for a child, should not cause frustration, problems, or injuries. I hope the book will assist all readers in locating the best toys and encourage safety and lots of high quality play.

The toy chests we recommend due to safety considerations and style are by American Toy and Furniture, Blazon Flexible Flyer, Julius Levenson, and the Welsh Company.

HOW THE TOY CHEST HAS
BEEN ORGANIZED

This sourcebook contains ideas and ways to select, use, and create toys. More than 150,000 toys are available in the American marketplace, manufactured by over 900 companies. So choosing appropriate toys isn't easy. As a child development specialist, teacher, and parent, I have been through the selection process innumerable times at toy stores, toy shows, and manufacturer's showrooms.

I have prepared this book with your child in mind. After evaluating thousands of toys, I hope I have eased the problems you (parents, grandparents, sales people, or others using this book) face when selecting toys, by locating those most suited to the age, skills, and interests of the children you love and care for.

I have concentrated on quality, safety, cost, durability, and the play needs of children. Ready-made toys can be expensive, so I have included information sources on how to make toys and playthings. Selections have been made based on my actual experiences with toys and interviews with people who have also investigated, compared, and tested toys. The goal is to show you how to choose the most appropriate toys, and provide you with basic information to assist you in the future.

THE TOY CHEST has as its primary focus the use of toys as an important part of children's play. Play in turn is seen as part of the child's learning and healthy growth. During the first five years, children are in the sensory motor development stage. The most rapid physical, emotional, mental, and intellectual growth of their lives occurs during the first two years. Babies hear, taste, and see objects for the first time. They want to touch everything and explore their own bodies. As they grow, they begin sitting, creeping, standing, and finally, walking. At each stage the child needs different kinds of stimulation, and toys can be an important source.

For instance, a baby spends many hours in his crib each day. Studies show that a mobile suspended across the crib can make this time more valuable for the baby simply because it provides something for him to look at. He is stimulated not only by the colors and shapes of the objects dangling from the mobile, but its slow whirling is a source of enjoyment before sleeping and on waking.

Toys continue to play an important role as children grow. Research indicates that older children need to vent their feelings safely when angry or frustrated. The pummeling, when necessary, of a friendly stand-up-knock-down figure can be immensely gratifying and useful to a child and save a lot of wear and tear on others.

Between the time of a child's first crib mobile and the time when he needs to knock around a plastic blob, a few years of intense exploration and experience have passed. THE TOY CHEST contains information on toys to help you select the right "tools" to stimulate your child and help him or her grow. Every boy and girl enjoys playing with many different kinds of toys as they develop from infancy to adolescence, and will play according to their needs and abilities at each stage of growth.

The core of THE TOY CHEST is organized by age groups: Babies, Toddlers, Preschool children, Primary-grade children (six to eight), and Older elementary school children (nine to twelve). To understand the kinds of play children engage in at each stage, specific pointers are given along with the suggested best types of toys for each level. Because of the rapid changes in merchandise from year to year, and the randomness of availability from store to store, we have used *types* of toys (balls, rattles, blocks, trucks), and suggested reliable manufacturers who make the different types of toys, rather than naming specific editions or brands of any toy. Then you can apply the suggested criteria as you make your selections.

Since it was impossible to name every reputable manufacturer for each type of toy (for example, hundreds of good infant rattles exist, made by over a dozen manufacturers), we gave you a good cross section of companies to choose from. If a company is not recommended for a specific type of toy, it does not mean the firm's products do not meet our standards. The company may be recommended for other types of toys. We also tried to avoid listing too many toys from the same companies, and to give instead a range of different toys from many sources. If your toy store doesn't have the item you want from one of the firms we recommend, they should be able to order it for you, or supply you with one of comparable caliber. Make your preferences known and get to know your local store.

Each of the age-related chapters begins with a brief description, followed by a suggested checklist of all types of toys included in that chapter. You can use the checklists for your own record keeping. Check off the toys your child has received. Tell friends and relatives who ask what you'd like your child to have at birthdays and Christmas time. You can avoid duplication this way, and assure the givers they will be offering a toy that's more likely to be really enjoyed.

Each toy is categorized as "Active," "Creative," or "Educational," depending on whether it has proven to be especially stimulating for the physical, imaginative, or mental development of the child. Although most toys do all these things to one degree or another, using the categories helps you be sure of a good balance of types. The categories are described fully in Chapter One, "Toys and Play in Your Child's Life."

The book gives tips on the way toys are to be used, stored, and rotated, as well as how to create play spaces inside and outside the house, and choose toys for travel and playgrounds. Since putting away his or her toys is an important habit for the child to develop early, ways to create willingness for this in your youngster are discussed.

Besides guiding you about what to look for in potential purchases, the book is loaded with ideas on how to encourage children to use toys to gain new skills and enliven curiosity. There is a section on how to find props around the house to outfit a "nurse," equip a "plumber," or help the "mechanic" to set up a mini-garage. The important information on toy safety you should know about is included, and there is a very useful section on toys for children with special needs, plus a section on television, toys, and advertising; substantial material on educational toys; and a tough-minded rating of some recent brand-name extravaganzas which might better be in the trash box than the toy box.

Finally there's an extensive reference section with information on recommended books, magazines, films, toy stores, catalog firms, manufacturers, museums, and other sources of information.

The book also contains brief, but wonderful observations and valuable pointers by selected experts based on interviews I had with each of them. Topics range on everything from "Where Teddy Bears Come From," to "A Swell Toy Store," "Collecting Toys," and "The Secret Thrill of Games," plus other special aspects of toys such as design, manufacture, and sales. The contributions from various toy people were included to answer the questions you have about toys. The list of contributors indicates their interests and area of expertise.

If you have questions, information, or want to share, you are welcome to write us at the Institute for Childhood Resources, 1169 Howard Street, San Francisco, CA 94103. We have a vast library and a long list of experts available to consult, but if your query requires additional research, a nominal fee must be charged. In any case, we would very much like to hear from you if any toys you read about do not measure up, and also about new toys you like so we can test them, and share the information. I hope you will enjoy THE TOY CHEST and find it helpful.

Special Contributors

Over 100 specialists in toys were interviewed in preparation for this book. Due to space limitations, I have selected 38 special contributors. The contributions touch all aspects of the toy industry and include topics of specific interest to parents and to people who buy, store, and collect toys. Some of the topics covered are: design, safety, sales, marketing, and services in the toy business. Each article in this section is filled with useful information about the many facets of the toy business. I would like to thank the following people for their interviews, which due to space limitations, were unable to be included. Murray Altchular, Richard Badler, Brenda Bozung, Adeline Daley, Alberta Darby, Gene de Christopher, Ted Erickson, Jack Fox, Ed Gandhour, Betty Green, Harry Guckert, Karen Holland, Chris Kamar, Joel Kaufman, Virginia Kempe, Beverly Kennedy, Harold Levine, Richard Levy, Ron Liedtke, Joanne McKracken, Victor Petrone, Cy Rothbard, Phillip Rubin, Anne Serio, Olympia Tresmonton, and Michael Wiesman. Many other informal interviews were of great value as the information was gathered for this book and were very much appreciated.

Alphabetical

Marta Arango	Toy lending library
Tom Arbuckle	Historic view of toy center building
Carol Blackley	Toy research
Meredith Brokaw	Toy store inside
Roger Burrill	Stuffed animal production
Bill Clarke	Train collecting
Dorothy Coleman	Collecting dolls
Bernie de Koven	Children and games
June Dutton	Snoopy and Company
Nancy Elsmo	Library services and resources
Nancy Everhart	Preschool activities
De Fischler	Public Action Coalition on Toys
Carolyn Foat	Children with special needs (Chapter 9)
Robert Forbes	Collecting toys
Linda Gold	Make your own toys—found materials
Mal Goldman	Educational toy store
Harold Goldstein	Selecting educational toys
Scott Goode	Selecting varied toys
Sally Grauer	Make your own puppets
Elizabeth Grotz	Toy testing
Sheila Harty	Media clones and corporate toys
Karen Hewitt	Cultural response to toys
Flora Gill Jacobs	History of Doll House Museum
Sandy Jones	Baby play
Manny Luhn	Toy store trends
Ian McDermott	Toy buying—FAO Schwarz
Glen Nimnicht	Toy lending library
Letty Cottin Pogrebin	Toys for free children
Roy Raymond	A Unique toy store
Nancy Record	Making toys
Ronnie Shushan	Games magazine
James Skahill	Manufacturer's representative role
Joanna Slonecka	Toy libraries—England
Edward Swartz	Dangerous toys
Doug Thomson	History of Toy Manufacturers Association
Tony Torrice	Storage of toys
Lois Van Guilder	US Consumer Product Safety (Chapter 2)
Joanna VanLevetzow	Toy libraries—Canada
Debbie Wager	Annual toy survey
Jeff Winokur	Make your own toys—found materials
Sarah Woodward	Children's advertising
Helane Zeiger	Toys that come back
Sy Ziv	Toy buying—Toys R Us

About Children

Sandy Jones	Baby play
Bernie de Koven	Children and games
Carolyn Foat	Children with special needs
Linda Gold	Make your own toys—found materials
Jeff Winokur	Make your own toys—found materials
Sally Grauer	Make your own puppets
Nancy Record	Making toys
Nancy Everhart	Preschool activities
Harold Goldstein	Selecting educational toys
Scott Goode	Selecting varied toys
Tony Torrice	Storage of toys
Letty Cottin Pogrebin	Toys for free children
Debbie Wager	Annual toy survey

Special Aspects

Sarah Woodward	Children's advertising
Dorothy Coleman	Collecting dolls
Robert Forbes	Collecting toys
Karen Hewitt	Cultural response to toys
Edward Swartz	Dangerous toys
Flora Gill Jacobs	History of DollHouse Museum
Nancy Elsmo	Library services and resources
Sheila Harty	Media clones and corporate toys
De Fischler	Public Action Coalition on Toys
Marta Arango	Toy lending library
Glen Nimnicht	Toy lending library
Joanna Van Levetzow	Toy libraries—Canada
Joanna Slonecka	Toy libraries—England
Helane Zeiger	Toys that come back
Bill Clarke	Train collecting

About the Toy Industry

Mal Goldman	Educational toy store
Ronnie Shushan	Games magazine
Tom Arbuckle	Historic view of toy center building
Doug Thomson	History of Toy Manufacturers Association
James Skahill	Manufacturer's representative role
Roger Burrill	Stuffed animal production
June Dutton	Snoopy and Company
Ian McDermott	Toy buying—FAO Schwarz
Sy Ziv	Toy buying—Toys R Us
Carol Blackley	Toy research
Meredith Brokaw	Toy store inside
Manny Luhn	Toy store trends
Elizabeth Grotz	Toy testing
Roy Raymond	A Unique toy store
Lois Van Guilder	US Consumer Product Safety (Chapter 2)

INTRODUCTION

Parents have spent over twelve billion dollars on toys each year for the past several years. In contrast, they spent only 50 million in 1950. The enormous increase is evidence of the greater variety, as well as increasing interest, that parents have in providing stimulation for their children through the use of toys. Over 150,000,000 toys, manufactured each year by over 900 different companies, exist in the American toy market. Choosing appropriate toys is difficult when parents, other family members, and friends are confronted by so many choices.

After talking with hundreds of toy company executives, reviewing catalogs and toy showrooms, classifying, and evaluating thousands of toys, I prepared THE TOY CHEST to assist you in the wise selection and proper use of toys.

I have intensively investigated the value of toys. I selected types which are durable, appropriate, educational, and emotionally satisfying to the child. Information about the child's development from baby to the age of twelve is organized along with the best types of toys for each age. The descriptions are designed to assist the adult in selection and ways to encourage the use of toys.

Interviews were conducted with over one hundred specialists in the toy industry, including designers, manufacturers, experts on dolls and other types of toys, and people who distribute, market, and sell products.

One of the most informative aspects of research for this book was going to the actual places where toys are designed, made and tested—the factory. I also visited over a thousand showrooms, shops, and stores. I gained enormous respect for most of the industry's commitment, creativity, ingenuity, and productivity to serve children. The toys I recommend and the companies that make them are dependable and innovative.

THE TOY CHEST has as its primary focus expanding the awareness of the importance of play, helping you to learn more about the potential uses of toys in play inside and outside the house, and ways to use toys as educational or creative devices.

Children appreciate order in their lives. Maria Montessori, the well-known early childhood educator, found children enjoyed and needed to have specific time to put away their toys in easy-to-reach storage areas. She discovered a great amount of learning took place during the effort.

Children benefit from freedom to play as they wish with their toys and the need to return them to a safe storage place. How to create this willingness and appreciation on the part of the child will be discussed. I have also included important safety information, to assist you in evaluating a potential purchase, so that the toy you bring home will be a safe one.

Most of all, toys are fun. Toys bring children hours of enjoyment and education. Reviewing the contents of THE TOY CHEST will make your selections not only safer, but also more enjoyable. The specific suggestions offer tangible pointers to guide you in choosing toys for your child through the years.

Toy companies, like any other business in America, are consumer oriented and responsive to demands of the marketplace. Toy companies try to respond to an ongoing and intense interest in the well-being and healthy development of children, yet they also are interested in making a profit. You must shop carefully to ensure the best value.

As a parent, I enjoy the use of toys to amuse, instruct, and stimulate children. As a psychologist and child development specialist, I question some of the assumptions, practices, and pressures of the toy industry on children. As a consultant to the toy industry, I see aspects of a service business attempting to produce the best products at the lowest possible cost to obtain the greatest consumer response and financial success. As a consumer advocate, I see problems with production design, costs, and advertising claims and methods. As a child advocate, I wonder whether children should be deluged with toys that have little meaning or questionable use, are ill-conceived, inappropriate, poorly-made, or improperly tested, or toys that do not meet the claims of their advertising and packaging. I wear all of these hats as I reveal the contents of THE TOY CHEST.

Sometimes serious flaws occur in production and need to be corrected, or products must be recalled. The toy industry has been criticized for its advertising practices, lack of safety standards, poor design, high prices, poor construction, and inadequate packaging of toys. It is my hope that this book may influence the design, safety, and other aspects of toy merchandising. It is not the purpose of this book to criticize the industry, but to expand awareness and understanding for parents and others who want to be responsible consumers or sellers of toys.

The critics who have maintained close scrutiny on the industry are for the most part to be commended for keeping the industry responsive to public pressure. I would like to make note of the watchful monitoring of television ads by Peggy Charren and Action for Children's Television; the careful surveying of products and price fluctuations in stores observed by the Americans for Democratic Action group in Washington, D.C., headed by Ann Brown and Debbie Wager; the legal aspects of damage done to children by dangerous toys by attorney Edward Swartz; the investigation of sexism in packaging and in the use of toys as researched by Letty Cottin Pogrebin; and the uncovering of the abuse of licensed products by Sheila Harty. Consumers appreciate these services, even though some in the industry may at times find them a nuisance. Because we have an open and competitive economy, sometimes the eagerness to make profits obscures the original objective or purpose of toys and the responsibility for making quality products.

As a parent or grandparent, you have an important function to obtain the best toys you can. As a member of the toy industry your responsibility is to produce products that can in no way harm children physically or psychologically.

Years ago, when my daughter Amy was born, I would have liked such a guide as this book provides. I knew instinctively that I was her first "big" toy, and through all the years, she has taught me more about play and laughter than anyone. For her time of learning and playing with me, I am very grateful. I hope the experiences and guidance I share will be helpful to you whether you are a parent, or a member of the toy industry.

Another purpose of the book is to serve as a bridge for the child and by sharing his or her point of view with adults. I intend to clarify some of the questions that often arise for adults when considering toys for children. I hope that by listening to the comments included by children, parents, manufacturers and others connected with the industry, we will assist in having more appropriate toys available.

I hope you will find THE TOY CHEST helpful in making toy buying easier and more enjoyable. I look forward to maintaining, updating and improving the information in THE TOY CHEST.

Let's Play!

Stevanne Auerbach, Ph.D.
Director,
Institute for Childhood Resources
1169 Howard Street
San Francisco, CA 94103

PART I

BACKGROUND

CHAPTER ONE

Play and Grow

THE IMPORTANCE OF TOYS

Play Is All Around You

Play is a natural phenomenon. It is essential for the healthy growth of children. Through play children interact with their environment, improve skills, and learn to express themselves. In playing with others, children gain mastery and learn social values and responsibility. The way a child plays when young reflects the way he or she will act in later life, since through play children express their unique ideas, feelings, abilities and personality. Children learn the give-and-take of life in relating to other children through play.

Young children play all day. Through play they explore their environment, expand their abilities, and learn new skills. From the first object the infant sees, feels, and responds to, through the games and toys a child uses alone or with others, we see toys are an integral and important part of a child's growth and experiences.

Essentially, a child is his own "first toy." An infant in his crib will play for hours with his hands, his toes, sunbeams coming in the window, and himself by babbling and "talking." As he plays, he gains awareness of himself and the world. He makes distinctions between color, light, and sound. He begins to separate parts of himself. He becomes aware of people around him. When you talk with your baby, make special sounds, make him laugh, you too are being an early and the best "Big Toy." He soon learns to distinguish between father and mother through touch, sound, smell, and the different ways in which each plays with him. A baby wants to play with each parent in this way. He begins to learn about the external world.

Although it is not possible to spend the whole day cooing, talking to, and playing with your baby, he needs as much of this stimulation as possible. You also stimulate

the baby's intellectual growth and personality by talking and singing. The baby might not understand the words, but when you take the time to interact, he will be more alert and learn faster. In the discovery of what he can and cannot do he learns his limitations, and begins to make distinctions and boundaries. Carefully chosen toys will assist in stimulating and satisfying your baby and can serve as a catalyst for the actively curious baby.

When you join in play with your child and his toys, additional benefits occur for both of you. A toy is an object for play and serves as a facilitator of play. Use a variety of toys with the baby, as its attention span is very short. It is not only the toy, but the baby that determines the length of time he or she wants to play.

1

As the baby's abilities increase, new and different kinds of stimulation are needed. When he begins to play with other children he learns to share toys, to give them away, and to fight about them. This is an exciting part of growing up for him.

When children enter nursery school, child care, parent cooperatives, or have visits away from home, they expand their newly developing social skills. They learn to obtain and hold the attention of others. They also become totally absorbed in the activity of play and in what they are doing. The ability to concentrate is an important skill, enhancing ,he learning process.

Importance of Play

Research related to play has been done in many areas. In the research on the Toy Lending Library Program conducted by Dr. Glen Nimnicht, for example, parents were instructed over several months on the values and uses of toys as they also learned about their child's development. In the Responsive Education Program a toy was introduced and the child was allowed—without interference—to discover for themselves about the toy's attributes. Dr. Nimnicht was one of my advisors for my doctoral work and stimulated my awareness of the attributes of toys as part of the educational opportunities available to parents and children.

In a study conducted by the American Institutes for Research in the Behavioral Sciences it was found that through loaning toys and providing workshops for parents that the children improved in speech, had more interest in reading, and gained in curiosity.

The parent education programs of Drs. Earl Schaeffer, Phyllis Levenstein, and Marilyn Segal have shown the importance of teaching parents how to play effectively with their child and that these activities benefit the child in language and expression. Dr. Joe Frost has shown the value of open, creative play spaces and the expanded involvement children have in free and imaginative play.

Child development research, such as the studies by Dr. Benjamin S. Bloom of the University of Chicago and others, show that the first five years of a child's life is the most rapid period of growth in learning, personality formation, and physical dexterity. The time the child spends playing with toys is essential to the fullest development of the child's mind, body, and spirit. The selection of the right toys is therefore extremely important. A baby spends many hours in his crib or cradle. Research has shown that an interesting mobile, hanging so the child can easily see it (but not directly overhead) will stimulate a baby's perception of color and form. The slowly moving objects are often a source of fascination and comfort for the baby.

It is essential to a child's mental and emotional growth to have both a variety of toys to play with, and caring adults to reinforce their playfulness, involvement, and interest in life around them.

Children become totally involved in what they are doing naturally. When they are playing there is less need for discipline. For instance children can play for hours with blocks, constructing and reconstructing buildings without disturbing anyone, or they can play with friends while talking and building at the same time.

As children play they learn about color, shapes, sizes, weight, and form. By testing reality and fantasy, children begin to grasp the differences between the two worlds. As they engage in play, they learn to make decisions and acquire the basic social skills they need, not only for school but for life. They learn to share, support, cooperate, and have fun with their peers. Other important aspects to know about the value of play are:

Children gain skills needed for concentration which they will later use in reading and math.

Play increases opportunities for communication.

Play contributes to the child's growth and development.

When playing, the child learns such skills as finger dexterity and eye-hand coordination in less time.

In addition, as a natural part of childhood, children need to have lots of time for pleasurable experiences. Play is good for children's emotions. He will gain pleasure and satisfaction from play. He learns to express his feelings. Children even learn to resolve differences while they are playing.

You can discover a great deal about a child by observing them at play. You can learn about a child's abilities, behavior, limitations, stress, personal preferences, and his or her entire repertoire of emotions.

Child psychologists use play therapy as a way to learn about the inner life of the child. It is not necessary for you to be a trained psychologist to observe whether your child seems stressed or creates an unusual situation in play. When angry or frustrated, children need to find constructive ways to vent their feelings. Hitting a friendly, large, stand-up-knock-down punching figure can be immensely gratifying to a child and save a lot of wear and tear on others. Foam bats are another safe and fun way to act out aggression. If negative behavior is frequent, (withdrawal, excessive aggression, low tolerance to frus-

as trains, automobiles, ride-ons, and crafts. Children need toys to play with alone and toys that they can use in play with other children. Kaleidoscopes, Viewmasters, electronic toys, and board games can provide opportunity for self-mastery and social enjoyment with others.

The Value of Toys

With the right toys, children learn sounds, shapes, colors, how to count numbers, improve manual dexterity, and practice eye-hand coordination, and gain many other skills. These skills improve as they have more experience; they learn to compare, contrast, talk, and use an expanding imagination.

Not every toy children use has to be bought or made. Almost anything a child finds engaging can be a toy, from the measuring cups or pots and pans in your kitchen to more complex toys which can be pulled or built up, make sounds, pop up, or form into shapes. Creative opportunities exist in all sorts of objects, such as shells, wood, fabric, and scrap objects. These materials can provide hours of pleasure for the imaginative, creative child.

As your child develops, which toys are best? Which ones will not only be fun, but will also help teach skills and stimulate? In order to answer these questions, you first need to understand the importance of play in your child's growth and how children use toys to explore their environment. You will want to have a variety of toys around for different purposes:

Activity	Examples of Toys to Use
ventilate feelings	foam bats
express creativity	clay
create learning opportunities	shape sorter
test skills	ring toss
expand communication	puppets
engage in social relations	games

Your child will enjoy going with you to toy stores and making selections. They like talking about toys and looking at them as well as playing with them.

Children of all ages enjoy a variety of toys from the major types included here. Such items as a plush or stuffed animal will be a favorite for many years. Others such as trains, model planes or cars, and other special items are often treasured and form lifelong hobbies. Children from infancy to age twelve usually enjoy the following:

balls	models
cars/trucks	puppets
construction sets	puzzles
dolls	ride-ons
games	stuffed animals
hobby sets	trains

tration as examples) or if you are concerned, you might consult a pediatrician.

Children are likely to form an attachment to a particular toy. It may be a rattle, a doll, a teddy bear, a telephone set, or something else. They like to probe, look in, take apart, and put together. They enjoy turning, twisting, pulling, and manipulating items. They enjoy devices that have a surprise or a challenge. Children enjoy mixing mediums together to create expanded play situations. Construction sets, cars, trucks, and dolls can be used together to make their own home or an imaginary village creating hours of fun.

Children enjoy experiencing the range of their abilities with different toys. Toys such as building blocks and construction sets enable them to explore spatial relationships, gravity, connecting things, as well as giving them a means of expressing their creativity. They will ask questions, try out different configurations, and explore all the possibilities their growing imaginations can come up with. Many toys exist which help improve children's abilities on this level.

A child will enjoy the simplest of toys, such as yo-yo's and tops, and will also like more complex toys, such

How to Select Toys

As you use THE TOY CHEST please consider the potential play value of toys. Base your selection on the following:
1. what you want to spend;
2. your child's age, abilities and preferences;
3. the availability of an item.

I have included in the book as examples only those manufactured toys that reflect the basic principles I feel essential to apply as criteria for all toys.

Basic Principles in Toy Selection

Suitable Design—A product that is suitable to the needs of the child and for the age range intended. Reflects the best possible choice for the item in concept, selection of materials, and color. Adequate and clear playing instructions are included if needed.

Quality—Determines the extent of the best materials used, how they were used, color, shape, and workmanship. The price does not always equal quality, but workmanship does. Most toys are created to give you basic or equal value for money spent, but this is not always true.

Durability—Indicates how well the toy lasts and if it is "child-proof" (not easily broken). The item is designed to be long-lasting and made of substantial, good quality materials. Match the object to your child's ability to use the toy sensibly. A small child can often wreck even well-made products.

Safety—If the object is well-made and designed, the basic safety of the toy is assured through testing and use. Does it have a UL (Underwriters Laboratories) or CSA (Canadian) stamp affixed? Potential hazards such as flammability must be checked before you purchase anything. What toy is selected and how it is used is the responsibility of the parent.

Toxicity—All items children play with must be nontoxic. This is crucial to consider when used by children under the age of 5. Materials used must meet minimum

5

safety and purity standards. Has it been tested? More specifics about safety guidelines are included in Chapter Two.

Educational—Any toy can be educational or used for learning, but sometimes the parent or adult needs to assist the child. It can be talked about or used to learn skills, or it may be a toy that is based on educational principles.

Creative—Toys teach many skills to children and give them opportunities to create stories, new games, and other surprising activities. When children have sufficient time to use their imaginations, they expand their creativity.

Cost—Toys can be expensive. If you shop wisely, you will find good toys in your price range. Comparative shopping often reveals wide price variations for the same item.

Play Value—The purpose of having a toy is to enjoy and have fun with it for as long as possible. Selecting toys with high, long-lasting play value is the objective of this book.

A Handy Checklist to Evaluate Toy Selection

This checklist will assist you in a simple evaluation of all prospective toys before purchase and assist you in thinking about the appropriateness of the toy:

1. Is the toy fun? The purpose of the toy is to entertain, amuse, delight, excite, and be enjoyed.
2. Is the toy appropriate for the child now? How will the child interact with the toy? In order to know the likes and dislikes of the child and what sort of toy he or she prefers, you must know and observe the child at play. Parents are usually the adults who know this information best, but other individuals that know your child should also be able to inform you (grandparents, child care or nursery school teacher, or baby-sitter).
3. Will the child know how to use it? Will the toy frustrate or challenge the child.
4. Is the toy well designed? How well is the toy made? Does the toy have any potential hazards?
5. Is there more than one use for the toy?
6. Will the toy be something that will endure? Is the toy durable? Children play hard and the toy needs to be

sturdy enough to withstand a lot of abuse and wear. Sometimes expensive toys can be as easily damaged as less expensive toys. Will the toy have long-lasting value to the child? Does it have lasting play value?

7. Is the toy appealing?
8. Does the toy offer an opportunity to learn or stimulate thought. What is the learning value of the toy? Although children learn from everything in their environment, toys enhance this learning. By using appropriate toys, children learn eye-hand coordination, develop attitudes about themselves and toward their environment and much more.
9. Will the toy help the child expand his or her creativity.
10. Does the toy match the package and the package match the toy?
11. Can I afford to purchase this toy?
12. Can the toy be cleaned and reused? If it is not washable, can it be cleaned another way? If the toy can be cleaned its longevity is tremendously increased.

An Inventory of Children's Skills

This inventory will assist you to identify specific toys matching your child's abilities and interests.

Skill or Interest	Matching Toys
building	construction toys
counting objects or numbers	number blocks
cutting and pasting	safety scissors, non-toxic paste
drawing	non-toxic crayons, pencils
enjoying friends	play games, stories
enjoying music	record or cassette player
exploring objects	blocks, magnifying glass
eye-hand coordination	blocks
grasping	squeeze toys
language	puppets, cut out pictures, paper dolls
learning science	tracing leaves, build bird house
modeling shapes	clay
naming colors or shapes	match-ups
painting	fingerpaints, watercolors
recognizing words	magnetic alphabets
recognizing objects	puppets, cut out pictures, paper dolls
shaking	rattles
sorting objects	puzzles

Types of Toys

The element of surprise and spontaneity is vital to the child's creative process. Self-discovery of a toy and the realization of its potential attributes assist children to grow, discover, and reach out—expanding their limits.

Types of skills and an example of the types of toys that can reinforce these skills are listed below:

Skill	Example
challenging their abilities	construction sets
communication	puppets
developing coordination	ride-ons
enhancing imaginative play	dollhouse
gaining new skills/ abilities	sewing cards
learning to build up/tear down	blocks
relaxation	bubble pipe
responding	pounding hammer and peg set
thinking	games

As toys assist children to think and learn, they also involve their *active, creative,* and *educational* skills. The toys selected in THE TOY CHEST have been chosen to be a balance of these types. They are rated within each section and some are in more than one category.

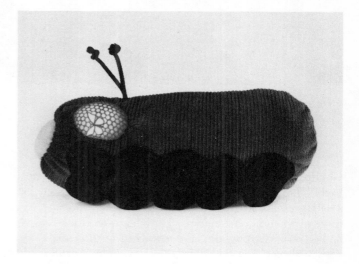

Active

Children need to develop and strengthen their physical body. They require time to exercise their bodies, develop small muscles in their hands and fingers, and improve their eye-hand coordination. They learn to climb, crawl, and move. Throughout the growing period they are constantly in motion. Some toys to help develop and improve physical ability are:

balls
bicycles, tricycles
punching bags
push-pull objects
pounding toys
ride-ons, wagon
table-top games
Throwing objects (aerobies, frisbees, beanbags)

Construction Play—Toys which help children build and create unlimited self-initiated activity. Opportunities to build are important for freedom of self-expression. Blocks, Quadro, and Lego are examples.

Adventure Play—Children need to climb, crawl, jump, and balance. It's good to do it outdoors, but it is also possible to provide indoor play environments for children which are fun and a challenge to their developing muscles. Included are long tunnels, slides, and play houses.

Coordination and Manipulative Skills—Opportunities to play with jigsaw puzzles, match-up sets, hammers, and screwdrivers assist them with eye-hand coordination.

Destructive Play—Sometimes children need to tear down or take apart objects. They enjoy changing something. Sand and clay lend themselves well to this kind of play, as do large toys designed to be taken apart.

Creative

Creative toys allow your child to develop imaginative play. For their full development, children need to play with blocks, boats, or trains. They also need to draw, paint, tell a story, or expand their description of an event by making something. They also play with dolls, doll houses, paper dolls, or act out particular events with their toys. Crafts and hobbies are another excellent form for the child's expression and self-development. Creative play allows your child's imagination, reasoning, and feeling abilities to increase. Some of the toys that promote creative play are:

blocks
coloring books
craft sets
crayons and paints
construction kits
dolls
doll houses and accessories (furniture, clothing)
hobby horses
miniature cars, trucks, planes and trains
mirrors
musical instruments
old clothes and costumes
play money
puppets
rocks, shells, and pine cones
spoons and utensils
stuffed animals

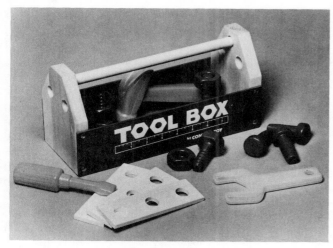

Dramatic play—Some of the toys that reflect the adult world are dolls, housekeeping equipment, tools, puppets, stuffed animals, play villages, automobiles, airplanes, hats, costumes, and mirrors. They are used by the child to mimic or alter the world as they see it.

Social development—Toys encourage cooperation and relating to other children. Housekeeping objects and blocks are the kinds of toys that enhance this form of play.

Artistic development—Art materials, musical instruments, and handicrafts are some of the items in this important area for their full creative development.

Educational

Toys can also stimulate your child's mental development. Children can use toys that provide challenges to their thinking and problem-solving. They observe and understand more through actual manipulation of objects. Examples of toys which stimulate mental development and help to educate the child are:

board games
books
checkers and chess
coins
construction toys
dominoes and cards
electronic games
magnetic alphabets
miniatures
pegboards
postcards
puzzles
science projects
stamps

Science and mathematics—Opportunities to understand and experience natural laws include use of chemistry sets, electric trains, engines, models, microscopes, telescopes, gyroscopes, telephones, telegraph sets, and magnets. Capsela (Play-Jour), tinker toys, and construction sets like Lego are examples.

Hobbies and special interests—Important as a child grows older are toys which encourage a special interest. Children like to make and create, collect and categorize.

Create New Playthings

Although toys assist children with their play, children can play effectively without toys, using their imagination and objects found around them. Children who live in parts of the world where they do not have ready-made toys use whatever natural objects they can find to play with. Folk toys were created by adults from wood carvings or other hand-made or found materials to provide the child with something interesting to play with.

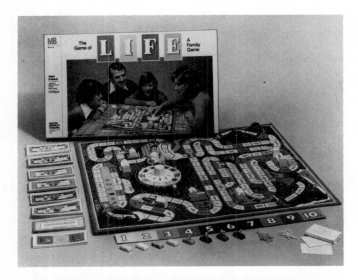

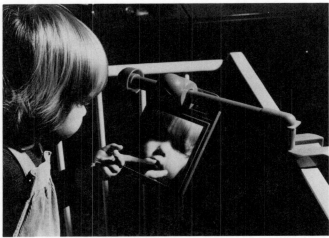

Children easily become the creature or character they pretend to be, and through play acting gain mastery of their behavior. By exercising their ability to make-believe, to use fantasy, to imagine situations and people, the child's creativity grows. Children create new situations and express their growing knowledge for themselves and others. Resources are given at the end of the book to locate many arts-and-crafts projects and creative activities you can introduce to your child and make yourself.

Where to Buy Toys

Toy stores vary in size, price, and service. There are discount stores in every community. Wise shoppers look for the best values. The local toy store which offers special interest items is also a good place to shop. In the process of becoming a better toy buyer, you will become familiar with the types of items available and the range of prices, both in the discount houses and the specialty stores. The smaller specialty store will carry selected items, quality toys from other countries, handcrafted toys, and educational toys that many of the discount houses do not always carry.

Because they are able to buy in quantity, discount houses will have better prices. However, the specialty stores will have other features to make them attractive, such as gift-wrapping, personal attention, sampling the items, and willingness to have or order hard-to-find items. Prices will vary as to location, store size, kinds of services available, number of stores in the chain, and rental costs. Your toy store can be a resource for a long time, so get to know the people and the items they sell. If there is a toy referred to in this book you would like to have for your child, ask them to order it or write to the company asking how you can get it. You may also want to buy toys at home through catalogs, certainly a convenient way to buy. Different ways to obtain toys are included in the resource section of this book. If you can't find what you want, write to the Institute for Childhood Resources for further assistance (address at the end of the Introduction).

Guide for Using THE TOY CHEST

Children need a variety of items to play with, from homemade to ready-bought items, the simplest to the most complex. The amount of money and energy you can put into providing your child with a variety of interesting and stimulating toys depends on your budget and the time you have for researching, shopping, and creating toys. Any time you spend will be that much more enjoyable if you inform yourself about what your child needs, what your child prefers, and what is available. The checklists in each section will assist you with your toy shopping and inventory types of toys you have available. I recommend a variety of toys from the different types suggested to provide the greatest variety of play for your child (creative, educational, and active).

Parents can create toys at home and certainly supplement ready-made toys. They can use found objects to make new objects. Children enjoy playing with anything that captures their imagination. Smooth wood (to prevent splinters), clothespins, clean fabric, spoons, unbreakable dishes, paper pieces, pictures from magazines, and home-sewn beanbags can serve as playthings. Parents who are involved with the Waldorf Schools, founded by Rudolph Steiner, spend time often creating handmade playthings. The school provides toys of natural woods and fabrics as part of its program. Many play groups and nursery schools are also involved in the how-to's of handmade toys.

Children like to dress up in costumes. Ready-mades are fine, as the children often can identify with the characters they represent. But home-made costumes are equally fun. You can make costumes from fabrics or old clothes you have about the house. Fabrics alone are often used by children to play with, draping, pinning, or knotting. Making capes, wings or tents will provide creative fun.

If any toy included in THE TOY CHEST is no longer available use your imagination and select a substitute toy of equal type. I included in my search items expected to be available over a number of years, but one never knows. Unfortunately good items sometimes disappear, even when popular, and become unavailable. However, the basics are always good. If you find a toy that is not included and feel it is worthwhile, please write. I will review new items and if suitable will include them in future editions of THE TOY CHEST. I would like to hear from those who have any special experiences about toys and your child. Thank you for delving into THE TOY CHEST. I hope you and your children will find the toys you want to play with.

CHAPTER TWO

Toy Safety

Selecting toys appropriate for age, interests, and play value for the child is a skill parents gain over a period of time through experience. You can help the process, however, by educating yourself about what is available, the factors which make a safe and well-designed toy, and the abilities which develop at specific stages of the child's development.

The long-range usefulness of a toy lies in its play value, safety, and ability to capture the imagination and interest of the child. Toy companies concerned about high quality are careful at all stages of their production, from their initial design phases through development and manufacture. It is estimated that to produce a multi-featured, complex plaything, the cost of product development, including the cost of safety testing, can range as high as 10 percent of net sales and could be half a million dollars or more.

For the past fifty years, the Toy Manufacturers of America (TMA), in collaboration with the National Safety Council and the American National Standards Institute (ANSI), have worked on cooperative ventures, including a national accident reporting service, a national clearinghouse for toy injuries, and standards for the coatings and finishes on children's playthings.

A very comprehensive volunteer safety standard established by the TMA, known as Products Standard 72-76 (PSF2-76), applies to all aspects of toy design, functioning, engineering, and production. It was drafted by the TMA in 1971, submitted to the National Bureau of Standards the following year. Others that participated in its development were the U.S. Consumer Products Safety Commission (CPSC), the American Academy of Pediatrics, the Consumers Union, the National Safety Council, several national retail organizations, and toy industry safety experts. It does not include bicycles, home playground equipment, skateboards, craft materials, art materials, or model kits.

What it *does* include is over one hundred testing and design specifications to guarantee that the normal use of a toy will not result in or cause an injury. Some of the tests that might be used for a simple plastic truck are: use and abuse tests, small parts, sharp points and edges, electrical-thermal-acoustical energy, wheel-pull resistance, projections, toxicity, and flammability. The majority of American toy manufacturers comply with these standards and incorporate them into their design and production.

An international committee of toy industries was established in 1975 by toy trade associations around the world. Its objective has been to bring together the toy safety standards in each country and discuss topics of mutual interest. The code regulates labeling on electrically-operated toys, chemistry sets, such toy features as points and edges, and requires that the label be clearly legible and printed in contrasting color.

The basic law covering safety of toys is the Federal Hazardous Substances Act and its amendments, in particular the 1969 Child Protection and Toy Safety Act. The 1973 law that created the Consumer Product Safety Commission incorporated the previous legislation. They have headquarters in Washington, DC and branch offices in major cities. Their field inspectors monitor domestic and imported toys, for electrical, mechanical, chemical, and flammability hazards.

According to a detailed study in 1973 by the Toy Safety Council, toy-related injuries are usually a result of destructive, careless, or aggressive behavior, rather than the design of the toy itself. Defective toys do exist, however. While children are hurt with ordinary household objects, such as pens and pencils, kitchen utensils, and guns, the statistics from hospitals and emergency rooms on toy-associated injuries among children under the age of 14 are astounding. It is imperative that parents be careful about the toys they do select for their children and educate children as to their uses.

13

To illustrate how one manufacturer plans, designs, and produces products, we have included interviews with several persons involved in toy safety testing. One of them is a tester with the R. Dakin Co. The company has high quality control, from design to product testing. Producing superior products requires standardization of products and careful management throughout the process. Products which are carefully tested and produced are not cheap. They are, however, usually more durable and well worth the investment. Parents have become more aware of this, as the competition for quality toys on the marketplace has increased and more quality toys are available.

Children can be hurt seriously by misusing toys or by playing with a faulty toy. Potential problems injuries have been reported with the following items:

bicycles and tricycles
blocks and stacking toys
caps, cap guns and darts
crayon and paint sets
fuel powered toys
modeling and construction materials
rocking horses
roller skates/skateboards
toy cars and trucks
toy guns with projectiles
wagons

In checking through the potential hazards of children's products for safety and guidelines, we have reviewed the U.S. Consumers Safety Commission on Hazards of Children's Products. The points reviewed are for your use in checking the potential hazards of any toy.

Toy Safety Checklist

1. Look for UL (Underwriters Laboratories) seal on electrical toys showing the toy has been checked for electrical safety.
2. Avoid toys with sharp edges and protrusions, such as a bird with a pointed beak that could be jabbed in an eye. Select toys with rounded edges and smooth surfaces.
3. Remove splinters or projecting nails from boxes or other equipment before giving them to a child.
4. Make sure plastic is used and not glass in toy car, truck, or airplane windows.
5. Avoid toys that are poorly constructed, such as a rattle that could break apart and tiny parts inside that a child could swallow, or noise makers and squeaker toys with metal mouthpieces that might fall out.
6. Avoid toys with detachable parts, such as dolls with button eyes that a child can put in their ears, nose, or mouth. Dolls with embroidered or firmly glued eyes are safer.
7. Check to see that stuffed toys are filled with hygienic material that is washable or can be easily changed.

8. Avoid dolls with fluffy trimmings that the child can pull off and put in his mouth.
9. Be certain paints on products are non-toxic. Paints on toys should meet Federal Hazardous Substances Act requirements.
10. Prevent use of loud caps and toy guns which can cause hearing damage. Avoid toys which shoot objects that can injure eyes.
11. Check the appropriateness of the toy for the age of the child. Avoid toys which are too complex for young children. Toys should match the child's age and interest. Follow any guidelines on or in the box. Packages and presentation of the toy in advertising

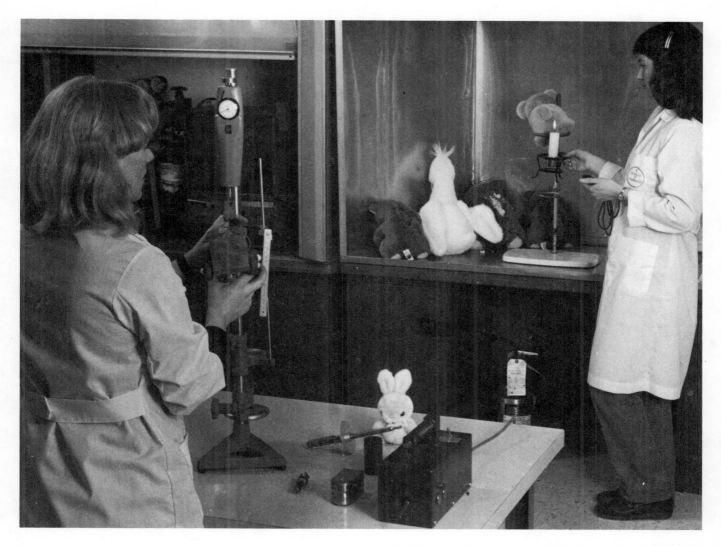

must use words, graphic materials, or statements that are consistent with cautionary labeling, age, grading, and instructions.

12. Show children how to use their toys properly and safely. Encourage children to put away their toys so that they will not be broken.

13. Examine toys periodically for sharp edges and points. Check for any damage and make repairs if necessary.

14. Toys constructed of new materials or reprocessed materials must be refined so that contaminants are not hazardous.

15. Materials should meet Flammable Fabrics Act requirements.

16. Food and cosmetics should meet Food, Drug and Cosmetic Act requirements.

17. Flexible strings attached to toys intended for crib use should be less than twelve inches long.

18. Flexible strings longer than twelve inches for pull toys should not have beads which can tangle and form a loop.

19. Ride-on toys and seats should be designed with sufficient stability and made in such a way as to minimize unexpected hazards.

20. The principal components should be labeled with the name and address of the producer and distributor.

Indoor Equipment Safety Checklist

When painting a child's crib or toys, use only paints that are labeled "lead free" or "non-toxic". These paints will not contain antimony, arsenic, cadmium, mercury, selenium, or soluble barium, which could be harmful to your child. Since not all paints are so labeled, look for and use only those that are marked: "Conforms to American Standard Z66.1-9: For use on surfaces that might be chewed by children."

Outdoor Equipment Safety Checklist

When a child starts using playground equipment, skates, bikes, or other outdoor toys, he should be old enough to know the dangers of such equipment and be taught to follow certain rules:

• Bicycles, tricycles, or sleds should not be used where there is traffic, and should be used carefully in areas where other children play.

• Roller skates should be taken off before crossing streets.

• Swings and other playground equipment must be firmly placed in the ground, away from walls and fences, and out of the direct line of pedestrian traffic. The equipment should be the right size for the child and assembled according to the directions of the manufacturer.

In shopping for a tricycle the CPSC suggests:

• Match the size of your child to the tricycle. If the child is too large, the tricycle will be unstable; if the child is too small, then the tricycle will be too hard to control. Low-slung tricycles which are close to the ground are more stable, but also are less visible.
• Look for treadles and handgrips that provide a good grip which prevent the child's hand or foot from slipping.
• Inspect pedals and handlebars for broken parts.
• Cover any sharp edges with heavy warp-proof tape.
• Do not let the bicycle stay out overnight as the moisture can rust many parts.

Teach the child safe riding habits

• Never ride in the streets or busy parking lots.
• Never ride double.
• Riding downhill can be dangerous and difficult to control or stop.
• Avoid sharp turns and to make all turns at low speed.
• Never ride down steps and avoid curbs.
• Keep hands away from moving spokes.
• Learn how to check the tires and keep them properly inflated.

Types of Testing

1. Temperature and other changes to be expected while using the toy.
2. Bathtub toys should be tested out in soapy water.
3. Toys labeled machine-washable should be subjected to at least six machine washings and tumble-dry cycles.
4. Toys should be tested for impact in simulated situations, such as falling from cribs. The toys should be dropped at least ten times from a height of four and a half feet.
5. Toys intended for infants and young children must undergo a bite test, twenty-five pounds for babies under eighteen months and fifty pounds for children under thirty-six months.
6. The seams of stuffed toys or bean bags must withstand tension tests. The appropriate amount of force should be applied in all directions.
7. Packaging should be free of hazards such as staples and pins.
8. Packages should be subjected to a number of tests to see if they will stand up under destructive forces of shipping and distribution. There are vibration, compression, and incline of impact tests.

TOY PROGRAM AND SERVICES

Lois Van Guilder

Consumer Affairs Officer
US Consumer Product Safety Commission

Toys are much safer than they used to be. We all remember sharp, cutting edges; vicious wires stuck out of a stuffed toy; dolls' eyes attached with easily removed pins or nails; rattles which broke easily and released tiny pellets a baby could choke on; or rigid wires that could poke out a baby's eye.

Fortunately toys are much safer now because of regulations. These regulations cover sharp points, sharp edges, electrically operated toys, pacifiers, rattles, lawn darts, clacker balls, sound level of toy caps and toy guns, lead paint, and toys with hazardous chemicals. In January 1980, regulations on small parts in toys intended for children under 3 went into effect to eliminate this choking or ingestion hazard (see CPSC Fact Sheets #47 Toys and #86 Baby Rattles).

But regulations can't do the job alone. Only parents can see all the toys which come into each home, supervise their use, and see that they stay safe.

This is what *you* can do to be sure toys bring happiness to children, not hurt them:
1. CAREFULLY SELECT TOYS to suit the age, interests, and the skills of the child. Remember that toys which may be safe for older children can be extremely dangerous in the hands of little ones. (For example, the popular space age toys with tiny weapons and easily

removable parts are fun for a 5 or 6-year-old, but could choke a 2-year-old). Read the age recommendations and believe them! (Age labeling is not required, but the toy industry uses it voluntarily.)

(See our brochure "For Kids' Sake—Think Toy Safety" for selection guidelines.) [listed in the bibliography]

2. Your job isn't done when the toy has been carefully chosen. There is also SAFE USE or misuse. Carefully read the instructions and be sure the child understands how the toy is to be used or not used. Add your own guidelines (like "never in the house") so there are no misunderstandings. Younger children may require supervision (depending on their age and the toy, of course). Everyone in the family must share seeing that younger brothers and sisters don't use things intended for older children. Small parts choke and kill young children. So do elastic cords. Be sure toys with these hazards are kept out of their reach! Never hang toys in cribs with elastic or long cords.

3. STORAGE is important too! The roller skate on the stairs joke is no joke! Storage can prevent deterioration, breakage, keep little hands from toys for older children, as well as remove the threat of tripping or falling over toys left out. Teach this to your children.

4. MAINTENANCE and REPAIR are all-important. Toys must be checked periodically to see that they haven't acquired sharp edges, points, etc. through use or misuse. Immediately repair them to keep them safe as they were when new.

5. And, finally, CORRECT DISPOSAL: When a toy isn't safe any longer or repairable, destroy it! Be sure it isn't discarded where it will be an attractive nuisance to some other child. The CPSC prints free materials which might be of help to you:

Brochures:
For Kid's Sake—Think Toy Safety
Holiday Safety Teachers Guide (Grade 4-6)
Leon the Lizard Guide (Preschool—2nd grade)
Merry Christmas with Safety (Holiday Safety)
A Toy and Sports and Equipment Safety Guide

Fact Sheets:
47—Toys
61—Electrically Operated Toys
84—Roller Skates and Ice Skates
86—Rattles
93—Skateboards

In addition to printed materials, the following can be ordered from some CPSC Offices.

"For Kids' Sake"—Toy Safety slide presentation with cassette

"Bubble, Bubble, Toys & Trouble"—10 min., 16 mm film.

17

You'll no doubt have many other ideas for a successful parent toy education program. For starters here are a few ideas that might fit your plans.

Local toy buyers might be part of your program to tell how *they* buy safer toys.

Each person could bring an example of a toy, show that they had made a good or bad choice, and tell why.

Have a "toy box survey" and bring in the broken and now dangerous toys turned up by parents or children.

The discussion part of your program could include brief descriptions of toy-related accidents and how they could have been prevented.

Take this program to your community when you decide where it can help other parents the most.

Let us know if we can be of further help to you. We want to encourage everyone to think PRODUCT SAFETY IS NO ACCIDENT, and your program will help spread the word. We would like to know how successful your program is.

CONSUMER PRODUCT SAFETY COMMISSION

Toy Regulations

The following CPSC regulations are now in effect.

1. Sharp points—(since December, 1978) Provides manufacturers with testing methods to ensure that toys and other articles intended for children under 8 years old do not have hazardous sharp points.
2. Sharp edges—(since March, 1979) Provides manufacturers with testing methods which they can use to eliminate hazardously sharp glass and metal edges from toys and other children's articles.
3. Electrically-operated toys—(since 1973) Designed to prevent electric shock and burn injuries which could result from poorly constructed electrical toys.
4. Baby rattles—(since August, 1978) Requires that rattles must be large enough so that they cannot lodge in an infant's throat, and they must be constructed so they cannot separate into small pieces.
5. Pacifiers—(since February, 1978) Pacifiers must be large enough so that babies cannot choke on them, and they must not come apart into small pieces.
6. Clacker balls—(since 1972) Toys to be manufactured in accordance with strict performance requirements so that the plastic balls will not shatter or fly off the ends of the cord.
7. Toy caps and toy guns (since 1972) To prevent hearing damage, the Commission has regulated the amount of noise that toy caps and toy guns may make. These regulations have been in effect since 1972.
8. Aluminized polyester film kites—(since September 20, 1979) Aluminized polyester film kites have been banned. They can become entangled in power lines and cause electric shock.

9. Small parts—(since January 1, 1980) Small parts must be eliminated from toys intended for use by small children under the age of three.
10. Lead in paint—(since February, 1978) Paint on toys or other articles intended for use by children must not exceed a level of 0.06%.

I appreciate the contribution from Ms. Van Guilder and the amount of useful information produced by the U.S. Consumer Product Safety Commission.

CHAPTER THREE

Toy Chest Closeup

At their best and worst, toys are a reflection of our society. From a tradition of simple and often home made playthings, toy buyers are now confronted with thousands of confusing possibilities. A simple rattle is now a multi-faceted plastic bubble with a handle that might break off and injure an eye. The teddy bear is now a hundred different teddy bears some of them potentially toxic. A simple rag doll created in rural Appalachia suddenly is promoted to become the national rage and eclipses all other dolls. In this nation of faddists, toys are the most trendy. The newest toy trend, carefully planned in the board room, is a well devised strategy, created not unlike the ad campaigns for the latest breakfast cereal. The latest and best is promoted to the child, but those of us who reflect may well ask what is going on.

When you hear news reports that adults are frantically fighting in a store over the possession of the newest rage, a soft doll, you might readily conclude toy trends have strong supporters from buyers. How can inanimate objects, created to be objects of love and affection for children, have so much influence? How do toys designed for the child during their prime learning and growing time become the newest symbol for hype? These questions arise and the answers are complex. Naturally parents want the best, newest, and popular item for their child. Sometimes, regardless of whether or not the child wants or needs it. For the most part, I feel the toy selection process should be a good balance of different types of toys, purchased all year around, and be appropriate for the recipient. Toys should not be given only at Christmas or on a birthday, nor should they be promoted to excess on television. I am not "against" any toy unless it

has the potential to harm the child physically, psychologically, or in any other way. I do think, however, that some of what appears to be innocent or momentary hysteria over any toy is not in the child's best interests. Many choices of toys are good for children as they vary so much in interests and abilities. All too often good toys disappear simply because the amount of sales is not high enough to meet a quota. I hope this will change. Like the backlist in the field of book publishing or the middle of the line offerings, many toys that are truly worthwhile should continue to be available if at all possible. Over the years they will prove to be a good investment.

I hope toy companies will continue to maintain their high level of product development, will seek new safe and creative products, and will continue their policy of responsible television advertising.

As a child advocate, I hope to raise sufficient issues so you will be a more perceptive shopper.

It is not just the "Hurried Child" that Dr. David Elkind so eloquently describes, but the "Hyped Child" that concerns me. The child who is bombarded from the moment he sits in front of the television with pressure that shifts his thinking from learning to pressuring Mom and Dad for "one of those," and then after he gets "it" his interest last for five minutes. The results of reducing the hype may be children who are not stuck on pressuring parents about "What did you buy me?," or "buy me X," but happily expressing "Thanks for thinking of me."

Our contemporary "disposable" society is doing a disservice to the child's natural potential. It is also a disservice to the large number of fine companies offering a full range of excellent toy products. These good, and

often better, offerings are frequently buried behind the BIG HYPE which gets all of the media attention.

I have been impressed by observing the process of bringing new toys to the market place. Most toy companies are to be commended for their careful efforts. Some products, however, should not be on the market at all. They are sold solely for the "fast buck," and may not be good for the child. Even if it is popular. We must ask ourselves if "slime" benefits children, or "drawing blood from a pen," even if it is pretend. Does the child benefit from toys that "blast, crackle, or pop," or toys that break ear drums, hurt eyes, or in any way damage the child's spirit, or mental well being?

These are the issues we need to examine closely. Certainly you have your own opinions. You may say, "I had a gun, why shouldn't my child?" or "I do not want my son playing with dolls," or "I won't let my daughter play with a dump truck." You may wonder if your children can become spoiled if grandparents buy them too many toys. I have spent a great deal of time thinking about these and other issues. I have listened to many people in the toy industry and surveyed several hundred parents. I have requested parents' and experts' comments on all of these questions. I have interviewed children who showed or talked to me about what they like and dislike. I have also spoken to successful toy people who have made large profits from some of the toys you and I may find objectionable. Although I can see their point and even why they feel as they do, I still have to look at these issues from the child's viewpoint. The child is not always able to know what's good. After all, anything you give children, good or bad, will be initially fascinating. They do not question

whether they should have cosmetics or guns, they just think the object is great, especially since it appears on television.

If harm may come to the child as a result we must take responsibility. This includes successful manufacturers who have their company's name and reputation on the line. Making a "fast buck" may actually be detrimental. Children need to be carefully considered when we think about producing their playthings. The criterion I feel for a product to be available and to be selected by the shopper is to examine if it is in the child's best interest. Let's take a close look at the questions asked most frequently beyond the usual "What is play?" Let's evaluate what is happening at the national level about toy testing, design, evaluations, market place strategies, advertising, sexism in packaging, and in the toys themselves, as well as how advertising stimulates certain predetermined behavior. Let's take a closer look for example at the potential damage to the child.

Toy guns are an example. They may give a child the idea they can be used as a "handy" way to resolve conflicts. They see them in use constantly on television.

Guns do not encourage conversation, negotiation, or compromise. Do we want trigger-happy children reaching for the cap gun or electronic blaster at the slightest provocation? Observe children at play in school and see how often they attempt to resolve their differences with a shove, kick, or the barrel of a toy gun. Within the world of toys I can trace other trends, see patterns, and be concerned. You will understand the trends more fully when you read about the history of the toys and the contributors to THE TOY CHEST. You will discover how much the toy industry reflects the growth of our society. These changes are from simple to complex, in quality from excellent to shoddy, and durable to disposable. Designs change from elegantly creative to efficiently functional. Values changing from family oriented to peer-group acceptance. These trends happen for many reasons.

Why is not as important as *how* we live with the negative qualities. It may not be possible to change all of the negatives. Buyers can be even more influential if they want to be. First they must be aware of the effects of "bad" toys on children. Then they must speak out! We must spend some time carefully thinking, observing, and re-

23

flecting on what is best for the child. What is good for our children is good for society as a whole. It has been shown in recent studies that even very young children are troubled by the world we live in. They express their fears in play. Children must not be hurried along in the process of growing up either by hype, power, greed, or superficial values. They must not be deprived of their essential childhood. If children learn to value what they receive and care about their playthings, they will take better care of themselves respecting you more as a caring parent. They will also appreciate what they are given, not as a right, but as privilege. They will be able to cope with life in a more sensitive and responsible way. They will have a happier, more productive childhood and be better able to cope with the future.

THIS CHAPTER IS DIVIDED INTO THREE PARTS:

A. SAFETY AND WELL-BEING OF THE CHILD

Examples: war toys, bad toys

B. INDUSTRY EXCESSES AND INEQUALITIES

Examples: girls' cosmetics, designer dolls, sexism, advertisement of many toys

C. GENERAL CONCERNS

Examples: educational toys and durability

A. SAFETY AND WELL-BEING OF THE CHILD

The first concern is that a toy may be physically or mentally dangerous.

War Toys

More than 19,000 children are harmed each year by the use of play guns, cap guns, darts, and other related paraphernalia. These items are dangerous and need to be controlled. Children do not need to stockpile replicas of MX missiles in their living room. Nor do they benefit from playing with real-life gun replicas. When children argue, usually it is with a television scenario in mind, where violence is used to solve many problems. Some of the toys children play with can injure, put out an eye, or permanently impair them or their playmates. Toy guns do not enhance childhood. They are not essential to the child's well-being, security, or emotional growth. The combination of toy guns and excessive television violence have done irreparable damage to a whole generation of children. If studies are accurate, young children may be observing thousands of shootings, murders, and other destruction before they are ten years old.

When children lack the manufactured variety, they make guns out of found pieces of wood or use their fingers and then engage in full play combat, but then the conflict is over. Children will in fact naturally act out aggressive behavior. It is part of their role playing. Canada, England, Germany, New Zealand, Sweden, and other countries have simply banned war toys altogether.

Children grow into the roles we create. If we want militarism, then our children will play soldiers. Recently the Peace Museum in Chicago created a highly successful exhibit of positive, peaceful toys and activities for children.

War toys and their related injuries are responsible for over one billion dollars in medical costs over the past several years. I have talked about these issues with

parents who expressed their concern when they see violent ads on television promoting this kind of toy. A child's sense of adventure is not improved with guns. They do benefit from conceiving and acting out adventures with their own props. The parents I spoke with felt very angry about this invasion of violence into children's television. As a result they monitor the programs and the ads. Some have written to companies protesting and some have organized with other parents. Most parents want to stop war toys. The irony is the very well financed toy companies say, "We are responding to the demand".

The issue is which came first, the product or the hype? Who are the parents who want guns for their children? Are they members of the National Rifle Association, the children of police or military personnel? Do they want their children to use in make believe play what they use in real life? Some adults do think arms are the way to show children to keep the peace. Meanwhile, how many more youngsters will be shot by someone thinking the toy gun was real, or injure a playmate by sticking them with their "plaything?"

While researching the root cause of violence in children, I was struck by the concept of the gun as being the reinforcer of negative behavior. The indications are that children, in attempting to resolve conflicts, will use a gun first before choosing other possibilities. Drs. C.W. Turner, D. Goldsmith, L. Berkowitz, A. Le Page, S. Fesbach, and A. Mendoza reported in their respective studies that the presence of guns increased children's aggressive behaviors. They reported a conditioning effect on children. Guns serve as a "retrieval cue" associated with characters on television.

In 1981, 156 children under the age of 12 were reported by the U.S. Surgeon General as having been killed due to use of handguns. Hundreds of children were treated for injuries, with some permanent eye losses. Children simply do not understand the difference between toys and the real thing.

Some scientists and pediatricians believe the long-term effects of playing with guns is serious and detrimental to children. In experiments with college students and the mere presence of a gun elicited more aggressive and destructive behavior.

In 1969 the National Commission on the Causes and Prevention of Violence found that watching violent television programs made it more likely that a viewer would behave violently. In 1972 the Surgeon General's Advisory Committee on Television and Behavior concluded that a

causal relationship exists between violence and aggressive behavior. In 1982 the National Institute of Mental Health published two volumes supporting overwhelming evidence that aggressive behavior is a result of watching television. Since 1946 a group of psychiatrists have worked to compile evidence on the impact of television on children. The conclusion is that television is definitely a contributing factor to aggressive behavior in children. The child identifies with the violent characters seen on television, reinforcing impulsive behavior. If all conflicts on television are solved with fists and guns, then in the playground differences will be solved that way also: with a push, a shove, and a kick in the face. Parents, it has been found, do not monitor their children's television viewing sufficiently.

The evidence is in, but the big advertising bucks and the violent mindless programs continue as if none of these findings had been made at all. Children are unable to protest and are victims of the industry. Good programs are possible, but do not seem to be being developed in sufficient number in the networks plans, budgets, or social consciousness. Too few programs such as "Sesame Street," "Mister Roger's Neighborhood," or "Wonder Works" offer humanistic entertainment for young chil-

dren. Considering the size of the toy industry, one would hope for greater responsibility among manufacturers to help sponsor worthwhile programs.

I have suggested to a number of manufacturers that they examine the possibility of creating non-destructive "peace toys" that enhance children's resolution towards aggression and conflict in positive ways. Everyone would gain from alternatives to "Destroy," "Kill," "I got you," "Bang, bang, you're dead." Choices we can make to encourage other forms of excitement are camping trips, adventure stories, treasure hunts, knock-down/pop-up punching bags (vinyl and inexpensive), bat and balls, and forms of fantasy play.

Bad Toys

In today's toy market, there is a tremendous number and variety of products. By scrutinizing the toys more closely, we see that many of them are cheap, shoddy, or dangerous. Costs are a big factor in the creation of bad toys. Economic pressures too often result in products that kill. When a child can be killed or permanently injured by badly designed toys we must speak out. The Consumer Product Safety Council ideally has a staff to test toys and prepare safety information for the public, and when necessary the power to recall bad products. Government cutbacks have affected these regulatory agencies. Funds have dried up along with international publications, staff, and people to monitor new toys and enforce regulations. Too many toys are released that are not checked carefully. Who does the parent go back to when a badly designed toy injures a child, the store, the manufacturer, or the government?

A special study conducted in Washington, D.C., by the Community Affairs Committee of the Americans for Democratic Action, has each Christmas for the last thirteen years created a shopping survey of the worst toys. Their address is listed in the References section. The study of toys each year is run by volunteers who take the time to shop, compare, and evaluate what they see. The bad toys they throw into the "Trash Box." They have other special categories for different types of toys.

Some examples of "trash box" toys have been:

Product Name	Manufacturer
Garfield Ride-On	Durham Industries
Manglor Mtn. Volcanic Fortress	Ideal
Happi Returns	Ideal
E. T. Finger Light	Knickerbocker
Wrapper Racer	Kuzan
Wacky Monster Writer	Lakeside
Baby Skates	Mattel
Freckles	Playskool
All Terrain Cycle	Processed Plastic Co.
Li'l Folks Metal Tools	Roth America, Inc.

Examples of GOOD TOYS for the Toy Box:

Product Name	Manufacturer
Cabbage Patch Kids	Coleco
Construx	Fisher-Price
Riding Horse	Fisher-Price
Sky Talkers	Fisher-Price
Gloworm	Hasbro
Care Bears	Kenner
Li'l Loggers	Kenner
Upwords	Milton-Bradley
Domain	Parker
Lights Alive	Tomy
Popoids	Tomy
Small Stuff Space Shuttle	Tomy

A toy that is popular and potentially dangerous is the ride-on. If it is made with the seat directly above the axle the child could tip backwards and land on the head or face. The ride-on often can flip backwards when the child is pushing on the back. One safe example is the Fisher-Price Riding Horse, or Combi Train. See the section on ride-on's for toddlers and preschool children for other safe products.

During 1983, the Consumer Product Safety Commission reported over 120,000 toy-related injuries plus 20 deaths treated in hospital emergency rooms. Despite the fact that falling toy chest lids were high on the accident list, the Commission, however, refrained from taking monitoring action. The title of our book has a double meaning, both as a cornucopia of toy offerings and as a caution to prospective buyers of toy chests, to be careful to obtain safety hinges.

If you shop at a store you trust, and the people who own the store are careful buyers of products, you should not have to worry about the toys you buy. Ultimately,

however, you are responsible for what you purchase and how your child uses or misuses the product.

Bad toys do more than fall apart. They injure and sometimes permanently damage children. Before you buy an item ask yourself:
1. Will my child benefit from this toy?
2. Is it well made and sturdy?
3. Are there any parts that can come loose or break?
4. Is it made by a company I can trust?

As your child plays with it make frequent checks for sharp edges, parts broken off, or corrosion. Your child will be safer if you inspect carefully what he or she plays with. Children also must learn to take care of their toys. This includes putting them away in a safe place after play. More information on safety is contained in chapter two.

Attorney and author, Edward M. Swartz, in his book *Toys That Don't Care*, gives details on the damage done to children by bad toys, and the often resulting law suits. After a death or serious injury a settlement in a law suit is small compensation for the pain of the family. In his book, Mr. Swartz says 700,000 children are injured annually. Certainly the reported injuries are only a fraction of the entire population, but he does make a specific point about planned obsolescence. When cheaply made toys break in a dangerous way, the child is in trouble.

B. INDUSTRY EXCESSES AND INEQUALITIES

Today's children learn about toys through other children, their family, and television. "Buy me that one, Mommy!" is heard over and over by parents whose children have been influenced by television to desire a specific toy. Sometimes the toy is right for the child and is genuinely suitable for age, interests, and abilities. Sometimes the toy is wrong. Advertising influences the child, but the parent is ultimately responsible for what toys the child plays and grows with. There is an enormous range of toys, both good and bad, on today's market. Parents must sharpen their skills of discernment before purchasing any toy. Observe your child carefully. Let the toys you buy for your child be ones that expand creativity or dexterity, and not ones that could potentially blind, stab, or maim.

The first TV ad directed towards children was created in 1956 by the Mattel Company to promote Barbie Dolls on the Mickey Mouse Club Show. The trickle became a flood. Toy advertising on television is now pervasive, persistent, and very big business. Critics such as Peggy Charren of Action for Children's Television, conclude that the hard sell of children is inappropriate and influences children in a bad way. Short of not having a television, it is not easy to shield your child from the flood of ads sponsoring children's television programs nor is it easy to shield them from the many adult shows they might watch.

For a time the television industry responded to increased public pressure over advertising aimed at children, established a code of ethics, and took action to screen ads. They were responding to public pressure. This response produced a television code that called for "Truth in Claims," avoidance of misleading phrases, compliance with legal requirements, and responsible treatment. Some of these actions resulted in stopping dramatizations that were not authentic, exaggerated, unfairly glamorized, or frightened children. More about these actions are included in the chapter History of Toys.

As of 1983, the codes and enforcement staffs were curtailed. This requires that parents and others be even more discerning consumers when buying toys.

Too Many Toys?

Can I spoil my child by giving too many toys? This is a question I am frequently asked by young parents. Children enjoy receiving gifts. They enjoy surprises. They need lots of loving attention as they grow, and to feel good about themselves. Playthings help make them feel good, but feeling good does not necessarily depend on the number and kind of playthings they have.

Giving toys should never be a substitute for you. If you give the child an excessive amount of toys without giving personal time, your child will know it. Children can easily become demanding and self-centered because of not getting what they really want, your personal attention. Gifts are even more loving when you come with them. To sit and play with your child, enjoy a board game, puzzle, have tea with a new set of play dishes, work on a hobby, model boat, or car together is often a rich moment between parent and child. It is wise to take the time to shop carefully and when you can, let your children go with you. They can see for themselves how many toys there are. They will understand your living room will never be that store. Do not overdo what you give your child in objects. Give your child what he needs, not what will impress, overpower, or control him with dependency.

Children can earn money from chores around the house to buy attachments or special accessories, or other special items that you feel are beyond your budget. Set a plan to buy toys not only at Christmas. Toys can be enjoyed all year round. If toy buying is spread out over the year, the toys can be rewards for work well done, doing

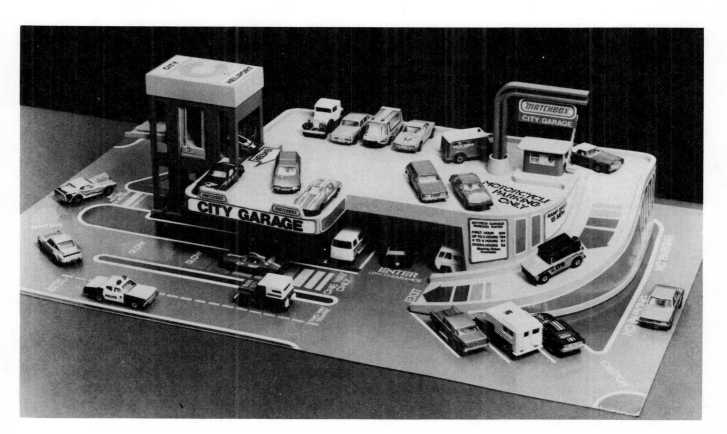

fine in school, trying hard, or just helping around the house.

Can electronic games be harmful for children?

Anything children do to excess is potentially harmful and can limit their potential. Some concern exists that electronic games can strain delicate eyes still undergoing formation. Electronic games can be, after a while, repetitious or boring. Often the child simply loses interest. It is best to balance the time children play with electronic games with other types of games, toys, and playthings. Children should interact with each other, not continuously with machines. Although computers are important, they should augment and never attempt to replace real people.

Many good and challenging games exist that allow children to test their minds, find expression, and learn skills. However, these activities must be balanced with others, inside and out of doors. It is not healthy for children to be plugged into an electronic world from crib to college.

Each child is an individual and some thoroughly enjoy the challenge of computers and electronics in all manifestations. Fortunately, computer technology has been rapidly developing and now provides a wide range of choices of educational software. Many games now have an educational basis. Using a computer as learning tool is becoming easier and can include the entire family. Most children will enjoy some aspects of computers and a basic understanding of them will help in the future. This should not detract from their time with sports, crafts, dramatics, and other activities. Diversity should be encouraged in school and at home.

Bernie de Koven, one of the contributors to THE TOY CHEST, has suggested ways to consider the value of computers in an article in *Popular Computing*, October, 1984. He suggests that through the use of a computer, a child gains skills that assist in the growth of mental capacities, even if they are not strictly according to pedogogy, or expectations of the school. A child will often exceed these expectations. A child gains skills in computing on many levels of activity and it can be beneficial. As long as the time spent with the machine is balanced, the computer as toy can effectively facilitate learning.

Girl's cosmetics

Children love to dress up, play, and act out fantasies. Make-up reinforces play and makes it more real. If your child gets into your cosmetics, you will probably be upset. There is also a possibility they may be allergic to certain ingredients. The walls might not come clean after being decorated with your lipstick or eyebrow pencil. It is a good idea to have make-up for them that is washable and hypo-allergenic. You can get these items at theatrical supply stores and some toy stores.

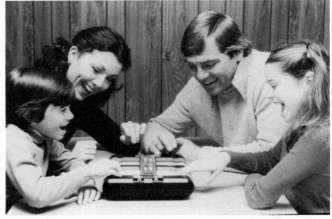

Girls' cosmetics have been heavily advertised. The idea is often not for play, but to exploit children. Entering into the world of girls' cosmetics is like entering an adult make-up salon. They are color-coded to match a girl's complexion and elaborate systems have been developed. It is interesting that the people who do this have advertising campaigns to match and are very designer or model-oriented. This is pushing girls too fast into being grown up. This is different from clown or costume makeup that is for play and having a good time. Creative and dramatic play is essential for their development.

Should little girls play with Barbie or Brooke dolls?

Barbie has been around for 25 years and is a classic designer doll. Brooke is a clone of the original fashion doll, along with Loni and a number of other designer/ dress dolls, made to capitalize on this trend. Girls like to play with these dolls. An active Barbie Doll fan club and collectors' group has been in existence for 20 years. Adults get very excited over all of the Barbie accessories, old and new. If the child is totally absorbed with the designer doll, to the exclusion of other dolls or playthings, then it can be overdone. Kept within balance, collecting can be a good idea. However, I am not sure that overemphasis on glamour and fashion is in the best interest of the young developing child. Many other forms of dramatic play provide more creativity and stimulation leaving time later for being "grown-up."

What about sexism in toys and packaging?

Many manufacturers have not fully recognized that young girls like to play with many of the same toys as boys. Certainly girls can be discouraged by the graphics of the package that depict only boys having fun with the toy inside. It's a good idea to have both sexes pictured on the box. We are all influenced by packaging. We may make too much of it because of growing awareness, but the non-sexism trend should also become more actively implanted in the minds of designers and manufacturers.

A recent study by Dr. Michael Lewis at Rutgers found that parents' attitudes are more relevant than the playthings themselves. Children make early identification with gender and sex roles. Most by the age of 3, clearly understand the differences between masculine and feminine. They found that the attitudes and ways that parents respond to toy buying will affect how the child reacts. The important aspect to reassure you about is that boys can play with girl-type toys with no change in their later sexual preference. For the first several years both boys and girls need to experience, dress up as, and feel O.K. about male and female and play with all types of toys.

Do not be alarmed about children trying on different roles. This is part of their socialization and is normal for the preschool child who learns continuously through play.

C. GENERAL CONCERNS

How important are educational toys?

Educational toys are specifically designed to teach a skill (such as eye-hand coordination), learn a concept, practice a pre-reading skill (such as up-down or left-right), gain mastery of colors, numbers, shapes, sizes, or challenge thinking (games serve as an example). Many wonderful products are available and have been for a number of years. The products have improved in many cases and more value is placed on their importance. Thinking, reasoning, and mental challenges are important for the child's mind.

I have had the opportunity of using educational toys in the classroom and creating new ones for my students as needed. "Feely" bags were created by filling bags with different objects for the child to guess what the item is by feeling with fingers, or "Senses"—plastic vials filled with different substances from "sweet" to "spicy"—to heighten the child's awareness of smells and descriptions. These experiences can be used to expand communication skills, stimulate poetry or art, or provide an enriched opportunity to share a fun concentration game.

Parents and teachers can see and try out products, and there are endless possibilities in this field. You will find many suggestions on specific toys and the most effective ways to use them. Your selection should always be based on what your child's needs and interests are. Children reach for what looks like fun and discover what they need for play from what is available. You can create many educational playthings and in the process learn a lot about play and toys.

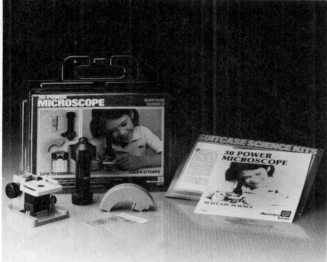

Creating positive learning experiences with toys

If you have purchased a stacking ring toy, for example, you might be able to use the stacking rings as part of a learning game. If you're talking with your child about counting numbers, see how the stacking toy can work itself in. You might use the pieces of the stacking toy together in a "one-plus-one-equals-two" method, or by identifying the colors.

Toys can serve many practical educational purposes if you create the opportunities. "Barbie" or other dress-up dolls can be a language opportunity for preschoolers when you go out shopping. "Let's get the doll dressed to go out," or "What does she want to get at the store?" are questions

to ask as examples of creating language opportunities between parent, child, and doll. A child can often share "feelings" with the doll easier than with a parent, and by listening, a parent can better understand what is difficult for the child to express.

Some Examples of Educational Toys

Infant	mobile
	musical toy
	cradle gyms
Toddler	stacking colored rings
	twist-turn shapes
	color shapes
Pre-School	puzzles
	oversize gears
	take-apart toys
	books
School Age	peg board
	construction toys
	games
	musical instruments
Older Child	construction toys
	games
	science toys

Is there any way to extend the life of a toy?

Too many toys are left in the toy chest unused. Sometimes a child finds another toy he likes better. A child may put aside a stacking toy, for instance, although he enjoyed putting the rings on a lot and for a long period of time. It is best to let that toy be stored in a locked toy chest and then revive it later. Put toys away so that the child does not become bored with the toy and doesn't damage it. When children actively play with fewer toys they tend to take better care of them and do not become overwhelmed or confused by too many things lying around.

Toys are given as gifts sometimes before the child is fully ready to appreciate them or has the capability to play with them. These items can be put away and brought out later or exchanged for a more current toy. Be sure your child has an easily accessible place to store his frequently used toys. They do not have to take over your living room. They can play with a few at a time and learn to replace them before taking out others.

The issues involving toys are even more extensive and have already caused a considerable amount of discussion. You may agree or not. I look forward to any additional information or experiences you can provide about any of these issues shared in writing. The purpose after all is to provide children with a safe and stimulating childhood. I hope, we are aiming toward the same objective.

PART II

SELECTION

CHAPTER FOUR

Toys for Babies

The Baby's First Big Toy Is the Parent

Becoming a parent for the first time is one of life's most exciting experiences. The first toys for the new baby are among the most precious items you will ever buy. Most people find they enjoy shopping for the baby, looking for ways to decorate the baby's room, and thinking about what toys to buy him or her. You will want to be practical about these purchases, and not overdo the number of things you buy beforehand. In fact, you will want to select the first toys carefully, using as your guide the basic abilities and needs of the baby.

As the infant grows, his abilities expand, and his needs change. So watch your baby explore and respond. Use the developmental guides in this book to assist you in understanding your child. Remember each child is a unique individual and often acts different from the "average" descriptions given for his or her age. You will notice on many toy packages the age range is given to serve as a guide for appropriateness. The notations are usually helpful to assist you in the selection process.

Before you go shopping for toys for your baby, remember that you are the MOST important BIG TOY to your baby. You are the special person who will feed, talk, sing, stroke, bathe, change, and play with your new baby. From you, your baby will have the first contact with the world. This is an important reason to take good care of yourself physically and emotionally, before, during, and after pregnancy. Having clear communication between you and your mate will help to resolve many of the

questions you will have. How well you are both prepared before having the baby is vitally important, since preparation will help you to raise a healthy happy baby, and to have more fun.

To prepare for the baby, you can visit other friends and learn from them what toys, activities and other ideas have worked well for them. You might want to create a notebook to write down and keep your good ideas for the baby. You will also want to read and learn all you can about babies. (See *The Whole Child* for more complete references and the suggested books in the bibliography.) Your baby will benefit from the extensive research conducted for many years in the area of child growth and development. New information has led to guidelines, books, toys and production of many excellent and carefully tested products. You can also learn to make useful and inexpensive toys for your new baby, and learn more about effective play. Instructions for creating toys are available in some good paperback books listed in the bibliography.

As you review information given on toys, you will be able to begin a place in your notebook for a BABY GIFT LIST. When members of your family or friends ask what you would like, you can consult your record. In one column, list the kind or name of the toy, next to it a check if received and the name of the person who gave the item. A thank-you note should always include specific mention of the toy and something about the child's reaction, as a particularly thoughtful gesture. A photograph of your baby with the toy would be a special treasure to the gift giver.

Early Shopping for the Baby

Timing is important. There is a relationship between your baby's development and the toys appropriate for his or her age and ability. Buying something before he or she is ready for it will only lead to frustration, disappointment, or boredom. It is better to wait and give the baby the toy when he or she is ready to enjoy it. You may want to run right out and start buying dolls as soon as you learn you are pregnant, but it is probably more sensible to purchase a soft, washable, baby-proof stuffed bunny rabbit or teddy bear instead.

When one couple, Tom and Arlene Davenport, learned they were to have a baby, Tom decided to celebrate immediately. He went to a store to buy something he wanted, a large set of Lego blocks, something he never got to play with when he was young. Actually, the time he took to use them and to create objects became a relaxing and enjoyable way for him to recreate and satisfy his own childhood needs.

Although it was a while before Annie, his two-year-old daughter, got to play with the first starter set of Lego, her daddy had a lot of fun with his early selection. Over the two years since the birth of Annie, Tom and Arlene have learned to shop selectively and have made many wise purchases. They obtained toys that will be used by their second child which is expected soon.

Whatever purchases you make, remember that you are the BEST person to make the final selection because you as the parent are the baby's daily observer. If you are not a parent and are using this guide to purchase a gift for a baby, you might want to ask the parents what they have not received of the different items included on their BABY GIFT LIST (see sample list).

By watching and testing, you will soon learn what works best for your own baby. You will find that, first and foremost, your baby needs you to play with. Be a creative "Big Toy" with your baby. This is a great opportunity to learn to play, talk, sing, and have fun with your new baby.

As you understand more about the needs of the baby and the right toys to select in response to his needs, you will notice that toys can be classified by type.

Active or Action Toys for physical development, eye-hand coordination, and strength.

Creative or Imaginative Toys for developing and expanding spontaneity and self-expression.

Educational or Learning Toys for mental development of thoughts and specific skills improving the mind. (Rapid mental growth occurs during the first two years.)

Many good toys have qualities in each of these categories which makes it difficult to present a rigid classification. You will see the possibilities for each type of toy and see how they merge into different areas through creative use. Also, it's impossible to separate toys for girls or boys as many items satisfy mental and educational needs of both sexes. Another difficulty is classifying the hundreds of choices within each aspect. Many dozen choices of well-made rattles exist, manufactured by a dozen companies. The store you use will have a good variety of toys to choose from in EACH category. The most useful service we can provide is to give you many ideas and a few suggested companies as examples. If any company is not listed, it does NOT mean they are not good, but simply not included due to space limitations. An attempt was made to limit the listings with many toys from only a few companies but rather to give you a sampling from as many different companies as possible.

38

Your toy store should be able to supply you with a good substitute if they do not carry the specific item mentioned, or will try to order it.

THE FIRST SIX WEEKS

Baby Is Ready for Gentle Play

Your baby is born with all of the senses necessary for play. He or she sees, hears, tastes, touches, and through observation and experimentation, begins to gain mastery over her or his environment. Important aspects of the environment prepare the baby for later introduction to toys. The way adults respond is critical to his overall development. The time this process of learning takes depends not just on the individual abilities of your child, but also on you and others who love and care for the baby. The way you play with your baby greatly determines his later effectiveness as a player. Loving, warm, and nurturing play teaches baby that the world is a loving, warm, and nurturing place. Babies who feel secure and confident reach out for pleasure and stimulation and for positive relationships.

From the moment of birth your baby is aware of his new environment: the sounds, the temperature, the way he or she is held and moved through space. From the moment of birth, how a baby is treated can affect her or him for the rest of his life. When Frederick LeBoyer introduced the idea of bathing newborn babies in warm water in his book, *Birth Without Violence,* some did not understand his belief in the need to reduce the trauma that accompanies birth. He substantiated his theories with photographs of newborns who received warm baths. These were smiling, quiet, and relaxed, while babies born from mothers treated with sedatives or in an insensitive way, were noticeably more irritable and unhappy.

LeBoyer pointed out in his next book *Loving Hands* the essential effectiveness of touching and stroking the baby. The infant picks up all his cues from touch through skin and other sense organs. Therefore, it is important to touch the baby in ways that are pleasant and soothing to him: giving him baths, carrying him close, snuggling with him, rocking him, singing to him, and wrapping him in soft, warm blankets.

Breast-feeding also brings the mother and baby closer together. In addition to the practical function of providing nutrition and passing on immunities, breast-feeding provides tactile stimulation. It is a perfect time for communicating with the baby. Ashley Montagu in his book, *Touching,* strongly endorses the effectiveness of touch for essential emotional support. Dr. James Prescott reinforces these theories with the crosscultural research he has conducted to verify the importance of touch.

The baby learns about love from early experiences and about trust. His next learning experiences are through observation and sound. The first month the infant will be sleeping and eating most of the time. Gentleness through touch and by singing and talking will convey to the baby that he is happily welcome. Because his eyes are not able to focus for the first few weeks, it is difficult for him to follow objects clearly. He does follow light and objects that make noises, as long as they are soft and gentle sounds.

The newborn is extremely sensitive to light and sound. (If the newborn is not startled by a loud noise, such as a door slam, a pediatrician should be consulted about the possibility of a hearing impairment.) Coming from a prolonged period spent in a protected, dark, and quiet place into a bright and noisy world, he can only differentiate shades of gray and white. During the first weeks the baby begins to separate colors and they hold absolute fascination for him. Think about how you felt the very first time you saw something that surprised and delighted you suddenly appear in front of you. The world should be a safe, colorful, and happy place for the baby. From these early exposures to light, color, and sound the baby makes continuous adjustments every day to the environment.

Gradually he learns to focus his eyes and attention on the designs on ceilings and walls. As he approaches four weeks old, he is more aware of his surroundings and as his eyes focus, the objects in his crib become more important. A colorful mobile, with or without music box, is pleasurable. He enjoys responding to the rattle and to your smiles and sounds. He turns to sounds. He laughs at the rattle. He makes gurgling sounds. He reacts to music.

The baby responds and turns toward light or sound. He stares happily at a colorful object moving slowly in the wind. He responds to the sounds of people, telephone rings, and doorbells. He looks into Mother's and Father's faces and smiles. The baby will move his arms and legs, but cannot grasp or hold on to objects for long. His eyes are moving and learning to coordinate so that he can follow a toy in front of his eyes moving slowly.

During the first few weeks talk, sing, and be in close contact with your baby. You will watch him as he begins to focus on objects and smile. You will notice when he makes new sounds, reacts to you or another person, or follows lights. You will see him respond to noise and footsteps. While changing or washing the baby is a perfect time to communicate gently.

Several toys have proven valuable for the baby's early development and are recommended choices to begin your BABY GIFT LIST. A good investment is a colorful mobile, especially one that can be changed with different objects. You might like to consider making one as well. (See the bibliography for books to assist you in creating toys.) A rattle is a good device to use as an "attention-getter." Other items to consider may be new and less familiar, such as a versatile crib bar which allows you to add and take off different objects. Perfect all-time favorites include soft, washable animals as they are enjoyable for the baby to look at and are satisfying to grasp and hug. During the first months, you will want to

consider a musical toy, such as a soft animal with a music box inside. Bath toys are fun and can be as simple as a sponge and don't forget the "rubber ducky."

Toy Suggestions for Babies in their First Six Weeks

A ctive
C reative
E ducational

Would Like	Received		Toy	Type
_____	_____	1.	Mobile	(E)
_____	_____	2.	Rattle (sounds plus)	(A)
_____	_____	3.	Stuffed toy (1-3) crib, kitchen, travel	(AC)
_____	_____	4.	Bath toy (1-3) floating rubber squeeze toy, sponge	(A)
_____	_____	5.	Crib and playpen toys	(A)
_____	_____	6.	Music box	(C)

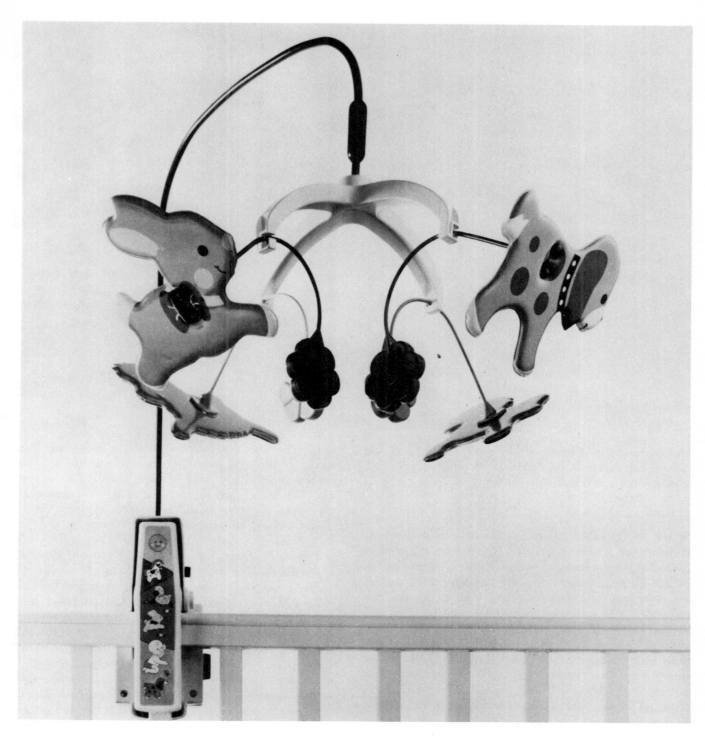

1. Mobile

A baby is attracted to color and movement. As a baby lies in the crib, its eyes focus on what is near. A simple and enjoyable first attention-getter is a mobile. The mobile is a series of objects held together by a bar and extended cords. The baby intently watches the hanging objects (figures of animals, fairy story characters, flowers, small balls, and other items) as they are moved around by air currents, and will enjoy the mobile for several months.

A variety of ready-made mobiles exist. More expensive varieties feature a music box that winds up and plays as the objects move around. An innovation to the mobile is one made by Semper. Its adjustable bar allows for different objects to be safely attached. The mobile can be changed by using other objects on the same bar. Put the regular mobile at the foot of the crib so baby can see it. For variety, you can trade mobiles with other parents.

You want to be sure to remove mobiles from the infant's grasp when he can sit up and extend his reach, since he will immediately pull down the delicate moving parts. The mobile can be moved away to another part of the room and left up as an interesting room decoration.

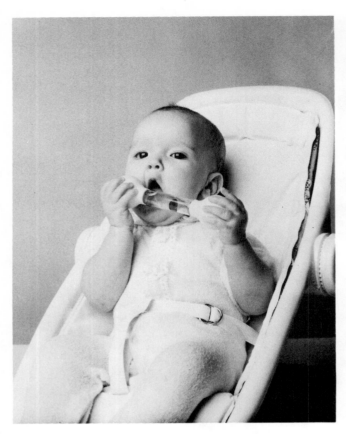

Mobiles made by Chicco, Child Craft, Child Guidance (CBS), Eden (musical), Fisher-Price, and Semper are among some you can choose ($10-30).

2. Rattles

Rattles get the baby's attention and have a calming effect. Perfect when a baby is irritated. He will be attracted to the soft shaking sound and will turn to it. Different rattles exist at all price ranges. Be sure to keep rattles washed and away from heat. Buying a rattle from a company you trust can assure you that it meets toy safety standards and will not fall apart. A rattle is useful when the baby is being changed as it can be calming and stimulating at the same time. Call the baby's name or use the rattle gently as you sing to him. Don't overuse the rattle, or any toy for that matter, or the baby will lose interest. Some rattles are designed for very young infants and come with teething rings and others are perfect for the older baby. Rattles come in a variety of materials, including plastic, wood, and cloth. Playskool makes a series of Happy Rattles with butterflies or bees enclosed in a safe transparent covering. Rattles are made by Ambi, Brio, Chicco, Fisher-Price, Kiddie-Kraft, and Plakie ($1-8).

3. Stuffed Toys

Soft animals are collected from the time of the birth announcement (or before) to adolescence and beyond. They are forever and consistently popular among chil-dren. The baby will receive several of these which can easily be displayed on shelves. Special soft toys are made for the infant so you want to shop carefully for this type. The "baby proof" soft toys are soft, cuddly, washable, and very safe. The toys should not clutter the crib. One is adequate for use as a visual object.

Stuffed toys grow with the baby. They will be held, put in their mouth, thrown, talked to, and generally enjoyed for a long time. They are fun to take on car trips and give you something convenient to amuse the baby with if he gets cranky. Babies fuss for attention and a combination of parent and soft panda is an endless treat. If you feel free to talk with the soft panda, later on the baby will also. You set the example for the baby and he will watch you for cues. A great deal of easy language will be communicated by an imaginative toddler who enjoys talking with his soft panda toy. The softness gives stimulation and comfort. Be sure that these first soft toys you buy are made for infants. Invest in a teddy bear which makes a "ma" sound when turned over, if you want a special gift. Softables by R. Dakin, and soft toys by Russ Berrie, Eden, Gund, Kamar, and Steiff are recommended ($5-30).

4. Bath Toys

Every day when baby has a bath is a perfect time for fun and pleasure. Using a sponge to squeeze water gently over the skin is fun and makes the baby laugh. Floating ducks, fish, or other bath toys are fun when you squeeze

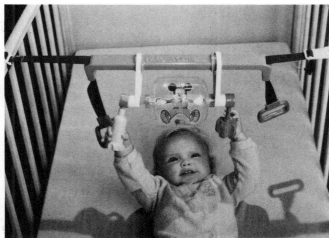

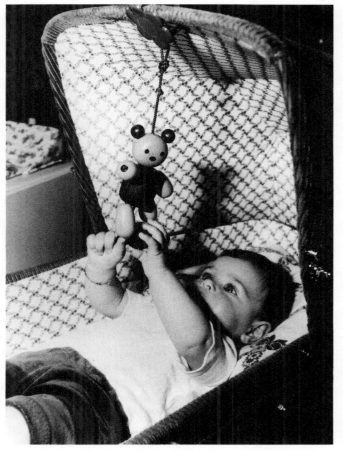

them and surprise the baby with a soft sound. Bath time should always be an enjoyable and relaxing time and can be more so with the addition of a few simple toys. A wide variety of bath toys exist in many shapes and styles. Some are made by Ambi, Child Guidance (CBS), Fisher-Price, Flakie, and Protecto. ($2-10).

5. Crib and Play Pen Toys

While the baby is lying in a crib or playpen you can introduce several other soft toys made specifically to serve as early stimulators. Many babies receive first year toys as gifts. I recommend that you review the list of suggested toys for the first year and not overdo your supply, such as three clutch balls, two mirrors, or too many of any one type of toy. It is variety that you want to stimulate all of the senses and promote growth. Try to maintain a balance of different types in each of the Active, Creative, and Educational categories. A number of excellent items are produced by Ambi, Chicco, Childcraft, Child Guidance (CBS), Fisher-Price, Johnson and Johnson, Kiddi-Kraft, and Semper. Each has a full line of first year toys ($3-15).

6. Music Box

An old-fashioned and still delightful custom is putting a music box in the baby's room. If the baby frets before it sleeps, often the music will relax and soothe her. Simple ones, safely sealed inside a soft toy, are available, or you may want to place one out of reach on a nearby shelf. You have many to choose from including those in separate boxes, mounted inside lamps, or connected to mobiles. Select a music box with care as with anything else you buy. When buying a gift for a new baby you can almost always be sure a music box will be a welcome and novel gift. Some large cities have stores specializing in the many different kinds of music boxes. Many toy stores also carry them, especially those of the stuffed toy types. Among the musical stuffed toys you can select from are those of Atlanta, R. Dakin, Eden, and Gund ($5-10).

SIX WEEKS TO SIX MONTHS

Babies Expand Play from Six Weeks to Six Months

You will enjoy watching the rapid changes and development of your infant during this period. She lifts her head and holds it up when lying on her stomach, and follows movement with more concentration. The baby will be smiling more, making many new sounds, and will watch intently as you move about. Talk and sing to the baby as much as possible.

The baby watches her fingers and puts them into her mouth; grasps a teething ring and swings it about; puts soft animals into her mouth: and experiments between playing with toes, fingers, and objects. The baby likes to explore everything so this is a time to be careful about what is left within grasp of the inquisitive baby. She will watch objects such as her mobile for long periods of time and will be delighted if the objects are changed once in awhile. When she fusses for attention you can distract and amuse her with a simple toy.

The changes are rapid in the first half year and each day you will notice added skills. The baby pays attention to its hands and feet and will shift attention from finger to soft teething ring and toy. She starts to differentiate between near and far. She will grasp a small object, the edge of the blanket, or whatever she can hold on to. Toys become more fascinating as the baby can hold toys and bring them to her mouth. She loves to look at a mirror and smile and make sounds. She will use both hands as she

needs to for balance. Babies like toys that can do something such as make a sound or movement. They need to be exposed to a variety of textures. Balance is the key to early stimulation—hard, soft, plastic, wood, and different materials. She will reach out and delight in games such as peek-a-boo when with responsive, familiar persons. She laughs easily and responds to people.

Toys during this period teach important basics. Your child will learn shapes, sizes, colors, and sounds. All of these stimuli assist your child in normal growth. They are important experiences which will enhance later learning. (If your child does not respond to sound, consult your pediatrician.) Play is one of the most important ways to learn the condition of your child and will give your child the basics of learning.

7. Soft Ball

Babies love to reach out and try to hold on to objects. A large soft foam ball with specially designed handles make it easier to hold. Balls are great fun. The ball will be thrown and received back with delighted squeals. Be sure it is not too heavy and large enough to prevent being put into her mouth. As the baby is able to sit up later, balls continue to be fun so they are a good investment. You will be able to find a variety of balls in many sizes, colors, and coverings to select from in the collections of Brimm-Shield, Child Guidance (CBS), Fisher-Price, R. Dakin, Kiddi-Kraft, Steiff, and Trupa ($3.50-10).

8. Cloth Blocks

Cloth blocks are a wonderful way to start learning about square shapes and have fun at the same time. The blocks are made of foam with a variety of coverings. Often they have pictures on the sides. They can be picked up. Some blocks are covered with vinyl and can be easily washed. Blocks are enjoyed both alone and together with you. In

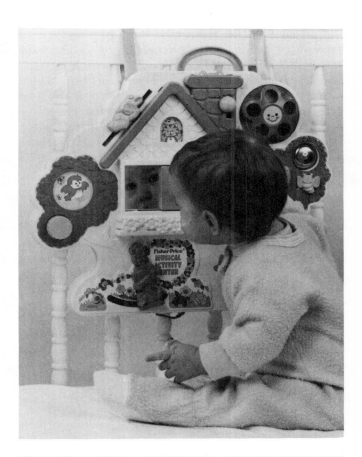

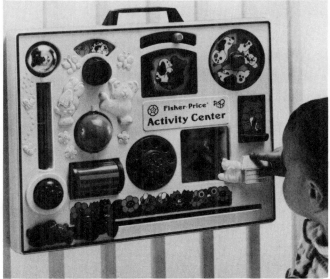

the beginning babies hold them and push them around. Later they will learn to stack them. They have many possibilities as they grow. They love to see the top one fall off and make the whole stack tumble. The choices for blocks include Child Guidance (CBS), Fisher-Price and Little Tikes ($5-14).

9. Teether

As your baby is teething and continues to suck she will also need to soothe and exercise her gums. She can do

that best with a sturdy and appealing teething ring. Babies enjoy having a teether and find it very satisfying. The choices available are plastic, rubber, or wood. They should be easy to hold. Plakie offers a full line plus you can select from Chicco, Fisher-Price, Johnson and Johnson, Playcraft, Playskool, and Semper ($2-10).

10. Crib Gym

As the baby begins to grasp, he will seek items to hold, push, and pull. A number of excellent crib gyms are available and will be used by the baby even before he is sitting up. They become more entertaining as the baby enters the fourth month. The crib gym is a securely mounted bar with interesting objects safely suspended within reach. It will delight the baby lying on its back for long periods of time. The range of gyms offered are from simple to more complicated. You will want to look and compare the choices. Those from Ambi, Child Guidance (CBS), Fisher-Price, Kiddi-Kraft, and Semper are recommended ($10-30).

11. Mirror

Babies love to look at themselves and carry on a conversation. They enjoy the opportunity to gaze at their eyes or noses for a long time. They should be allowed to follow their fancy whenever they want to study their images. This is one of the important early self-image devices which can help formulate positive feelings about oneself. Mirrors must be unbreakable and the edges completely enclosed. Have it nearby to use when changing diapers, talking, or changing clothes. Ones that are safe are Child Guidance (CBS), Fisher-Price, Johnson and Johnson, Kiddi-Kraft (can be suspended from its frame), and Semper (suspended on wheels) ($10-20).

SIX MONTHS TO ONE YEAR

Baby's Changes from Six Months to Twelve Months

Your baby is now rapidly growing, doubling his birth weight, and learning many new skills and abilities. He will want to grasp your hands and lift his head. He likes to roll over and begin creeping, crawling, and wriggling about. You will have to pay close attention to what gets put into his mouth and where he moves himself, as everything happens quickly. As the dexterity of the hands increase, your baby will be putting things into his mouth and experimenting. He likes pulling socks and booties off. He enjoys taking things apart and putting them together.

He likes to play games and make imitative sounds. Remember during this period to play finger and peek-a-boo games, enjoying the baby's responses. Don't forget to take pictures during this first year. Photographs taken of the baby and the objects he plays with will bring both of you enjoyment and delight in the future. A scrap book of pictures and remembrances of the baby is fun to keep.

During these six months, the baby is moving along at a rapid physical pace. You will see him move from standing up to being able to walk holding on with two

Toy Suggestions for Babies in their First Six Weeks

A ctive
C reative
E ducational

Would Like	Received	Toy	Type
_____	_____	7. Soft Ball	(A)
_____	_____	8. Cloth Blocks	(C)
_____	_____	9. Teether	(A)
_____	_____	10. Crib Gym	(AE)
_____	_____	11. Mirror	(C)
_____	_____	12. Link Rings	(A)

12. Link Ring

Shapes that link up are made of preformed durable plastic and allow the baby to easily pull them apart and put them together. They enhance eye-hand coordination and provide a single, yet enjoyable challenge to the curious mind. They are among the most useful toys available for the six month old. This toy is intriguing and provides busy fingers something fun to try to pull apart. Good link rings are made by Kiddi-Kraft and Playskool ($2-5).

hands. He will be able to go from lying down to being able to sit up. He changes from being an infant with no language to a baby who has the ability to build, push and pull objects, grasp, and hold onto things. He now has the ability to crawl.

The baby's language develops at a rapid rate from the first sounds of "mama" to several words in short sentences. He is able to identify sounds, look for things, and demand attention. You will also notice that some-

times your child is shy around strangers, but when he knows somebody he will react with great joy and animation. He has difficulty making a separation from his mother.

The baby likes to make things happen with his toys. He is delighted when bells ring or wheels turn as a result of his actions. He likes to play games like looking for things that disappear. He has learned to stack boxes, turn pages, and reach for things. He also does not like to stop while playing and will fuss profusely. He enjoys "reading" (hearing words read aloud) with an adult and loves to turn pages. This activity with baby close in your lap is one of the greatest joys of being a parent or grandparent. Chil-

dren have an enormous interest in hearing and responding. They have to be held and talked with. Talking and singing with your baby continues to be important throughout the early years.

As your baby is approaching one year, you will see him sitting up, standing while holding on, and increasing his mobility. As teeth have come in during this period, the baby's teething ring is well-used and satisfying. You will have many things to pick up as the fun thing to do is drop items and watch mommy and daddy pick them up. You will want to "baby-proof" the house as the baby doesn't know that objects are breakable or hazardous.

Toy Suggestions for Babies Six Months to One Year

A ctive
C reative
E ducational

Would Like	Received	Toy	Type
_____	_____	13. Assorted kitchen items	(A)
_____	_____	14. Flutter balls	(A)
_____	_____	15. Large puzzles	(E)
_____	_____	16. Nesting blocks	(A)
_____	_____	17. Push/Pull toys	(A)
_____	_____	18. Shape sorting box	(E)
_____	_____	19. Soft dolls	(C)
_____	_____	20. Stacking tower	(E)

13. Assorted Kitchen Items

Someone always asks me, "Can't you use simple objects like kitchen utensils?" I always say, "Yes." The items available are relatively inexpensive and you might consider buying several six or nine inch plastic bowls, plastic measuring cups, and a sponge. Somehow, when all else fails, these most common items seem to do the trick for a fretting baby who wants something interesting to do. As the baby grows the bowls will continue to be useful in many ways. Water play is always fun and they use their imagination with the bowls, cups, pots, pans, and other simple, available, and real household items throughout the next two years. Be sure you decide which items you want to be for baby and keep them separate and clean ($5-10).

14. Flutter Balls

A large clear plastic ball with a form of a butterfly, bee, or other object inside to move about. The shape captures the attention and helps the baby learn to focus. The ball shape allows the baby to move it about and make it respond. This ball encourages active play. Fisher-Price offers one as does Playskool ($10).

15. Large Puzzles

Some excellent puzzles offer a picture with a few pieces cut out. Some almost one year old babies enjoy putting pieces down, especially if lines are drawn on the board for clues as to where to put each piece. Available through Lauri, Playskool, and School Zone ($5-10).

16. Nesting Blocks

Another enjoyable activity for the baby is learning to stack and fit things inside each other. These blocks offer a learning activity as the baby puts the plastic cups inside each other and sees how they fit. These provide good practice in eye-hand coordination. This is a toy the baby will use for a long time. Later, the child will fill them with sand, water, or whatever is at hand, and invent new uses. Ambi, Brio, and Johnson and Johnson are possible choices ($5-10).

17. Push/Pull Toys

As the baby learns to move about, he enjoys pushing or pulling an object that moves along the floor. You can begin with a push/pull toy the baby can use from a sitting position. Remember, occasionally the toy can get to your ears after awhile. Once babies start to walk and move, these push/pull toys are a great way for them to announce their efforts. They enjoy the response of others to their activity. Brio, Child Guidance (CBS), Fisher-Price, and Playskool are among the possible choices ($10-20).

18. Shape Sorting Box

The shapes are geometric ones that fit through openings cut out of the top of a large square box. The baby enjoys putting the shapes through holes and makes happy sounds as he drops them in. This is a toy that can be too difficult for your baby at first, so don't worry if your child is not initially interested. Watch what happens four or six weeks later. Each child will select their own best toy, so have different ones available to give them the greatest choice possible. Shape-sorting boxes are offered by Ambi, Child Guidance (CBS), Fisher-Price, Playskool, and Semper ($10-15).

19. Soft Dolls

Many beautiful dolls have been created to satisfy all possibilities. Recently, manufacturers have produced many excellent dolls that are perfect for babies as they are soft, simple, washable, and cuddly to play with. They have no buttons to come loose and have faces sewn on with soft fabric bodies. The seams are tight and the stuffing is made of quality, washable materials. Choose from those by Child Guidance (CBS), R. Dakin, Fisher-Price, Gund, Kamar, and Steiff ($5-70).

20. Stacking Tower

A wonderful toy to teach a number of skills—colors, shapes, sizes, and numbers. This toy is versatile and will be enjoyed for a long time. Colored donut shaped rings made of strong molded plastic are stacked on a dowel. Stacking towers also come in wood. You will find this is a toy that grows with the child and has many possibilities. Offered by Ambi, Eichorn, Fisher-Price, Johnson and Johnson, and Playskool ($5-15).

As you explore any toy you are thinking of obtaining for your child, keep these types in mind. I have discussed the different skills you want to develop to assist your baby with learning. During the first year, all of the senses are bombarded. As your baby learns through his senses, his sight, hearing, taste, touch, and smell expand. His imagination increases dramatically and you will be part of his experimentation and creative fun.

During the last six months of the first year, he is happiest with toys that allow him to discover his abilities, such as grasping with fingers and seeing relationships between what he does and the responses he gets. The toys which allow for action, creative play, and education will bring hours of pleasure and support for his fullest development.

EXAMPLE OF PARENT INFORMATION MATERIAL

Visual Display and **Mirror Marvels** for the Johnson & Johnson Baby Products and The Play and Learning Booklets

A Play and Learning Booklet contains suggestions for play activities with the **Visual Display Toy.** But all babies are different. Some will enjoy a certain game before the time indicated: others might prefer to wait a few weeks or months. And many of the games will be enjoyed for far longer than the age range suggested. As he grows older, your baby might like to play with familiar games as well as new ones, especially when you add interesting variations.

One more thing…Games are almost always more fun when they involve conversation. Talk to your baby while you play, tell him what you are doing and why. This will help him understand language, and draw connections between words, actions and objects. In addition, talking helps gain and hold your baby's attention.

Let your baby know how much fun you are having when you play, by smiling, hugging him, laughing, and generally carrying on in a playful manner.

The young baby explores primarily with her eyes, and spends most of her waking hours looking at her immediate surroundings. So use the Visual Display to brighten up her crib or cradle. When in her bed, your newborn's favorite position is lying on her stomach or back, with her legs drawn up and head turned to the side. If you set up the panels on her mattress she can look at them when she's alone. During these early months, she can best focus on objects about 8 to 12 inches from her eyes.

You might first introduce the panel containing the target, a girl's face, and butterfly. The Visual Display panels are designed to match your baby's growing interest in visual exploration. A very young baby is most attracted to pictures of simple shapes which contrast sharply against the background. She tends to look at the outlines of the shape rather than at the center. As she grows, your baby will look more at the center of the picture and become increasingly interested in complexity and detail. She begins to look at the very simple pictures for shorter periods of time and concentrates longer on the more complex pictures found on the other panels.

Even though the simplest set of panels will probably be your newborn's favorite, she enjoys looking at the other panels as well. After a while, you may notice your baby pays less and less attention to the set of panels containing the target. Babies like variety, and this means it's time for a change.

If you substitute the sun, red and yellow "arrows," and cat, you'll see a renewed interest. In fact, it's a good idea to change her "Crib Pictures" fairly frequently, sometimes using a new set of panels, other times re-introducing a familiar one. After a few hours' absence, even the simplest panel seems new again.

Mirror Marvels—Babies are especially fascinated by mirrors. So add mirror games to your playtimes together. Play with the mirror continues to interest babies for many months.

Sit or hold the mirror panel in front of your baby's face so he can stare at the "other" baby, reach for his image, pat his friend, or even bestow a kiss, especially with your encouragement. You can take a more active part by pointing at his reflection and saying, "I see John. Can you see John?" Then hold the mirror so both of your faces are visible. "Now I see Daddy, too?" While your baby looks at himself, point to and name the different parts of his face. Or with both of you looking, point to his facial features, then your own.

Of course, at this age your baby enjoys exploring the Visual Display in his own ways when he plays alone: working the hinges back and forth, trying to pick the pictures off the panel, talking to his friend in the mirror, maybe even putting the edge of the panel in his mouth. The mouth, like the hands, is a sense organ, and your baby learns about size, shape, and texture by mouthing. When his Visual Display becomes dirty from all this handling, just wipe off the panels with soapy water using a soft cloth and rinse well.

CHAPTER FIVE

Toys for Toddlers- One to Three Years

Think of all the ways you can amuse, educate, and enjoy your growing child. Remember you are the best guide to your child's selection of toys, play and educational opportunities. You will want to continue to expand your understanding of the child's development, as the child will be greatly influenced by what you do. You should want to observe your child at play, to learn what he or she can do at different points in time, and how they react to toys and to other children.

Sally Jones wanted to do all she could for her toddler. She bought many toys that appealed to her. But when she got home and introduced them to her child, Ryan, he just looked at them and turned away to play with the cat. Sally was feeling frustrated and uncertain about what to do. We sat down and talked about it. Sally learned several things about Ryan that have helped her understand and play with him better. She learned through her reading about the child's natural interests and energy cycles each day. She learned how to introduce toys one at a time. She learned ways to increase her patience with Ryan. Sally and her husband Bob also learned to store Ryan's toys, and not let his play space get cluttered with too many objects (which can be frustrating when a child wants to explore in an open area). She realized that Ryan wasn't rejecting her, he was just more fascinated with a live creature and its responses. She began to use the toys she bought selectively. She increased the amount of time she spent talking with Ryan. Bob learned with Sally about where Ryan was in his natural developmental growth

pattern. They began to play with him more, talking, and getting his interest. They then showed him a puzzle if he really wanted a quiet activity. When Rayn discovered how the pieces fit together, he was so delighted he emptied the frame and did the puzzle again and again.

We discussed the changes at this age, which are that at one year the baby has grown to about half again its birth length and triple its weight at birth. Her skills have increased as she is gaining control of the head and body, arms and legs. She has many new abilities, and is rapidly crawling and sometimes walking.

She loves to crawl and will climb on furniture easily. Her attention span is not great. She is mostly interested in watching, exploring, moving, knocking things over to see reactions. She is making new sounds and creates words like "bye, ma ma, da da, dat." Her understanding of words has expanded and she learns your tone and meaning and is aware of your feelings.

She has developed many skills and loves to play games (patty-cake, peek-a-boo, clapping to music). People and animals fascinate. She loves to make sounds and act silly. She wants to laugh and giggle, and loves to be surprised. Parents fascinate the toddler and remain in this enviable position for the first three years of the child's life. Parents will continue to be the child's best "play mate" for many years. Adults often enjoy being silly with little children. If they will allow themselves to talk and behave in funny ways they will hold the appreciative attention of the child.

The toddler is very much attached to the people closest to him or her. The relationships formed at these earliest months are basic ones for emotional attachment of the child. Having fun with her parents is a delightful experience. The basic development of the emotional connection and the friendship between toddler and her parents allows her to move into the larger world of friends and other players. Parents who play and respond are more important to the child's health and well-being than any toy or object which can be bought at any price.

Understanding your child's moods will help a lot. Some days your child will be stubborn and fussy, sometimes she will be quiet, sometimes very active, or sometimes very intent on examining objects closely and sometimes not showing any interest. You will see her moods reflected in the activities she selects.

Time has no importance to a child. She is absorbed in the activity of the moment, whether it is pouring water, rolling a ball, playing with a doll, or watching a pinwheel spinning.

As a toddler, she begins to explore her physical abilities: she pulls herself up to sitting; if supported, she will pull herself up to standing; and will walk about holding onto the hands of others. It is not wise to force a child to walk before she is ready; to put too much weight on her legs before her bones are sufficiently strong to support her may cause problems later.

The world is opening up. It is hers to explore and discover, but she needs to be carefully watched. She has a natural curiosity and, if not carefully supervised, can injure herself badly. For example, she will open bottles or boxes without knowing the nature of what she is touching or tasting. Anything that is potentially dangerous should be placed well out of reach of the child or be in locked cabinets.

Here are some activities that are frequently observed:

The toddler loves to play with household objects such as dustpans, brooms, plastic dishes, pots and pans, and cups.

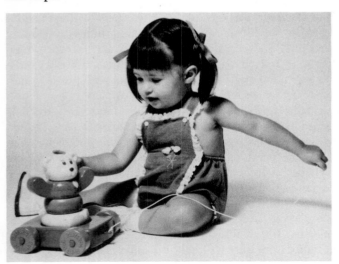

The toddler imitates the actions of others and tries them out for herself, drinking from a cup, talking on a telephone, hammering with a hammer.

The toddler sees differences between herself and others and between objects.

The toddler loves to experiment with objects to see what they do. She will notice some things bounce, other things make noises, other things light up, etc.

The toddler loves to fit things together, stacking blocks, toys, and cups are some of the objects toddlers like to assemble.

Toddlers enjoy quiet play with things to look at. They love picture books and to talk about the pictures, to point at them, and learn new words.

They like to listen to music. They like to imitate sounds you make and try to understand what is being said. Records and tapes will be imitated as well, so they are nice to play to your child.

They are excited when they recognize their favorite toys or animals in the books they look at.

They love to travel and go to different places. It is a good idea to take a few favorite toys along in a bag when you travel. Be sure to always use the car safety seat and seatbelts according to instructions when in the car.

Toddlers like:
to squeeze objects (like sponges)
to play with water
to dig in sand
to build things
to create art
to look at and paste up pictures
to take walks and go on rides
to throw things
to play with animals

As play is essential for learning, toddlers will be acting out their feelings, fantasies, and experiences during play.

They will engage in parallel play at this age, playing alongside of other children, sometimes doing the same activity, but at their own pace. However they do learn from each other about ways to play. This learning continues as children expand their experiences and understandings. They follow each other, eager to get responses. Although they enjoy contact with other playmates they will be possessive of their own toys and may fuss sometimes if another child grabs one of them. If your child is aggressive and tends to pull things away from other children, help her to understand sharing and cooperative play. Toddlers get into fights very easily, but these are soon forgotten. Have sufficient objects for them to play with individually and to share as they can.

This is the time for parents to connect playgroups with each other, and for children to begin to socialize. If you notice your child is shy or withdrawn, encourage her to play with puppets and dolls. Slowly she will play with one child at a time. It won't always go smoothly, but it will be a good learning experience for the toddler and the parents.

Toddlers quickly gain muscle control and soon walk, run, bounce, jump, throw, climb, and dance. They love to talk and sing. They will continue to explore and expand their understanding of the world, with loving encouragement and support from the adults around them.

You can organize your toddler's playthings into the following categories:

Active for physical development, eye-hand
   coordination, and strength
Creative for developing or expanding spontaneity and
   self-expression
Educational for learning and stimulating mental
   development, thoughts and skills

Many toys have been created for the toddler. Each year these toys are improved and refined. We are very fortunate to have available so many excellent products. If these are used selectively, with appropriate attention to the child's needs and interests, you will succeed in the goal of developing the child's mind, sense of joy, excitement about life, and of having fun alone and with other children.

You may have created toys for your child when she was an infant. You can still enrich your child's available playthings by making items which will teach skills such as eye-hand coordination, creativity, and physical development. There is a great deal of satisfaction that can be derived from making your own toys and it will enhance your role as the child's first teacher.

The growing child is happily engaged in doing, exploring and learning new words. Play and the discovery of playthings is a creative activity. She comes to learn about cause and effect (she hits a mallet and a peg falls into the hole, or pushes a button and a small doll pops up. She turns a handle and music plays and a jack-in-the-box pops up, etc). She delights in seeing what she can do. So will you.

A ctive
C reative
E ducational

Suggestions for Toddlers 1—2 Years

Would Like	Received	Toy	Type
————	————	1. Art supplies	(C)
————	————	2. Balls	(A)
————	————	3. Bath toys	(A)
————	————	4. Blocks	(A)
————	————	5. Books	(E)
————	————	6. Dolls	(C)
————	————	7. Pail and shovel	(A)
————	————	8. Pounding sets	(A)
————	————	9. Push/pull toys	(A)
————	————	10. Puzzles	(E)
————	————	11. Ride-on toys	(A)
————	————	12. Ring stack	(E)
————	————	13. Shape-sorting box	(E)
————	————	14. Stuffed animals	(C)
————	————	15. Surprise box	(E)

Note: These first 15 are also used over the next year and modified by the child as he or she grows more confident and skilled.

1. Art Supplies

Creativity begins early and, if nurtured, becomes an enjoyable part of the child's experiences. Art is a re-creation of what is seen or thought. Children have their own unique way of seeing and feeling, and when they create a picture, don't ask them, "What is it?" because you may not be able to figure out what they have drawn. Instead ask, "Can you tell me about your picture?" If you respond in a positive way they will feel encouraged and be happy creating new pictures and art objects. Their work can be done with crayons, finger paint, paints, clay, or cut-and-paste collages. Also, coloring books, fat crayons, or magic markers should be included. You can find art supplies at toy or stationery stores. You may want to color or paint along with your child, and the child will enjoy your company once in a while. Don't worry if you haven't done it for years; the memories will come back once you have a crayon in your hand. You may want to obtain an easel (with one or two surfaces (blackboard or cork is often found on the second side) and should be able to find paper and other supplies easily. Art supplies are made by Binney and Smith, Galt, Kenner (Play-Doh) and Reeves ($1-5).

2. Balls

Balls offer a lot of play time activity for developing children and will be among their favorite playthings for a long time. Balls come in many sizes and colors and they offer many different activities: rolling, bouncing, throwing, and catching are all important skills for youngsters' coordination and dexterity. You can choose the size and color. They are among the most expensive and fun toys you can buy. You do have to be cautious about balls in the house, though, but plush, soft, light balls are less likely to cause damage. The hard rubber or beach balls are better played with outdoors. You can make or buy a soft fabric clutch ball or texture ball. Since balls come in all sizes, you will want to have a variety: tennis balls, rubber balls, beach ball and light hollow balls. You and your toddler can have a lot of enjoyment rolling a ball to each other and, out of doors, throwing it gently. He will also find it delightful to play with balls with his siblings or friends, for they make good activities for every child. You can make a hoop from a large waste basket to throw a soft ball through as a fun rainy-day indoor activity.

Varied balls are offered by Parker (Nerf Ball), Atlanta, Barr, Brimm-Shield, Hallmark, Kathe Kruse, Playskool (Flutterball), Preston, and Wells ($.50-$8).

3. Bath Toys

Bath time is one of the most enjoyable times of the day for the child and can be even more so with a few water-safe playthings.. Select a toy or two at a time. These can include balls, rubber animals (The Immortal Rubber Ducky), and other floating toys, such as boats. Manufacturers are rather ingenious in this area and have created a

good variety of floating toys. If you want to indulge in one of the activity boxes for the tub wall, it will keep the child busy pouring water and making wheels turn. It's a good idea to 'rotate' the activity box, take it out for a while, store it and then put it back. Children get bored if something is around too much. Washcloth puppets make an added surprise and are good for sneaking in a cleaning up.

Bath toys are made by Battat, Chicco, Child Guidance (CBS), Fisher-Price, Lakeside and Mattel ($3-$12).

4. Blocks

One item that children find hundreds of uses for throughout their childhood are blocks. They offer children flexibility and creativity. Children build, create and use their imagination with blocks. They will find uses such as building structures and knocking them over. They will make things that fit the play of the moment: tunnels, carports, airports, farms, and houses. Several excellent books have been written on the use of blocks in the play of children (see bibliography). Blocks are a basic item in most nursery schools and child care programs. Children play with blocks from the toddler stage through kindergarten and later. A young professor of English who had completed two novels told me that blocks were his all-time favorite toys because he could use his imagination to the utmost when playing with them and he felt they had a special influence on his own creative process as a child. Many other teens and adults shared these experiences.

Start with small wooden, cardboard, or sponge blocks that are easy for the one-year-old to grasp. Look for blocks with alphabet letters and pictures. At first the toddler will make small stacks, but, as she learns and grows, will create more elaborate structures.

As the toddler approaches two or two and a half, you will want to give her some larger blocks: wooden, cardboard, or foam are good materials varying in weight. Many types of blocks are available on the market, so you will have a good variety to choose from.

This is another activity in which you and your child can have a lot of fun playing together. Just get down on the floor and your child will be delighted.

Blocks are made by Amtoy, Bandai, Fisher-Price, Galt (soft and hard blocks), International Play, Little Tikes, Mattel, Norok, Palo, Playskool, Semper, and TC Timber ($7-$25).

5. Books

Certainly books are a very important part of playtime and learning of children, but they are often forgotten. Books are essential throughout the child's development. The first picture books with large colorful alphabet pictures, animals, or objects are enjoyed by children over and over again, especially if you read books aloud to them. Remember to talk about the stories. You will also find the toddler "reading" to her baby doll and stuffed animals.

You will find the choices are great in the area of first books with large pictures and colorful, washable pages. You will want to get books that match favorite dolls or toys the children play with such as Paddington Bear and others. Children love to hear stories while they are playing with a doll or toy. Books can be saved for the next child or given to other children and certainly make wonderful gifts. Publishers for young children include Abingdon, Crowell, Dinosaur, Dutton, Golden Books, Grosset & Dunlop, Harcourt Brace, Macmillan, Morrow, Price-Stern-Sloan, Random House, Viking, and Walker ($1-$6).

6. Dolls

From the time the child is a baby until she is a teenager, dolls will be an important part of her play. Fortunately many excellent dolls exist and are easily available for making a selection. You will want soft and cuddly dolls for the young child. As she gets older, you will have many more for her to enjoy. She will hold, cuddle, talk and play endlessly with these little friends. Dolls help boys and girls learn to socialize, take care of one another, and release emotions. You do not have to spend a lot of money for expensive collector dolls for the very young child. You can create your own soft dolls if you like to sew. The bibliography in the resources section offers many excellent books with directions on how to create dolls. Dolls are fun for children of all ages and they will allow creative play between children at different ages.

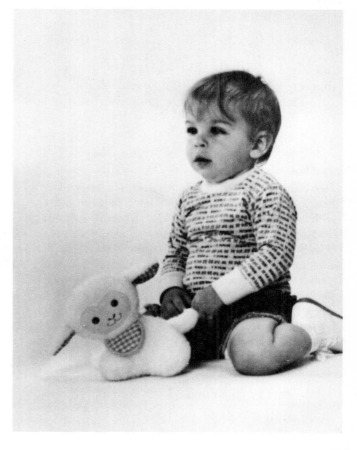

Many accessories go along with dolls, including clothes, beds, carriages, play sets, and other articles. Shop carefully for these as you can easily overdo it if you acquire too many things too soon for the young child. Keeping things simple is best for the toddler. Once the child is walking easily, a sturdy doll carriage is fun for outside play. Putting "dolly" to bed when the child is ready for bedtime can assist in the bedtime ritual and will help both you and the tired toddler.

Dolls are created by Amtoy, Aviva Hasbro, Badger, Brio-Scanditoy, Effanbee, Eugene, Fisher-Price, Goldenberger, Hasbro, Horseman, Kamar, Marlon Creations, Mattel, Small World Toys, Stupsi (Anderson-Swazy), and Uneeda ($5-$30).

7. Pail and Shovel

Old favorites are sometimes forgotten, with all of the glamorous toys available. Basics are important because they do not lose in style or in value. The child needs quiet time to dig, and play in dirt or sand and water. A shovel and pail offer the child objects to use when doing these things and something to carry the dirt, sand or water in from place to place. Establish an area in your yard that will not interfere with your growing plants or other places you do not want messed up by this free-form play. If you do not have a space at home, create time for this activity at the park or in a clean sandbox. A child needs some place where he can make a mess safely and not be scolded. He needs to dig and get dirty for the fun of it. This is a natural part of childhood and a constructive one at that. If the child works it out in the garden he will feel better and relate to taking care of things indoors without fussing. These items will be the least expensive of the toys you buy and will be used for many fun-filled hours. A pail and shovel teaches the child many tangible skills.

Manufacturers for these items are Battat, International Playthings, and Small World Toys ($2-$6).

8. Pounding Sets

The toddler delights in seeing the results of her actions. She likes to do something that gets a response. What better fun is there than knocking a peg through a hole with a hammer? This toy also has the advantage of developing eye-hand coordination, while allowing the child to ventilate feelings. The noise will delight her and keep her busy for a long time. You may not always like the sound, so you can let her play with this item outdoors. The toy is made with extra strength and can definitely withstand the pounding of the toddler. You may want to try it too. Your child will laugh with delight. This is a toy she will use for some time to come, so you can be reassured a pounding set is a good investment. If your child does not like to hammer now, put it away and bring it out later for her birthday or another occasion. Children will vary as to the activities they enjoy and will change in their interests rapidly. Be patient with your child and be careful she does not use the hammer on anything break-

able. Parents must teach the proper use of any tools especially at playtime.

Pounding sets are made by Brio, Child Guidance (CBS), Fisher-Price, Galt, Micki (Anderson-Swazey), Palo, and Playskool ($5-$12).

9. Push/Pull Toys

The growing toddler is exploring the world rapidly, crawling, pulling herself up to sitting and standing, and finally walking. She will enjoy pushing and pulling objects along during this period. Some of these items are animals on a platform base attached to a string and equipped with wheels. She will grip the end of the string and learn to make the object move, discovering her actions result in a response from the toy. There is a big selection of push/pull toys available on the market today, of all shapes, sizes, colors, and actions. This is a toy that your child will enjoy for a long time.

A variation of the pull object on a string is the wooden rod attached to a large clear ball that is filled with small balls or figures. The rod toys make noise when pulled or pushed around the house, but children clearly enjoy this toy, watching the balls flip around and make sounds. If you can stand the racket, it is a good toy for your child.

A variety of companies make these items in this country and abroad so you have many to select from. Be sure the plastic is non-breakable and the balls cannot be swallowed if somehow the outer ball is broken.

Make sure the object is on a stand that is firmly secured and does not have parts that can break off. Throughout this section you will want to refer back to the section on safety and pointers on toy selection so that you will always think safety before you give your child any time.

Push/pull toys (on a stand or with a stick) are available from Ambi, Brio, Educalux (International Playthings), Eichhorn, Fisher-Price, Galt, Hasbro, Johnson and Johnson, Kouvalias, Papa Dons, Playskool, Tomy, and Walter Wood ($7-$20).

10. Puzzles

Children enjoy puzzles, from the first one made up of four or five pieces through the complicated jigsaw puzzles later on. You will find many good ones for the toddler. Puzzles should be clear and easy to follow. The first puzzle should be one that is a whole picture and is easy to lift in or out. Some puzzles have the picture underneath the pieces that come out. Puzzles are available in wood or cardboard and must be made of non-toxic colors. A puzzle with a knob on the pieces is useful and especially so for any child with a disability. Your child will have lots of experiences with puzzles in child care or nursery school so don't buy too many, as they tend to lose appeal quickly. You might swap puzzles with other parents to offer more variety to your children.

Puzzles are made by John Adams, Brio, Colorforms, Davis-Grabowski, Fisher-Price, Galt, Lauri, Marlon, Playskool, Simplex, (Battat) Small World Toys, and Willis $3-$10).

11. Ride-on Toys

The hobby horse has been a classic toy for many years and is available in many variations. At age one the child will enjoy getting on a ride-on toy and moving with it. If you have neighbors below you sensitive to noise, add carpeting to muffle the sound of the ride-on toy moving across the floor. Your child's feet must be able to touch the floor to make it possible for her to move around on it.

Ride-on toys have a variety of features, some of which make one a better buy than others. You will want to shop around for the one that is best for your child. You might prefer the kind she can sit on and rock. A hobby horse on a pole is great fun as the child begins to walk and move around easily. Also available is a train children can ride on, a truck, or an animal shape. It is nice if a storage area is included on the back and the child can pack items to take along on the "trip." If the rider makes sounds or has a horn or bell or other features, so much the better.

This is a toy that can be passed on to siblings or the children of friends, so it is best to buy a sturdy one to last through the wear and tear of daily play.

Ride-on toys are available from John Adams (Hobby Horse), Combi, Child Guidance (CBS), Galt, Grandads Toys, Fisher-Price, Hedstrom, Leismann America, Little Tikes, Micki, Playskool, Tomy, and Velvet Stable (Hobby Horse) ($10-$30).

12. Ring Stack

A toy that definitely has appeal for a toddler. A cone tops a base with six colored rings fitted over each other to form a rainbow of colors. The rings teach color, can be used as teethers, and can be moved around for various purposes by the child. Children enjoy sitting and putting the rings on the stack and rearranging them by dumping them and starting over. This toy is made by several manufacturers, so you can decide which one you prefer. Several versions exist that are made of wood. These are perhaps not as tasty as the plastic, but you may prefer them aesthetically. This is a very durable toy in plastic, so you can select the one that seems most appealing. Children when using the ring

stack are gaining skill in eye-hand coordination, perceiving shapes and relationships and learning numbers.

Ring stacks are made by Brio, Child Guidance (CBS), and Fisher-Price, ($4-$8).

13. Shape-Sorting Box

One of the kinds of toys that came through the work of Maria Montessori is the shape-sorting box, based on her observation that children loved fitting objects into similarly shaped receptacles. The box has been redesigned and simplified. Learning shapes, fitting objects, learning by trial and error, and other coordination skills are practiced. By matching the shape of the piece to the shape of the receptacle in the box, the child learns to discriminate and learns similarities and differences. Introduce one shape at a time at first. It is an excellent toy, as it is educational, holds a child's interest for a long time, and is easily learned.

The shape-sorting box is available from Ambi, Bandai, Brio, Childcraft, Child Guidance (CBS), Fisher-Price, Galt, International Playthings, Micki (Anderson-Swazey), and Palo Imports ($10-$15).

14. Stuffed Animals

Children have a great fondness for their favorite stuffed animals and other soft toys. These are items that can please a tired child, provide cuddly affection and offer a very excellent transition toy when mommy and daddy have to be elsewhere. A fussy child soon quiets down when a favorite teddy bear or stuffed animal is offered. Stuffed animals made of a good quality plush, carefully stuffed, and subjected to a thorough testing for safety are

widely available. You can be confident about most stuffed animals. There are many types to choose from, but don't overdo them as clutter just confuses the toddler. Putting the extra gifts away in a closet is a good idea until the child is ready for a new item. Rotating toys is a good idea for items lose their appeal with too much exposure. Favorites are Snoopy, lions, soft puppies, bears, and rabbits. If you find a child is allergic to stuffed animals, a leather-covered monkey will be a good substitute (Kamar and Sandy Vohrs Leather Zoo).

Stuffed animals are made by Animal Fair, Aviva Hasbro, Russ Berrie, California Stuffed Toys, Commonwealth, R. Dakin, Determined Productions, Fisher-Price, Fun Farm, Gund, Kamar, Playskool, Princess, Rushton, Small World Toys, Tomy, Trupa, and Charles Zadeh ($5-$25).

15. Surprise Box

An ingenious toy that allows the child to do something with switches and levers that make a door open (pull, push, turn) and figure pop up similar to a Jack-in-the-Box. The fun of this toy is it allows children to see the immediate effects of their actions and feel safe. They laugh and enjoy the reaction of the toy to their manipulation of the switches. They can be so intrigued that they will play with the toys for hours.

Surprise boxes are available from Child Guidance (CBS), Fisher-Price, Galt, and Johnson & Johnson ($10-$15).

Optional recommendations for this age group: Stack and Bolt from Kenner (finger dexterity & coordination). Pound a Round from Child Guidance (CBS) (coordi-

nation). School Bus from Amtoy (teaches lacing, snaps, zipper). Threading Cubes from Galt (teaches sorting, stacking, threading).

SECOND YEAR

As toddlers play, they manipulate objects that relate to their physical characteristics. By two-and-a-half, they pay more attention to the function. By the end of the first year, their imaginations and attempts at make believe become very important. They will prefer dolls, wagons, stuffed animals, and trucks. Later, they will want toys that are realistic, with workable parts and pieces.

The toddler moves through rapid growth, and a great deal of new learning occurs during this time. By your understanding these changes and the activities they prompt can enhance their growth, you will prepare your child from the next stage of development. The grounding of support and encouragement he gets from you will help him in preschool, relating well with other children, and

learning easily and happily.

By the time the child is two, he is mobile, curious, active, and into everything. He is very interested in his surroundings, learning rapidly and loves to explore. He has many questions.

Toddlers need to participate in many activities, but with supervision. They are learning by climbing, exploring, placing and replacing objects, and moving. From these actual experiences, the child benefits, mentally, socially, and physically.

Jean Piaget, a Swiss psychologist says intellectual growth is dependent on dealing in an active way with objects and people. The toddler learns about life through his environment and a great deal of social and imaginative play. He acts out parental behavior and language. He acts out roles and activities (mothers, fathers, shopping, doctor, etc.). You will want to create "prop boxes" containing costumes, hats, shoes, bags, fabrics, and other "play things." Toddlers delight in making up characters. This enjoyable play activity continues throughout the first five years and beyond. (See suggestions for this type of dramatic play in chapter 11.)

Suggestions for Toddlers 2—3 Years

A ctive
C reative
E ducational

Would Like	Received	Toy	Type
_____	_____	16. Blackboard and Chalk	(C)
_____	_____	17. Bubble Pipe	(A)
_____	_____	18. Figures	(C)
_____	_____	19. Household Objects	(A)
_____	_____	20. Jack-in-the-Box	(A)
_____	_____	21. Musical Instruments and Music Box	(C)
_____	_____	22. Pegboards	(E)
_____	_____	23. Puppets	(C)
_____	_____	24. Telephone	(C)
_____	_____	25. Tops	(A)
_____	_____	26. Transportation Toys	(A,C)
_____	_____	27. Wagon	(A)
_____	_____	28. Wooden Beads	(E)

Reminder: Other toys your child has played with earlier, such as bath toys, blocks, books, dolls, stuffed animals, etc. are still interesting and enjoyable.

16. Blackboard and Chalk

A favorite creative toy, and one that can be used for a long time, is a blackboard. It offers a chance to draw pictures over and over. The child can also draw water pictures on it with a brush. A blackboard should never be used with crayons. Show your child exactly how to use it. Children sometimes cannot tell the difference between paper and a blackboard so the board could easily and quickly become filled with crayon markings. You should explain the use of the board and show them paper and crayons nearby and hope they will remember the difference. I ruined one blackboard myself as a child, so I can warn you not to spend a lot of money on the first slate. As your child matures and learns the difference between paper and the blackboard, you can substitute a larger and better board. They are perfect as a wall hanging at a height they can easily reach or use a portable type.

Blackboards are available from Brio, Child Guidance (CBS), Eichhorn, Micki (Anderson Swazey), and Playskool ($3-$13).

17. Bubble Pipe

A long time favorite and probably the least expensive item on the list, and definitely one that your toddler will enjoy for a long time. You will want to get a pipe that makes a lot of bubbles. You can make a soap solution from mild soap and water and put it into a plastic container. Children love to make bubbles outdoors and delight in having others watch them. You can get the type of pipe that you blow through or use as a wand.

Bubble pipes are made by Battat, Pustefux, Small World Toys, Wham-O, and Wells ($2-$5).

18. Figures

A very popular item are sets of play people and animals made from plastic or wood. These figures are used for imaginary play and offer a lot of enjoyment for children who love to create stories around the figures. Some of the figures come in already created sets such as a village, hospital, farm, or school. Get large figures if the child is still putting everything in his mouth. Some of the playsets come with small figures, and several children who were too young to be playing with them have put them in their mouth and tried to swallow them. Ultimately any toy can be dangerous if used improperly, so throughout your child's play try to introduce the toy if needed and pay attention to the label on the package suggesting the age range of use, but most of all, you must know what your child can safely play with. We need to strike a balance between protection, freedom of self-discovery, and negligence. Children have accidents just as we do. Although we can wish we could protect them so that nothing serious would ever happen to them, many accidents can be avoided with planning and preparation.

Figures are made by Fisher-Price, Little Tikes, and Reeves ($2-$5).

19. Household Objects

Children love to play with realistic household objects and they have a lot of fun with them. Select small, light weight, and inexpensive pots and pans. Put covers on top or stack them inside each other. They will make a racket but children's fun cannot break anything and they learn a lot. They create imaginary play and can have a lot to say as they "cook" with these versatile objects. Try a rolling pin, wooden spoon, or non-breakable measuring cups for a child who likes to imitate you and your activities. Allow the child to roll out extra crust or clay while you are making a pie. A wooden spoon can be used to stir up a bowl of whatever, with plastic bowls to hold it, and a plastic container for leftovers, or for storage of items that should be protected from spreading out all over the floor. You can also obtain a play iron and ironing board (a play set is preferred).

Plates and cups are available in sets and allow for great domestic play. The child will create "tea parties" with them for friends and dolls. Include plastic spoons, forks, and knives for the completion of the play meal at the play table. If you have any extra, let the child use placemats and napkins. Your toddler will be very delighted.

You can find household objects made by Galt, International Playthings, Galt, South Bend Toys, and Wolverine ($2-$15).

20. Jack-in-the-Box

Surprise is what the child enjoys, especially when he discovers that by turning a crank he can make a figure pop up with a sound. It's fun and she will delight in watching the figure jump up. You do not want the figure to scare the child, but rather to delight her, so introduce it slowly and without too much drama so as not to frighten. Once he gets the idea, he will look forward to turning the crank and will laugh when the figure pops up. Different Jack-in-the-boxes are made, so look around so you are sure to get the one you want.

Several are made by Child Guidance (CBS) and Fisher-Price ($6-$10).

21. Musical Instruments and Music Boxes

If a child is exposed to music of all kinds he will enjoy listening and dancing to music. From the baby's first experience with a musical wind-up teddy bear or a music box, he or she is fascinated and delighted with pleasant and not-too-loud musical sounds. A music box which they can turn on themselves is a delight, especially around naptime. You will also find excellent to use a few selected instruments like bells, tambourines, or drums. The child may play along to music that you play on a record player, cassette, or radio. As the child grows, introduce more music and you may find that she has a natural talent for playing and learning music. Experiences in music will be important to the child and be enjoyable for learning movement, singing, and in being with other children. If you dance about as you clean up, or listen to music for relaxation and enjoyment, the child will learn that this is a natural and fun thing to do.

Instruments are available from Child Guidance (CBS), Fisher-Price, Palo Imports, Playskool, Proll, and Rhythm Band ($4-$15).

22. Pegboards

Using a peg board is an activity that gives mastery over simple tasks, and a sense of completion and accomplishment upon seeing the results. Like blocks, pegs are perfect for teaching manual dexterity. Pegs can be small for older children, but they also come in larger sizes and different colors for younger ones. They fit into holes drilled into boards. Children can arrange them as they want. You can also arrange them in a row of colors with

the child. As he grows older and understands colors and numbers, he can concentrate on the task by making a whole row of the same color. Easy Grip pegs are made by some manufacturers, but are usually only available in school supply stores. The placement of pegs is a good eye-hand coordination exercise.

Pegs and boards are available from Brio, Educational Teaching Aids, Galt, Ideal, and TC Timber (large ones) ($5-$10).

23. Puppets

Puppets aid in teaching verbal, social, and communication skills and can be helpful in learning in general. Since puppets are soft, pliable, and used when the child wants to communicate or play imaginatively, they provide a lot of fun. Children use puppets throughout their growing years for acting out stories they can make up themselves. They also have fun with puppets alone or with other children. Puppets are a wonderful way to release upsets or feelings, and they offer the child great opportunities for

communication and exercising imagination. You can find many puppets for purchase, but I recommend you start with simple hand puppets that are not too complicated. If Sesame Street characters are your child's favorites, then select one or two from the many choices available from Oscar, Kermit, Big Bird, and friends. Children delight in puppet play as they play together and later on will make up a dialogue. Be sure eyes are sewn on securely and are not removable and that other small parts on the puppet cannot come loose. You can also make your own puppets. In the bibliography section a number of good books are listed that contain information on how to make them.

Puppets are made by Animal Fair, Child Guidance (CBS), Berling Spielzung, R Dakin, Furry Fold Puppets, Davis-Grabowski, Eden, Fisher-Price, Free Mountain, Gund, Puppet Workshop, and Steiff ($3-$10).

24. Telephone

Language is expanding daily. The child listens, observes, and practices everything he hears. A telephone is a good device to assist in developing language skills. A toddler imitates others and will imitate their telephone use by making sounds, pressing buttons, dialing, and talking. He will walk around the house with the phone dragging after him and will have a good time watching you make up calls and talking to people. A variety of play telephones with bells or silent and talking are available. You may want to play with your child by using it together. This play results in a talkative child who will want to use the real one sooner. A toddler will also enjoy hearing someone, a parent or grandparent perhaps, talk to them and having a conversation using the phone.

Play telephones are made by Brio, Child Guidance (CBS), Fisher-Price, and Playskool ($3-$10).

25. Tops

This is a long-time favorite that children always seem to enjoy. They come back to it when they want to make it turn, go on to other activities, and return again and again. Some tops just spin and others do it to music. Several types exist, so get a large one that your child will find easy to turn. Children enjoy knowing the effect they can have on an object and immediately seeing the results. This activity also helps in developing fine motor coordination.

Tops are made by John Adams and Small World ($5-$10).

26. Transportation Toys

With a wide variety to choose from, you should have no trouble in finding your toddler several great vehicles. He will enjoy them for a long time. The sturdier the toy the better. You can find out how sturdy it is by carefully looking at it and testing the potential vehicle. Most of the companies who make toy vehicles take great pains to be certain their products have smooth edges, are easy for young children to operate, and have a solid center of balance.

You can select a fine truck, a train, or any number of other vehicles, depending on your preference and what you think your child will like. Children will play with these vehicles in many ways and use lots of imagination and sounds when doing so. They create activities around the vehicles and become very absorbed in operating the vehicles during their play. If the vehicles are going to be taken outdoors and played with for a long time, you will want to get hard plastic ones or ones with a rustproof finish. Features are important, so be sure the ladder on the firetruck lifts up, the doors to the cab on the truck open and close, and the garbage dumpster lifts and dumps. Also make sure the cars are large enough and sturdy. After you have compared types you can also ask the storeowner if they have any suggestions. The vehicles can be expensive if you want good quality, so you want to investigate thoroughly. Girls and boys play with vehicles, and both will enjoy them in play activity.

Vehicles are made by Amloid, Brio, Buddy L, Child

Guidance (CBS), Ertl, Grandad's Toy Shop, Ideal, Little Tikes, and Norok ($20-$25).

27. Wagon

As the toddler begins to move about easily under his own power, he loves to push or pull something, and most of all he loves to pull something with his favorite stuffed animal, doll, or set of playthings. A wagon, in wood, metal or plastic, is exactly the vehicle for this purpose, and is an item he will enjoy for a long time. Be sure to get one that has secure wheels and offers enough space to load up. A variety of wagons are made by a number of companies, so you will have a good selection. Don't start him on one that is too big, as it will be frustrating for the child. This is definitely a good investment that will provide lots of playtime.

Wagons are made by Blazon-Flexible Flyer, Child Guidance (CBS), Grandad's Toy Shop, Little Tikes, Micki, and Radio Steel ($10-$25).

28. Wooden Beads

Large wooden beads will provide manual activity for the toddler and enjoyment in creating a necklace and other items. Your child will enjoy stringing beads as soon as he can concentrate enough to get the thread through the holes. If he doesn't seem interested, put the beads away for several months. The sets of beads usually come in different basic colors and shapes, so when playing with them, the child is learning these concepts and also gaining mastery of eye-hand coordination. Be sure to make a large knot at the end of the string so the beads cannot fall off at the end. You can show your child how to string a few so he gets the idea, but then let him discover how to make the rest. He may add about five or ten beads and then may lose interest for a time. But he will come back to the beads many times if you do not push this kind of activity. If you make a necklace for a doll and put it on it, he will get the idea and may make one for each of his stuffed animals.

Beads are made by John Adams, Child Craft, Child Guidance (CBS), Galt, and Playskool ($5-$8).

Optional Items

Dapper Dan and Dressy Bessy from Playskool (dressing skills).
First Wheels from Mattel (train set, adventure).
Giant Links from Childcraft or Playskool (dexterity).
Play Sets from Micki, Anderson-Swazy, or Little Tikes (communication).

Rocking Horse from Country Wood Shop (adventure).
See N Say from Mattel (educational fun).
Shoe lacing from Galt (dexterity).
Snap lock beads from Fisher-Price (dexterity).
Wood pieces from TC timber (creativity).

Some Play Tips for Toddlers

- Use sponges, plastic cups, and washcloths, plus a few small floating toys in the bath tub for variety.
- Use a board on a slant to give the child an incline to use with cars and trucks.

- Create time for music, active movement, and outdoor play every day.
- Allow the child a chance to cook or bake when you do. Give her small amounts of ingredients, a plastic bowl, and a wooden spoon. She will imitate you.
- Be sure to talk a lot, sing, and have fun with your growing child.

Please let us know if you have found other toys that you would recommend or have had problems with.

CHAPTER SIX

Toys for Preschool Children—Three to Five Years

Preschool children move rapidly through their growing period. Each day their physical and mental abilities increase. They have a lot of energy for running, jumping, and all aspects of play. They also enjoy the time taken by an adult to sit and read a story to them. They will follow the pictures, and their ability to listen and comprehend improves immensely. They are beginning to identify words and acting out stories with puppets by themselves and with friends.

When Barbara and Tom Whitten talked with me about their four-year-old, they were concerned about the child's shyness with other children. Barbara was concerned that her daughter, Peggy, would not make social adjustments well in the nursery school she was to be enrolled in shortly. I suggested taking time to play with puppets as one way to encourage the child to expand her own voice and to feel more comfortable in her communication skills. In addition, they could spend more time reading to their daughter so she would become more familiar with books and talking about stories. I also encouraged them to invite one child over to their home for their daughter to play with so she would be more at ease and less overwhelmed when she started nursery school.

Soon Peggy began opening up in conversation and had more to talk about with her parents and other children. The adjustment to nursery school became easier as a result of the support she received beforehand. Her parents also learned more about the child's development. With that understanding, they began to relax more in dealing with the stages their daughter was moving through.

Preschoolers love creative playthings: fingerpaints, chalkboards, and drawing equipment. They enjoy playing with dolls and puppets. They like to look at interesting objects.

This is when children enjoy constructing and gaining in their ability to use the materials they play with. They become more involved in complicated dramatic play and fantasy play. They enjoy their ability to create characters in their lives and to draw from their own experiences with their families and friends in their play. Dress up dolls with zippers, laces, and snaps help them expand their self-help skills.

They enjoy the ability to use ride-ons and tricycles as they gain in gross motor skills. They like ride-ons that look like horses, cars, motorcycles, trains, or spacecraft. They like to pull wagons and have objects inside the wagon to pull. (However you may want to watch them carefully because they tend to wander off easily.)

Their imaginations are expanding, so puppets, dolls, and telephones take on new meanings and enjoyment for them. They love dress up and enjoy having various play clothes and fabrics and hats to put on. They like to play "store," "house," and "going on a trip" with their friends.

This is the time when children are usually at play with other children in groups. The play in nursery schools, child care centers, Head Start centers, or in playgroups at home. Children at this age are continuously experiencing new toys and new activities. They play regularly with their friends, and though they may fight or have disagreements, these are of brief duration as they are learning to share activities, and toys and to take turns.

Preschoolers use more outdoor equipment than before: swings, ride-ons, and climbing materials. They can concentrate on tasks for a longer period of time, and become more specific in their activity. They are learning to adapt to their friends and to act in a more socially acceptable manner. They are becoming more able, independent, and skillful.

Some of the quiet activities they enjoy are games, puzzles, sewing, and building with construction toys. The best games are those that allow them to learn, have a good time, and are not too difficult.

Boys and girls develop at about the same rate during this time. The expansion of legs and muscles is a noticeable part of their overall physical development. They can build with blocks and throw balls, but they cannot yet do what a five-year-old can in terms of small motor skills. Some toys are inappropriate now, but will be more suitable to use later.

The child during this period can do many things: run, jump, climb, and bounce. They have more strength, durability, adeptness, coordination, and ability to repeat movements.

Children need many different kinds of experiences. They enjoy creating all kinds of new things from raw materials, such as shells, stones, paper, and pipe cleaners. Various materials hold different promise. The child explores each piece to find out their different properties and uses. (Refer to chapter 11 for more ideas on found materials and the bibliography for suggested craft activities.)

Their drawing ability becomes more focused and their ability to perceive objectively improves, as does their ability to render their perceptions. They find great delight in new sights, sounds, and smells.

They are learning the alphabet by now. Having some individual, colorful magnetic letters on the refrigerator door encourages them to make up words easily. In general, children who are exposed to lots of books and magazines learn to read faster and better.

Children have some difficulty in understanding concepts of time, space, and quantity. It is important not to push them to learn these concepts before they are ready to grasp them. Just allow them to experience time, space, and how many, and they will learn what they can at their own pace.

Expressions of anger and frustration through play is very necessary. Puppets, dolls, and dollhouses make this safer and more comfortable for the child. When the child was younger, he or she may have expressed anger through temper tantrums. Later, as he becomes more sophisticated he can susually handle any anger through verbal means. The child has to learn when he has hurt another child, deliberately or accidentally, and understand what the limits of behavior are, on the playground or wherever else he may be playing. He will express his feelings in play easily. By observing and listening you can learn more about the issues he is coping with and assist if needed.

Preschoolers should have ample opportunity to express themselves creatively in dramatic or imaginative play. Their relationships with other children improve and grow more creative. They enjoy more of this kind of contact. They love pretending to eat, drink, or sleep. They can be even more dramatic in their play if they have a variety of costumes, play hats, make up, and props for play acting.

Imaginary companions are common for this age. They often are found with the first-born child or only children. Imaginary playmates emerge as a natural part of active imaginations and will be around for awhile. Do not be alarmed, since imaginary playmates are part of normal emotional growth.

The more preschoolers interact with other children, the more they learn to share and make friends. They connect with children they feel safe with and form close friendships.

Jane and Paul McKnight, noticed that their two- and four-year-old liked many of the same activities, but they also were having many conflicts. The difference in their abilities frustrated the younger child, who tried to copy the older child. I suggest that this is exactly what happens to children who have siblings. They could enjoy playing together if they were encouraged to cooperate and were presented with less competitive activities they could both do together. By providing them duplicates of their favorite dolls and obtaining a few extra supplies, the parents eased the competition. The children began more positive play in close proximity.

Three to Five-Year-Olds

Three and four-year-old children are able to do many activities. They have a wide range of skills and energy levels. They understand what is being said by others, but will vary in their own ability to talk and express ideas. They love to be read stories. They will have their favorite stories and ask for them time and time again, so be prepared. They play lots of make believe games, like being the characters in the story, or mommy, daddy, baby, and others significant in their lives. This is why play groups are so important at this age, as it gives them a chance to play actively with children they know and trust. Preschoolers will learn even more in these groups than they can alone or with just one or two playmates. Playgroups will be beneficial for everyone. Some of the play children become involved in includes: jumping, running, climbing, riding, rolling, and building. In addition, they have time for a balanced very active play with looking at pictures, listening to music, resting, cutting, pasting, playing with puzzles, drawing, and snacking. The children are positive in their outlook, but sometimes shy around strangers.

The child will find his own pace in his activities. He also needs you or his teacher to make sure he doesn't get overstimulated and tired. He can now do more with his hands, and he enjoys discovering puzzles that are more complicated, art activities, and simple crafts. These are good activities to do at home to achieve a balance in the active day.

The three-year-old will ask a lot of questions, so be patient with his curiosity. He wants to know everything as his world expands. He is interested in what is happening around him. He will feel good about himself and want to do things that express his growing confidence and reflect this improved self-image. His most important achievement will be to feel good about himself and have the sense that he can do things. Try not to overdo the no's and the restraints. He accomplishes many physical skills with balance and strength. He will usually go along with you and his friends and not be hard to get along with. In six months the picture will change and he will begin to establish his own identity and say "no" a lot, so it will be harder to get him to cooperate. It is a natural shift in the developing personality, so don't be worried or wonder "where your nice boy went."

These personality changes will continue throughout childhood and are simply what is happening within the child. Your understanding of what is normal, such as an outwardly secure child suddenly becoming insecure and uncertain, or a happy child becoming moody, or an easy child becoming stubborn, are all part of the changing and shifting patterns of growth. However, the changes are also indications of potential problems, so try to pay attention to these often subtle changes. Inconsistency is a natural part of the adventure of raising children. They outgrow these temporary changes so please be understanding, and try not to take it personally.

The child's emotions shift rapidly from happy to sad, from quiet to active. Your understanding of these changes is important. Also try not to fight with your child; see if both of you can be winners. Provide alternatives and positive support. Small toys can be rewards for a child's efforts to be helpful or other good behavior worth noting. He needs to win as part of his building strength, power, and self-esteem.

The child enjoys playing with other children and can do so easily at this age. They listen to each other and tend to respect their playmates' property without pulling things away from them. If a child does forget, gently remind him that the truck belongs to Johnny.

Children want to get along with each other and try to understand how others feel. This is a milestone in cooperative play and in getting along with others. For the most part, they get along with other children and talk together, cooperate in sharing toys, and have a lot of fun playing with toys, play clothes, blocks, and other activities. They do imitate each other and learn a lot from each other's behavior, interests, and responses. They copy each other's silliness and delight in taking turns at the imitative-type games they make up.

By understanding the variety of play the child likes at this age you can more easily plan the types of toys you want to have available at home, in the play group or at the nursery school. The child is physically very active: climbing, playing with large blocks, tricycles, and wagons. He likes to create things with fingerpaints, paints, soap bubbles, clay, collages, yarn pictures, and cut-outs.

Preschoolers get very involved in their play. They like to feed, dress, bathe, and take care of their baby dolls. They will wheel the carriages, and take very good care of things involving their stuffed animals and dolls.

You will see rapid changes between the three-year-old and the three-and-a-half-year-old in terms of physical coordination and emotional behavior. These are temporary changes and require patience and skill in handling on your part. Be assured that your child will be fine after six months of growing and catching up to himself.

During this entire period children enjoy having stories read to them. You can continue to teach and reinforce skills, such as recognition of colors, sizes, shapes, words, and numbers. Explain toys and games to them. You can assist your child in practicing what he is learning. Remember to talk a lot to him. Ask him questions and discuss things, such as about the weather, flowers, and stories.

You can play games with your child. Close your eyes and ask him to tell you what is in the room. Take time to sing. Make up stories. Imagine things and laugh about them. Begin a picture and let him finish it. Create things together from clay or construction toys. He will delight in your participation in games and activities.

You can continue with some of the toys he played with earlier, but others may now be old, too familiar, and in need of replacement. Again, do not have too many toys and games cluttering the floor. Find good ways to store them to avoid confusion. If his toys are easy to get to and put away, it will be a lot easier to take care of them. They will last longer and he will have less frustration when he wants to find something. Excellent ideas for storage are presented by Tony Torrice, an outstanding designer of spaces for children, in Part III. Preschool is an exciting time for children. Play is a central way to relate with and learn from others. Excellent preschool toys are available and you will be able to select from among many choices. The balance between active, creative, and educational is important.

1. Art Supplies

Creativity continues to be important to your growing youngster. Art expression is an enjoyable way for him to express himself. You have a lot to choose from: paint, fingerpaint, clay, paper, glue, pictures, yarn, and scissors. Have a supply of these materials convenient, in a place where they can be located easily, but used under supervision. There's no telling what can happen if you leave children alone with paints or something equally messy. However, you don't have to stop everything you are doing to supervise them. For example, clay can be used by children while you are nearby cooking. Ask them to tell you about what they are doing. Put their art work on display; they will feel pride in what they have done and want to do more. Give them time to finish the project they

Suggestions for Toys 3–5 Year Olds

A ctive
C reative
E ducational

Would Like	Received	Toy	Type
_____	_____	1. Art Supplies	(C)
_____	_____	2. Balls and Beanbags	(A)
_____	_____	3. Beads	(E)
_____	_____	4. Blocks	(A)
_____	_____	5. Books	(E)
_____	_____	6. Construction Toys	(A)
_____	_____	7. Dolls	(C)
_____	_____	8. Housekeeping Toys	(A-E)
_____	_____	9. Musical Instruments and Music	(C)
_____	_____	10. Play people & objects	(C)
_____	_____	11. Puzzles	(E)
_____	_____	12. Sand and Outdoor Toys	(A)
_____	_____	13. Stuffed Animals	(C)
_____	_____	14. Transportation Toys	(A)
_____	_____	15. Tricycles	(A)

are working on, and also try to be understanding if they get tired and don't want to finish it.

You can obtain art supplies in any five-and-ten store, art stores, and some toy stores. You don't have to spend a lot of money to get a good variety of supplies. Once you have the materials, a good idea is to organize them in boxes. Avalon and Binney & Smith have excellent art sets with paints, crayons, and suggested activities. Try and locate plain, unglued or non-stick white shelf paper or brown wrapping paper for paint activities; you can make a roll of paper go a long way. You can find large shapes, as in Colorform shapes, or rubber stamps to print and make patterns. Your child will love them and use them again and again. Locate a good supply of clay, Play-doh, or Plasticene, or make your own play dough:

2 cups flour
1 cup salt
½ cup water
kneed until smooth

An Etch-o-Sketch (Ohio Art) is also an enjoyable activity at this age. If your budget can handle it, a good sturdy easel will be used a lot and for a long time, or create one. A blackboard and chalk are also useful. You can encourage art by painting with sponges, brushes, fingers, and other materials.

Art supplies are available from Avalon, Binney & Smith, Colorforms, Fisher-Price, Kenner, Reeves, and Stampos ($1-$15).

2. Balls and Beanbags

The child at this age enjoys throwing balls and beanbags. Children can have a lot of fun playing together with beach balls, large sponge balls, and Nerf balls. All sizes are enjoyable and relatively inexpensive. If they are not lost outside they will last a long time and provide a lot of entertainment. They are great for large muscle development and for movement, coordination, and social play. Balls are available from many companies.

Beanbags offer skill building, and coordination. A simple game of throwing the bag into a target (an empty trash can or cardboard container) from gradually longer distances is a good game to play indoors on a rainy day.

You can make or buy beanbags. Just be sure to make the bags very secure or you will have beans flying everywhere.

Look for balls from the following companies: Atlanta, Barr, Hallmark, Preston, and Salver. ($1-$6).

3. Beads

Large wooden beads are now easier for children to manipulate. They will enjoy stringing them to make necklaces or just ropes of beads. Beads are good for teaching colors, shapes, coordination, fine motor ability, and learning to count. Playing with beads is a quiet indoor activity, good for a rainy day. Beads are also a good balance for the rough and tumble play preschoolers are usually engaged in. Be sure to tie the end of the string with a large knot so the beads do not slip off. You will notice in activities such as this that as the child grows in his ability to manipulate, to use, and coordinate the movements of his fingers, he will enjoy them even more than he did a year ago.

You can obtain beads from John Adams, Childcraft, Child Guidance (CBS), Galt, and Playskool ($5-$8).

4. Blocks

Blocks are one of the best investments you can make. The simplest items can give a child so much to play with and stretch their imaginations. Blocks come in all sizes and materials: from small wooden ones with alphabet and pictures, to foam and large plastic forms. Children will

select from the blocks they have available and create wondrous constructions, playhouses for their dolls, garages for the cars, and imaginary buildings that may not be explainable, but are beautifully constructed. Again, I'd like to remind you to ask them to tell you about their creations, but do not interfere. They will build and destruct at their whim. This ability gives them the feeling of great power. Be sure to have a place for them to store their blocks or everyone will be tripping over them, and that's no fun.

Blocks offer creative, active, and educational play, all in one kind of toy.

You can obtain blocks from Amtoy, Bandai, Child Guidance, Dolly Toy Co., Eichhorn, Fisher-Price, Galt, International Playthings, Little Tykes, Mattel, Palo, Norok, PlaySkool, Semper, and TC Timber ($7-$25).

5. Books

So many times the most obvious types of play are forgotten when we rush to buy new things. We may overlook the very essential basics that have great value for long-lasting benefits to children. Books are among your child's best friends. Through books, rather than television, he will have his creative mind stimulated. His imagination will be ignited by reading. He will absorb ideas and become a better learner. With books he will gain skills he can use for the rest of his life. He will recognize pictures, and point to objects he knows and likes. He will learn from your reading aloud and become familiar with words, sentences, conversations, and descriptions. Finally, as he matures, he will learn to read for himself.

This can be among the most enjoyable activities for the two of you. A perfect way to quiet an active child before nap or rest time is to give the child opportunity to do quiet, non-stimulating activities. Putting things away, brushing teeth and hair, listening to music, and reading are better just before bedtime and create a restful time for the child.

So many wonderful books exist. Whenever possible visit the nearest library or bookstore with your child. He will learn to love books, especially those that have illustrations which depict what is familiar and comfortable to him. If given puppets, or soft toys, the child will act out the stories you read to him, as well as create his own version of stories he has heard. I like to combine books with toys whenever possible. Good examples are Paddington Bear, Snoopy and Raggedy Ann & Andy. You will find that children can enjoy more complicated and longer stories at this age, and they will readily share their feelings and experiences. The child will become familiar with the story and probably want you to read it the same way each time. They know a good thing when they hear it. They love to hear funny stories and stories which reflect the growing experiences that they are going through. Books are being made to be more toy-like, playful, and child proof. Research indicates that children whose parents take the time to read to them as children have fewer problems in learning to read later on. Become familiar with the books before you purchase them, which is a good idea before you purchase anything. Examine the book for illustrations, text, message, and see if it is a book your child will comprehend. For very young children, try to get washable, sturdy books. If you receive a gift of a book you do not feel is right for your child, try to exchange it for one that is more appropriate. Be sure to have a place in their room or play area where children can put their books and store them.

Books for children can be obtained from Bobbs-Merrill, Doubleday, Delacourte, Grosset and Dunlap, Harper and Row, Lady Bird, Little-Brown, McGraw-Hill, Follet, Knopf, Random House, B. Shackman, and Western Publishing. (See reference section for children's books related to toys and play.) ($2-$10).

6. Construction Toys

Like blocks, construction toys allow children maximum imaginative activity and the chance to create. You have a wide choice in this area, since construction toys come in plastic or wood and in many shapes. This type of toy will allow your child to build or create what he wants. Try not to interfere or give him directions unless he asks you a question. Occasionally join him in play and do a construction while he is busy making his own. He will enjoy your company. He will find what you make will be very nice and will tell you so. He will also enjoy your positive comments on his creation.

Construction activities provide learning and coordination skills. The child will create, take apart, and start all over again. Let him have plenty of time for creative building, who knows, he may become a designer or architect someday. Your daughter benefits equally from these experiences. She may have the same aspirations to be an architect or engineer. One never knows what experiences may prompt a child's decisions and shape the rest of their lives. These are times that allow them to expand mentally, physically, and creatively.

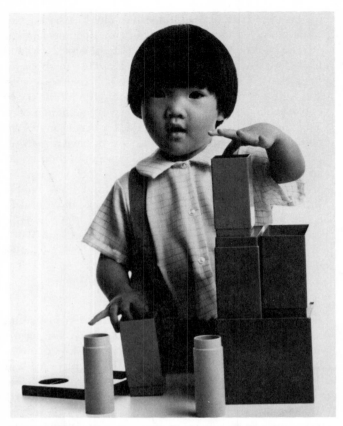

For this age I recommend starting with selections from Brio, Child Guidance (CBS), Fischer-America, Lego, Playskool, and Tinker Toys, ($5-$25).

7. Dolls

One of the most phenomenal parts of the entire toy industry is the number and variety of the types of dolls available. They range from soft fabric dolls, small figures and variations of shapely designer dolls, to robust baby dolls and costumed creations. The numbers of dolls available are amazing. The play value for dolls is also endless. The collecting possibilities of dolls are beyond imagination. In researching this book I spoke to many specialists and several of the observations of the very best in the country are included here. The interviews with doll specialists were very useful. Doll collectors' groups are found throughout the U.S. and Europe. This is an active hobby for many people who study about dolls regularly. You may want to select collector dolls as part of your child's toy treasures.

For practical everyday play the basics are best. A baby doll with a soft touch and simple features, which is easy to dress and undress will delight your child for a long time. Soft rag dolls like Raggedy Ann and Andy will also be thoroughly enjoyed. The special curvy designer dolls are best saved for later on.

Dolls are another item you can make for your child. A number of books are listed in the resources section to give you some directions on how to make dolls. Later on you may want to invest in a doll house, doll accessories, and other artifacts. I suggest you create a bed for the baby doll, a cover, and maybe a chair and table for your child and dollie to play together. He or she will enjoy playing Mommy or Daddy and putting the baby to sleep, eating with the doll, and talking to the doll. A lot of housekeeping learning derives from caring for the doll and is a natural part of the play of children at this age. I feel that boys and girls both need experiences in playing with dolls, which helps them to act out their feelings. You will find your child talking to the doll and making "dollie" very real. And it *is* very real for the child.

You have many excellent dolls to choose from. Companies are Amtoy, Badger, Fisher-Price, Effanbee, Eugene, Hasbro, Horseman, and Ideal. Equipment from Empire of Carolina and the Welsh Company ($5-$30).

8. Housekeeping Toys

A natural part of playing at the preschool age is acting out familiar roles. This happens as part of play time at home, with friends, and at nursery school or childcare center. Acting out different people, situations, and places are the way that young children learn, develop language, and gain skills in social interaction. You can help them to enjoy this time by providing simple props: broom, dustpan, a few pots and pans, dishes, play stove, table and chairs, eating utensils, plastic bowls and cups, playclothes, playtool sets and whatever else you might have that is extra, available, and useful. Hats of various kinds can help them create many changes in the types of people they act out. You need to have places to store these objects, as you do not want them scattered all over. If the child can have one place that is his exclusively, it will help satisfy his needs and keep his playthings from being underfoot. Don't let the amount of this household equipment get out of hand. Be selective. Children can have fun with a small number of objects. The rest is their imagination. Props such as just bowls and wooden spoons, for example, can go far. If you

can't or choose not to buy a lot of this equipment for home use, don't worry, there will be plenty of these objects to play with at nursery school or at a friend's house. You may have only limited space, and that is a legitimate concern. (See chapter 11 for other suggestions on objects for play at home or at school.)

When you are cooking, let your child participate by giving her or him small amounts to mix, cut out, or roll. Children enjoy proximity to you, enjoy talking, and doing imitations of the activities you are doing. When it comes to preparation of items like pancakes or french toast, why not let the child learn to mix the eggs and milk and then flour. She will enjoy eating the food even more later on because she helped make it.

Household items can be obtained from Child Guidance (CBS), Galt, H-G, International Playthings, South Bend Toys, Tupperware, and Wolverine ($2-$15).

9. Musical Instruments

This is definitely the time to expose your child to musical experiences. Ideally, this is what has been happening since they were babies and toddlers. They need to hear a variety of music. Whatever your favorite music may be, share with them a variety including the classics, folk music, and children's songs. So much music exists by so

many excellent musicians. It is an art form they need to hear and experience for their own personal growth. Music is good for children; they like to hear it, move to it, dance, sing, and clap to it, and play music themselves. You may get the idea of the type of instrument your child would enjoy learning by exposing him to different possibilities and watching his reactions. If you can, let him have a record player or a casette player. Many good sturdy ones for children are available. An assortment of musical selections to play is essential. They can help you choose the things they want to hear if you ask them: later on, as they gain more experience with music, they will develop a taste for their own favorite kind of music.

Children need to learn not to touch other people's musical equipment or instruments without asking first. They naturally want to touch pianos, and pluck guitars (any musical instrument will fascinate them), but it is also a good idea for them to understand what to do first and be guided to an instrument they can handle and enjoy.

A good first keyboard is made for children by several companies. Percussion instruments (drums for example) and recorders are also good choices. Instruments can be obtained from Child Guidance (CBS), Fisher-Price (who also make a great cassette player), Playskool, Proll, and Rhythm Band ($4-$25).

10. Play People and Play Sets

Miniature play people offer enjoyable creative times and many play opportunities. The figures come in a wide range of choices, including western, medieval, everyday scenes in the community. The commercial play sets are very well done, and you can also make your own.

Cardboard will be a constant creative element because it is so versatile. Try to locate figure sets that have boys and girls, men and women, and animals, and offer a lot of flexibility. Some miniatures are available in entire sets. You can have a wonderful time collecting these items if you are so inclined. This may be too young an age to start serious collections, but the pieces can be enjoyed and treasured. They make nice gifts to start a child collecting. A number of companies have good play sets and the characters to go with them. By the time you add small cars, trains, and other play materials (like blocks) you can have a small village or other location. The child will have a lot of fun alone or with friends creating action and movement around the sets.

Play sets are available from Fisher-Price, Majorette, Little Tikes, and Playskool ($2-$10).

11. Puzzles

As the child matures, he can use puzzles that have more pieces and complexity. Puzzles are great entertainment on rainy days and for quiet times. If the child is sick at home, use puzzles for an interesting bed activity; they are a good substitute for TV watching. Television is not mentally challenging. Puzzles will teach finger coordination, dexterity, and logic.

Choose puzzles that children of this age can realistically complete. They will be frustrated if they are too complex. The number of pieces expand proportionately to

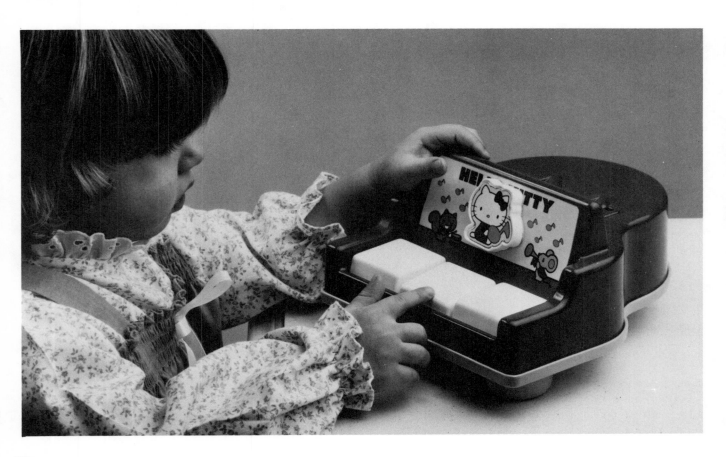

age and ability. Give them time to complete the puzzle, a table surface to lay the puzzle on, and leave to come back to at a later time, if they don't finish it.

They also may ask for help at times, and you could sit down and play along for a while. Let them figure out how to solve the puzzles for themselves. Again you have to judge what is possible and what is not yet within your child's grasp. This is a good item to recycle as the mood and inclination strikes your child.

You can find puzzles made by Acre, Brio, C. Salco, Fisher-Price, Galt International Playthings (CBS), John Adams, Playskool, and Willis ($3-$10).

12. Sand and Outdoor Toys

Children need to play in dirt, sand, and water. They need at least a bucket and shovel. The rest is optional. You will find that wading pools, rubber balls, hoses and large plastic containers are the simplest most and pleasurable playthings for children in the backyard all summer long. If you want other objects, you can get a number of toys made especially for out-of-doors; watering cans, funnels, egg beaters, and plastic pitchers are good playthings. As long as the items cannot easily be broken or won't splinter, select what you feel will be fun for the child. I recommend that you buy selectively, and only what your child really needs. He or she will have a chance to play with more diversified objects at nursery school, so it isn't necessary to have everything at home.

Playground equipment at home should be simple and consist of swing, slide, and ladder. Look at the references in chapter 11 for outdoor play equipment.

13. Stuffed Animals

Long-lasting, cuddly, and emotionally satisfying, the stuffed animal is a most wonderful toy. Like "dolly," "teddy," or "friend" can be held, cuddled, and taken care of. It can also be held for comfort if the child is upset, the mother is going away, or a difficult transition must be made. All in all, a stuffed animal offers a lot of play value. You may enjoy stuffed animals too, so buy a few for yourself. After all, why should children be the only ones to have stuffed animals?

You can get stuffed toys in all ranges from simple to complex. There is enough variety to fill Noah's entire ark, so select carefully. Your child can play with them in small groups and may line them up for different play situations.

Stuffed animals are carefully designed, well made, and inspected before they are distributed, so you can be assured that, for the most part, they are safe. Be sure the eyes are permanent and other parts cannot fall off or be pulled out. I have personally seen the great pains manufacturers take to protect your child from anything potentially dangerous. They have a reputation to uphold and they care about your child. There have been a few accidents in the past due to carelessness in inspection or design so a rigorous safety inspection is standard. If ever

there is a problem with any defective item, take it to the store you bought it from.

Stuffed animals can be obtained through Animal Fair, Axlon, California Stuffed Toys, Charm, Commonwealth, R. Dakin, Determined Toy, Fisher-Price, Gund, Kamar, PlaySkool, Princess Rushton, Russ Berrie, Steiff, TFA (large, soft auto replicas), and Trupa ($5-$25).

14. Transportation Toys

Children never seem to tire of pushing their boats, cars, trains or trucks around on the floor, tables, or outdoors, making sounds and generally have a good time. This type of play is very important to them and is a significant part of their peer play. They take on different personalities as they play, driver, airline pilot, or truck driver, and develop their own realistic sounds and dialogue from what they have heard in direct experience, from friends, or from what they observe.

Be sure when you buy transportation toys they have designs the child will enjoy, have parts that work, and are what the child wants. Children seem to learn fairly early what is the most popular vehicle and will be influenced by their peers.

Transportation toys provide endless hours of fun and children learn a lot from the roles they portray. You may want to start collecting trains, parts, and tracks for the child who seems to be really fascinated by trains. These are popular collectors' items and a hobby you can enjoy along with your child.

Look for vehicles by Amloid, Brio, Buddy L, Corgi, Ertl, Gabriel Child Guidance (CBS), Haviland, Ideal, Matchbox, Kusan, New Generation, Norok, and Westwind ($4-$20).

15. Tricycles

The first tricycle is a thrill for the young child. As children become adept they will want to expand their travels, but be sure they are only in safe areas and that they know how to handle themselves as they ride. They need to be courteous to other children, and be able to stop the tricycle.

Your child may want a tricycle with a picture of his favorite television character on it. He and his peers are often greatly influenced by television advertising. You have to decide how much licensed material you want on the daily items your child plays with. Many children seem to have the same amount of fun on tricycles that are not decorated. You can use your own judgment, as well as compare prices and quality. In any case, you will want a bike that has good sturdy construction, can stand up to rough riding, knocking over, and a lot of use.

Companies that make tricycles are: AMF, Colman & Hirschmann, Ertl, Hedstrom, Huffy, and Tomy ($25-$50).

Additional appropriate toys to consider from previous lists:
Blackboard and chalk.
Bubble pipe.
Pegboards.
Telephone.
Wagon.

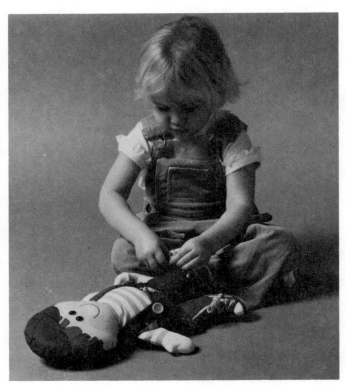

You may also consider:

Big Bounce (GPT), a trampoline.

Bowling pins and ball.

Candyland Game, a basic first game, (Milton Bradley).

Cash register (Blue Box, Chicco).

Color-recolor TV showtime (Avalon).

Creative Constructive (Learning Materials Workshop).

Dressing frames, shoes, dolls or pictures (Child Guidance, Fisher-Price, Playskool).

Funnel Tunnel, a long fabric tunnel for outdoor or indoor play (Carlin).

Games of cards for colors, shapes and other skills (Child's Play).

Kaleidoscope.

Jump rope.

Junior Stilts (Childcraft).

Lacing cards.

Large cartons.

Magnetic letters for refrigerator (Cadco, Fisher-Price).

Picture Lotto.

Pinwheels (Amuse Me).

Quadro Large Construction Pieces (Davis-Grabowski).

Ring toss game.

Rocking Animal (Commonwealth).

Shape Tac Toe, shapes to fit. (Bandai).

Teach-a-Time Clock (Child Guidance).

Tent or covered bridge table.

Tipi (Nomadic Tipi Makers).

Tool Kit (Blue Box).

Trains (Marklin, Child Guidance, Little Tikes).

Video Programs (Vestron).

Viewmaster.

V-2 engine, a see-through engine (Amloid).

Some Tips for Parents of Preschoolers

- Create play clothes and prop boxes with hats, etc., for dramatic play.
- Create opportunities for them to use large muscles in climbing, crawling, pushing, pulling, jumping, and throwing.
- Create an art supply box and collage (available used and recycled cards, magazines and other objects to cut and paste).
- Create opportunities for them to attend peer group activities, child care, or regular play groups.
- Save assorted boxes, which will be used for everything from stores, houses or climbing.

CHAPTER SEVEN

Toys for School Age Children- Six to Eight Years

An exciting new milestone in your child's development is approached as your child begins kindergarten and first grade. Again her world expands daily and brings new friends and new lessons daily. Many changes have occurred in the past five years. She is growing more independent. How well she adjusts to the new changes is definitely based on the groundwork you have laid down. She thrives on the experiences in play groups, with her playmates, through your guidance and careful selection of toys and playtime. Her toys will become even more interesting, more complex, and more diversified in the next phase of her growth.

She should have more to say about the selection of her playthings now, but she will still need your guidance and direction. Although she will have very definite ideas about what she likes to play with, she will appreciate your assistance and influence. Children like to conform to their peer group in many ways, but you will have to make the final decisions based on your evaluation, budget, and the appropriateness of the toys you buy. Just because "her friend Janie has one" doesn't mean you have to rush out and buy the same thing. Your decision is as important for this age as when she was younger.

Her large and small muscles have become very well coordinated. She is active and likes to engage in a lot of outdoor activities with her friends. If given the opportunity, children at this age enjoy climbing, tumbling, swinging, throwing balls, jumping rope, riding bikes,

and swimming. They also have fun running, tossing frisbees, and flying kites. Creating opportunities for plenty of safe outdoor play is important to balance the increased mental work they are doing in school.

In school they are learning to read, count and do many other tasks. You need to check the kind of outdoor play they have at school. If necessary, try to help to improve the equipment available. Take your child for visits to zoos, parks and to the country as often as you can. Children need a balance in their lives provided by natural surroundings. Learning will come easier if they have been exposed to alternatives. What they learn outside school enhances and is as important as the classroom.

At age five they are growing the slowest physically up to that time. Your child needs frequent rest periods. She may overexert herself and needs to be reminded to slow down for a while. She acts out a lot of what she sees around the home. She may be somewhat quieter, sometimes reluctant to reveal how she is feeling to anyone.

She usually gets along well with her playmates. Her preference is to have a few friends she can depend on and feel comfortable with. The personal changes and the way she relates to other children make kindergarten a particularly important transition time. This is a time that requires sensitivity and tact on your part.

She should be able to dress and undress herself easily. She will feel secure as school starts if she has had careful preparation. She needs to learn to follow directions, respect other children, and learn how to share a variety of playthings.

If you provide good materials for play and learning at home you will be assisting your child. It is easier at school for her to play with puppets, blocks, and other materials if she has had enough time to experience them at home and feels familiar and comfortable with them. Don't forget to continue to read stories to her. You can make up stories or write down sentences she makes up. Put her colorful pictures on the wall on display. Also continue to keep her playthings in good condition, not cluttered, and easily accessible.

Play games with your child, such as checkers and simple board games. She will enjoy playing with you. She needs time with her friends for games, creativity, construction, role play, and musical experiences. Providing balance and variety will continue to be important.

This is a good age to introduce simple scientific and natural materials as her understanding of these areas increases. Magnets, stethoscopes, and magnifying glasses are some tools she will enjoy. She will become interested in the clock and weighing scales. Many of the toys she played with when she was younger will continue to be important. She will have increased skills in using beads, which become easier to string. More complex block constructions become possible, and she can do more craft and art activities. She will continue to dress up and actively express herself.

These interests will continue as she becomes six. She is just now more capable, stubborn, and opinionated. This is a more difficult period and many emotional changes occur. The child becomes the center of her own activity and is mostly interested in herself. She tends to be defiant, and does not listen to directions easily.

Defiance and stubborness will make her hard to deal with at times, and it is essential to understand these phases for your own balance and patience. She is not always secure, tends to be afraid to make mistakes, and is quite sensitive. Your positive guidance will help considerably. She is also curious, asks a lot of questions, and is interested in learning.

The six-year-old period is an active time between the quiet five-year old and restrained seven-year-old. The six-year-old likes to do a lot of creative craft and art activities. She practices at home what she has learned in school. If you can create a space for these activities so much the better for everyone. Try to find a place just for the supplies, and make sure they are handy and where the child can reach them.

Imaginative play continues to be important, as do books, games, and experiments. Encourage your child to practice the skills she is learning at school by reading at home, creating hobby projects, and developing her interests in science, nature, and biology. Find time to take walks, exercise and make things together.

By the time the child is seven, she is even more independent and capable. Seven-year-olds are more apt to try to do things perfectly, over and over, and are totally involved in what they like to do best. More competition exists between children. They like to act out fantasies and play action games. Their peer group becomes more important than ever and a lot of play activity centers on her friends.

They also like to be alone and do things by themselves. They like to alternate play between inside and outside. Children improve their motor skills with many of the games they play. They focus on one activity for a while, lose interest, and then go on to the next. A definite

separation happens between the boys and the girls and the types of activities they do with their friends. They like to build and create structures and constructions. They continue developing skills with their hands. They also need reassurance and time to practice their new skills, as they sometimes feel uncertain. They are reinforcing the skills to tell time, count, read, talk, and write. They look for challenges, but also are very sensitive to criticism and may feel badly if picked on too much.

As the child becomes eight, the ability to coordinate the body and rhythm increases. The eye-hand coordination is smoother. It is easier for the child to read and write. Often she tries moving faster than she can to complete the work or activity she is doing. She likes to play more games that involve small-muscle coordination.

The need to be part of the group continues to be important. She enjoys being part of a group and being involved in group play. Sometimes the group breaks up over small fights. She may need mediation and someone to help at those times. She is also closer to one or two special friends. She needs a pal to have fun with, to create and play with.

She is interested in expressing herself through playing, writing, music and performing, and will do so spontaneously. She is active and likes to engage in a variety of activities. She is also very sensitive and feels a lot of empathy for her friends and for characters in a story or on television.

1. Art Supplies

As the child becomes older, so do her skills for artistic expression. Some children have a natural inclination towards creative pursuits and will enjoy drawing or making clay models. If your child has talent or seems to express herself well in these areas encourage her by getting the materials she needs and having them available. She will need crayons, pens, paint, paper, and other materials. A number of books are available to assist you in helping your child in art pursuits (see bibliography). Starting young is as important in art as in musical training. Once children start creating they will want to continue, especially if the results are pleasing. Display the work on walls, make a place where they can work

Suggestions for Children 6—8 Years

A ctive
C reative
E ducational

Would Like	Received	Toy	Type
_____	_____	1. Art Supplies	(C)
_____	_____	2. Bicycles	(A)
_____	_____	3. Books	(E)
_____	_____	4. Construction Toys	(A)
_____	_____	5. Dolls and Dollhouses	(C)
_____	_____	6. Electronic Games	(E)
_____	_____	7. Games	(E)
_____	_____	8. Jump ropes	(A)
_____	_____	9. Kites	(A)
_____	_____	10. Musical Instruments	(C)
_____	_____	11. Puppets	(C)
_____	_____	12. Puzzles	(E)
_____	_____	13. Tools	(C)
_____	_____	14. Transportation toys	(C)

creatively without getting on top of you. Artistic creations and crafts are a good balance between work at school and the active play with their friends. Creativity is an important substitute for television.

Art supplies are available from art supply stores and some toy stores. Makers of supplies are Adica Pongo (DAS), Avalon (stitchery, latch hook). Binney & Smith (color supplies), Fisher-Price, Galt (easels, supplies) ($2-$10).

2. Bicycles

A bicycle is a long-lasting investment. It can provide wonderful recreational opportunities for your child and means to get around with his friends on different outings. After seeing the flying bicycles in the movie E.T., a bicycle that only goes along the ground may not be enough for your child, but for now it's the best we have. Many excellent bicycles exist to match your child's ability, and interests, and your budget. You could write the Bicycle Association listed in the Appendix to learn more about selecting a bicycle. Your local bike store will be able to help you in the selection. Children should learn safety and how to ride properly. Riding is a responsibility they must take seriously for their protection and the safety of others.

Bicycles are produced by Fuji, Hedstrom, Huffy, Raleigh, Schwinn and Sears ($50-$200).

3. Books

As your child enters school, books are increasingly important for his education and also for recreational reading. You can continue to read to him and enjoy the stories yourself. Books are constant friends who provide informa-

tion and insight. Encourage him to keep track of the books he reads, to write a few sentences about them, and why he likes them. Book reports are still done in school, so this is good practice. Encourage him to collect paperbacks and books that are of interest. At those times when he needs to be quiet, the books will be good company. Have him read aloud also. Many excellent books for all interests exist. Trips to the library should be part of his regular schedule and obtaining a library card is advisable.

Books are published by Bobbs-Merrill, Delacourte, Doubleday, Follet, Harper and Row, Knopf, Little Brown, Marvel Books, McGraw-Hill, Random House ($2-$10). (See resources section for more books.

4. Construction Toys

Construction toys are an excellent opportunity to develop eye-hand coordination and to create something challenging. It is satisfying for your child to have something to show. Constructions are fun for children to do together. Many construction sets of all kinds exist. Usually construction toys accumulate. You may think your child has enough to start a small log cabin in the backyard. You will want to have adequate storage and places where this material is accessible, and not under everyone's foot.

The child will find many possibilities in materials by Fisher-Technic (model construction sets), Child Guidance, Tinkertoys, Korver-Thorpe (Froebel Blocks), Learning Materials Workshop, Lego, Magic Castle Molds (shapes for sand creations), Play-jour (Capsela), and Schafer (Playmobil) ($5-$25).

5. Dolls and Dollhouses

As girls get older their interest in dolls, doll accessories,

look like a very crowded doll convention. Encourage her to care for her dolls and keep them in good condition.

Some companies to look for when selecting dolls are, Alexander, ANDA Co. (twin doll beds), Effanbee (twin dolls and many others), Empire, Fisher-Price, Goldenberger, Jesco, Mattel (Barbie, Ken, dollhouses and accessories), South Bend (carriage and strollers), Uneeda, Vogue, and Welsh ($8-$35).

6. Electronic Games

An innovation here to stay and worth noting. I have a few objections: possible boredom and excessive use. After a while the child learns the key to the game, it gets monotonous, and he wants a new game that has more figures, noise, and action. I prefer interaction between human beings and the warmth it generates. I am not saying electronic games are bad, just that they are mind-limiting, eye-straining, and often teach some skewed values. The skills the child learns from some games are good for military purposes, but would not necessarily add to the child's intelligence and emotional growth. I understand that the child will play with them because they are a trend, and it is very hard to resist trends. I suggest you limit the amount of time spent in this activity and encourage a diversity of activities and interests. Allowing lopsidedness in any area is not helping the child to grow fully. While electronic games and computer software can give the child learning experiences, not all contribute to his or her development. I can recommend some of these games for children. You can add to them as you examine the newest choices. Some examples are Epyx, Kadon, and Tigen.

SAMPLE LIST OF ELECTRONIC GAMES ($25-$150)

Astrovision	Galaxian Professional Arcade
Atari	Video computer system
Coleco	Basketball, Hockey, Soccer
Entex	Baseball, Football
Magnavox	Odyssey
Mattel	Football
Milton Bradley	Super Simon

From the experienced reviewers of *Family Computing*

If you live with younger children, look for programs to help them grow accustomed to the computer. Especially good are packages they can use without the aid of an adult. Mickey's Space Adventures from Sierra On-Line, starring the famous mouse; Facemaker from Spinnaker, for kids up to age 7; Early Games for Young Children from Springboard Software; and Kids on Keys also from Spinnaker were judged winners in this category. (Jan 1986)

7. Games

So many different kinds of games exist for older children that you will have a lot to select from. You have your

and doll houses continues. Starting a collection begins to be of interest at this age. The number of dollhouses, furnishings, and accessories to select from is outstanding. Many dollhouses come ready-made, or you can make one yourself. Selectivity is important (a child usually just plays with her favorites), otherwise her room could begin to

choice of table top games, board games, and electronic games. Some of the current electronic games are listed above. You will want to have several board games on hand that will be great for a simple, quiet, and fun evening.

Despite the glamour and innovation of Pac Man and Joy Sticks, the results are pretty monotonous, and gobbling up opponents after a while loses its appeal. We need to be wary of technological fads that do not teach positive values to children. We need to have more non-competitive games that allow children to learn and have fun. Don't overlook games that offer a lot of challenge, have staying power, and require individual ingenuity.

A Guide to Selecting Games

Milton Bradley Company

Games are an important part of growing up. Games help teach young people how to count and read, how to think ahead and make decisions, how to cooperate with other people, how to compete, how to win gracefully and how to lose cheerfully. Because adults often forget some of these lessons, games are important for them, too. Games have one other important benefit that we often disregard.

Milton Bradley established his company in 1860 because he believed that learning could be entertaining, and that recreation could be educational. In old-fashioned 19th century New England, where hard work was valued and play frowned on, this kind of thinking was rather revolutionary. Today the Milton Bradley Company still tries to inject some educational value in its games.

There is a test anyone can use when examining a game, it's the same 4-question test Milton Bradley uses when inventing its games.

1. Is the game challenging? If the game doesn't make you think or plan ahead, if it is too easy to win or ends too quickly, if the game does not leave you with some feeling of accomplishment, then an important part of living is missing. Games reflect life, and achievement is an essential part of each day.

2. Is the game too frustrating? A game that seems unbeatable is just as bad as one that is too easy. No one likes to be discouraged. A game must be carefully designed to give the player a fighting chance.

3. Is there a reward? What is the point in playing the game? Is there a goal, a finish line, a clear-cut point where someone is declared the winner? Playing until

the game beats you or until you fail is frustrating. Modern psychology tells us that much can be learned with rewards.

4. Does the game have "repeat-play value"? A good game won't collect dust in the closet, having been played only a few times. Each round should be fresh and interesting, and continue to challenge and entertain each time it is played.

SUGGESTED LIST OF GAMES

ARC	Giant Cube (30 games, 16″ square)
Bandai	Air Traffic Controller
Creative Publication	Helix (a tic tac toe variation)
Entex	Escape
Fun-Da-Mentals	Robot
Great Games	Kangaroo, Dominique
Hasbro	Ring Toss, Tic Tac Toe
International Playthings	Marble Chute
Just Games	Reactrac
Lakeside	Isolation
Milton Bradley	Inner Circle, Twister, Yahtzee
Parker	Big Boggle, Can't Stop, Careers, Club, Parcheesi, Risk, Sorry, Wildfire
Pentagames	Quintessence
Pressman	Master Mind
Selchow & Righter	Scrabble
Star Game Company	Leverage
Whamo	Frisbee, Hacky Sack
World Wide Games	Table Golf

8. Jump ropes

The jump rope is a classic. It has been used by little girls and big burly athletes alike for generations. Some of the games children play have been around for years; for example, "Over The Stream-Under The Stream." Being a member of a rope-skipping group is good for social development. Children talk and learn to take turns as part of their activity. In addition, they are developing their coordination, muscular strength in their legs, and sense of rhythm and timing. You could try it too (to see if you can still jump like you used to.) It's lots of fun and good exercise.

Jump ropes are made by Galoob, Hedstrom Jak-Pak, and Schaper ($2-$5).

9. Kites

What mystery and fascination kites hold for children! They have a great deal of fun learning to fly them and feel a sense of power and mastery when they learn to make the kite swoop and dive and climb in the wind. Flying a kite is a perfect way to have fun with your child out of doors. It gives you a great opportunity to teach a little science as well.

Kites today are a far cry from the paper and balsa wood cross that most of us were familiar with when we were growing up. (The old stand-bys exist, but there is just a lot more to choose from.) Kites are available in many sizes, shapes, and materials. Some make outstanding room decorations on the days when it's not windy enough to fly them. There are special kite stores you can visit which are a delight to the eye with the colors and designs on display. This is something that you can also make for your youngster that he will appreciate and enjoy. And together you get the fun of making it and watching it fly!

Kites can be obtained from Davis-Grabowski Go Fly A Kite, Hi-Flier, International Playthings, and Tide Rider ($5-$20).

10. Musical Instruments

It is never too early to start learning music. Having music as a natural part of their lives is important for their expression and self-confidence. Children are often quite talented, and music helps them express themselves and gain friends. One group of children I know created a band with an appropriate name (Sibling Rivalry), and were recognized for their talents among their peers. They had a lot of fun making music together. Some of the members went on to professional music careers.

Music should be introduced as early as possible. If the child shows some interest and talent, make sure he or she has good instructors who like teaching children and is allowed to practice. You may have to remind them to practice but never force or coerce them. If they want to be good at music, they will play music in preference to other things. Just make sure that they don't do it so much that they isolate themselves from others and stay indoors too much.

Musical instruments for children are available from Bliss Musical Instruments, Chicco, Fisher-Price, Hering Harmonicas, and Yamaha ($5-$25).

11. Puppets

Puppets continue to be fun for children. At this stage they usually move hand-held puppets, and, if given a chance, will enjoy the marionette-type puppets, make up puppet shows, and create characters for their dramas.

Puppets can be fun for a child to amuse a younger brother or sister. Encourage children to express their dramatic sides; they will gain valuable experience and will feel less shy in school when they share them in front of other children.

Puppets are made by Animal Fair, Country Critter Puppets, Creative Art Activities, Gabriel, Furry Folk Puppets, Gund, Lauri, Inc., Mighty Star, and Velvet Stable ($5-$25).

12. Puzzles

Puzzles are a good quiet activity and one a child can continue over a long time. As children grow older, the puzzles they enjoy increase in complexity, difficulty, and the number of pieces. A great variety of puzzles exist, so it should not be hard to find one to match your child's abilities and interests.

Puzzles are made by Come Play, Hasbro Bradley, Ideal, and Milton ($5-$10).

13. Tools

Why not provide your child with some real tools: a hammer, nails, a set of screwdrivers, rulers, and boards? The child-size kits are available, but children often grow bored with them and want the real stuff. When you are ready to buy, be creative and look for sales and go to the five-and-ten or flea markets. If you are working on a project, let your child help so he can get some experience and learn the proper ways to handle tools. It benefits the child to understand how wood gets cut and how buildings are constructed. A trip to a construction or remodeling site is interesting and educational for you and your child. When he reads or hears about building in school, his comprehension will be much better as a result of his experiences.

Tool kits are available from Child Guidance (CBS), Davis-Grabowski Fisher-Price, Hasbro, Shmuzzles, and Skilcraft ($1-$10).

14. Transportation Toys

As the child matures, his knowledge and selectivity in the transportation vehicle field increases. Where once a car was a car, now a car is a Mustang, Corvette, or Firebird. Peer pressure is terrific at this age. You may find that your child wants to collect HO tracks and trains or a fleet of ships. These items can be very costly and how much you buy is a decision you have to make, depending on what you can afford and what other things you may want to purchase for your child. One way he can collect, is to build his own models, which will give him the fun of creating and cut the heavy expenses. He or she may need your help in the beginning, but don't do it for them: let them enjoy and feel proud of what they do. Start simple to avoid frustrating your child. Remote control cars are fun for this age and also for the older child.

As the child matures, his knowledge and selectivity in the transportation vehicle field increases. Where once a car was a car, now a car is a Mustang, Corvette, or Firebird. Peer pressure is terrific at this age. You may find that your child wants to collect HO tracks and trains or a

fleet of ships. These items can be very costly and how much you buy is a decision you have to make, depending on what you can afford and what other things you may want to purchase for your child. One way he can collect, is to build his own models, which will give him the fun of creating and cut the heavy expenses. He or she may need your help in the beginning, but don't do it for them: let them enjoy and feel proud of what they do. Start simple to avoid. Remote control cars are fun for this age and also for the older child.

A SAMPLING OF TRANSPORTATION TOYS—
($3-$15)

Britain's	Farm, service station equipment, cars
Buddy L	Super Dump Truck
Corgi	Fire engine
Darda	Demon cars
Ertl	Farm, service station equipment, cars
Eugene	Magic soft skin baby
Euro	
Imports	Models, cars, ships
Lionel	Train sets
Marklin	Train sets
Match Box	Die cast cars
Mattel	Hot Wheels
Shinsei	Radio controlled cars
Tonka	Racing set

ADDITIONAL SELECTIONS FOR SIX-TO-EIGHT-YEAR-OLDS

Abacus (John Adams).
Balls, bats, mitts, face masks, helmets, etc.

Boola Ball (Ball Dance Co.).
Bop Bag (Carlin Co.) hit it and let it return.
Bulletin board—burlap or cork is best.
Coin-changer (Harmony).
Dominoes.
Dress-up mirror.
Flexible Flyer (Sno Nut).
Ice skates.
Juggling balls or scarves
Kaleidoscope.
Lotto.
Quadro (Davis-Grabowski) construction.
Microphone (LJN) cordless mike for performing.
Paper dolls.
Play houses.
Play mats.
Sewing cards and embroidery.
Stuffed animals.
Tape recorder.
Target games.
Tipi (Nomadic Tipi).
Tool box.
Typewriter (Wesco) Petite Elite, comes with replaceable ribbon.
Vegimals and soft collectibles (Freemountain).
Velcro bat and ball for games.
Video Stories (Vestron) children's video.
View Master stories and travel.
Weeble Bop Bag (Hasbro).
Yo-yo's.

CHAPTER EIGHT

Toys for Older Children

Children are constantly changing. Sometimes the changes are very rapid; other times the changes are less noticeable. Physical growth slows down in these years, and they seem to reach a plateau. Some parts of their bodies may be out of proportion and, as a result, children may appear awkward. Adults often act toward children as the child appears outwardly. If a child is large, active, and well coordinated, adults will respond to him as if he were older and quite capable. But he is not always able to handle those assumptions about what he can or cannot do.

The older child's world is becoming richer in school activities with a wider circle of friends. School is full of new material and many lessons. Afternoons may become filled with after-school activities, clubs, sports, and other group activities.

If older children are not involved with school, groups or clubs, or watching television, they benefit from having a variety of games and other playthings around them. Although while at this age they are rapidly moving toward adulthood, they still enjoy playing with toys that are fun for them. Many of the activities they engaged in when younger are still fun for them, but take on greater levels of sophistication. They usually like to play various games with their friends.

Older children become sensitive and caring in their peer relationships. Their friends are becoming increasingly important to them. There is a tendency for girls to mature more rapidly in verbal ability, and boys to excel in mathematical ability and construction. Differences in how we socialize children to sex roles become more apparent. Boys like to play roughly. Boys and girls give each other positive and negative feedback.

Older children are especially fond of creating and constructing things themselves. Offering them oppor-

tunities to work with art materials, tools, and wood, and models and other pursuits is beneficial. Children can make their own toys at this age if given a chance to obtain supplies and some clear instructions.

After they get home from school they may need to have time to relax and play quietly. Opportunities to read are important at this age. Books and magazines should be at hand and appropriate for them. Many excellent newspapers and magazines for and by children, are available.

As this is a time when children are very involved in close relationships with peers, they will have secrets they would like to keep from their parents. They dress and talk alike. They learn a lot by imitating each other.

They may want to watch a lot of television. They need to be encouraged to explore other activities. A balance would be to play with friends, toys, games, and have outdoor activities so they stay active, natural, and lively.

They do like active play: roller skating, ice skating, baseball, street games, rhyming games, basketball, and bicycling. They often like to continue their play with dolls, and playing house to express their life at home and school. This play increases in collecting.

Children learn through play the skills they will need in school. They gain muscular coordination, perceptual development and other necessary skills. For example, in reading, children need good eye-hand coordination, visual and auditory discrimination, and the ability to shift their attention from parts to the whole and then back again. As they play, they learn to move things apart, put them together again, and develop coordination. Through puzzles they learn sorting, matching, color, shapes, sizes, sequences, etc. In science, they develop skills in understanding, observation, description, testing facts and theo-

ries. In matching sets, organization and classification of sequences is learned. In constructive play, they take things apart and learn to visualize in spatial terms.

When the child is nine, you will observe that he does things with tremendous concentration and involvement, sometimes overextending his abilities. He becomes more competitive and likes sports, adventures, and playing outdoors. He is now well coordinated and has fine motor control.

The nine-year-old gets along well with his friends, usually, and likes being part of a group such as Scouts, Little League, or the swim team. He likes to create clubs with secret passwords and meetings known only to members. He likes belonging to his peer group and values his friendships. But, he is also apprehensive, worrying about not being accepted, getting along with peers, learning how to work things out, and not failing.

The ten-year-old may sometimes be awkward and clumsy, but wants to get along and tries hard. A definite difference appears in language use between boys and girls. Girls are usually more advanced verbally and more poised. Boys and girls definitely notice each other, but then they separate by sex into their own groups for play. They get along well in their teams and find getting along with each other is very important. They make up rules for the group to follow, and tend to play hard and fair. They want to accomplish good things and are eager to help and

be of service. They are very curious, creative, and aware of each other.

The eleven-year-old continues to be part of his or her group. The group is a very important experience for the child. Older children like to be independent and earn money for their special needs. This is a good time to create special jobs for them around the house for which you can pay them. Girls tend to be somewhat taller than the boys for the next two or three years. They are active, talkative, and playful. They are eager learners and tend to copy each other. They need time to pursue their own interests independently from the group, so music, dance, or creative activities will be helpful for special times away from the group.

By twelve, maturation of the child really begins to show as he or she rapidly approaches early adolescence. This means a shift away from peer pressure and to intense feelings of hero worship or for one other person who they will want to imitate in style and habits. If the model is a good one, the changes will be manifest and their behavior will show improvement.

They also need to have the continued friendships of peers. As children relate to one another and to their common interests when playing, they also need much understanding and assistance from their parents. They need support, communication, and guidance as they move ahead in their development to the next level of

Suggested Toys for Children Nine to Twelve Years

Would Like	Received	Toy	Type
——————	——————	1. Arts & Crafts/Hobbies	(C)
——————	——————	2. Books	(E)
——————	——————	3. Dolls	(C)
——————	——————	4. Electronic Games	(E)
——————	——————	5. Games	(E)
——————	——————	6. Miniatures	(C)
——————	——————	7. Musical Instruments	(C)
——————	——————	8. Puzzles	(E)
——————	——————	9. Scientific Materials	(E)
——————	——————	10. Transportation Toys	(C)

adolescence. You as a parent will continue to be a vital factor in the child's happiness and well-being. You will need to make many decisions based on your own values about friends and personal styles. Some of the changes that the child is undergoing are still within your ability to guide or to help. The child will tend to be more emotional and this may be a difficult period in your relationship with him or her.

If you can, continue to stay in contact with your child through informal play and other activities like games or hobbies. You will continue to have a child who is happy and positive, a player in his everyday life.

Older children begin to babysit and care for small children to earn extra money. He or she will happily use toys with the little children they are babysitting. This is essential training for their role as parents later on. While they instruct young children in play and toys, they will reflect upon the kinds of experiences they had with you, as the first person they related to in play. The guidance you have given them on the pathway of play has been a vital part of their life with you and will continue to be in their lives apart. Through play experiences with their peers they will learn to adjust to the world. As players, they will learn to handle life and all of its many challenges.

1. Arts and Crafts/Hobbies

Being creative is great for relaxation and for expanding individual skills. Children can sit still for longer periods of time and focus on making something they will enjoy wearing, hanging in their rooms, or giving to a friend, parent, or grandparent. It doesn't matter what the specific art or craft is, as long as they have something that is satisfying to them. Some examples of crafts they can do at this age are: weaving, quilting, doll-making, collage, clay, or modelling. Many kits are available with instructions that will give them a taste of what the possibilities are. When I was a teacher I found that my weaker readers improved when I gave them hobby kits which required them to read instructions in order to build model cars or planes. They enjoyed the activities and discipline became less of a problem. Crafts take some skill, but the results can be very beautiful and rewarding. These activities are perfect to take along on vacations, to do on rainy days, or when there is nothing else to do. Be sure they have these opportunities and do not let them get caught up on only a few aspects of toys. Balance in play is important.

You can find good selections in crafts and art supplies from Adicia-Pongo, Avalon, Binney & Smith, Craft Master, Rose Art, and Woodkrafter ($5-$25).

2. Books

Books continue to be important and satisfying. Children learn a lot from books. Let the child read to you. Children like to read aloud if given the time. Also this is a more constructive activity than watching TV; it stimulates the mind, imagination, and develops dramatic and communicative skills.

One important function that books take on is giving information to the child that you may have difficulty talking about. They need information on sex and their bodies: hygiene, hormonal changes, growth, and other natural functions. They can read these books and ask you questions. It's very important to make time to discuss books and how they feel after reading something. They need to check out their experiences and will turn to you to talk about them. Remember your own childhood; wasn't it a long intricate tapestry of sensations and feelings from being an infant to a pre-adolescent? There were new changes taking place in your body and the arrival of strange emotions, moods, and urges. It was confusing at times. Having information helps the child feel more secure: he can face the changes and deal with them in an effective fashion if he knows what is happening.

Books are published by Bobbs-Merrill, Doubleday, Delacourte, Harper and Row, Little Brown, McGraw Hill, Follet, Knopf, and Random House. See publishers in the resource section for additional listings ($3-$10).

3. Dolls

Older children still play with dolls, and they especially like dress-up dolls. The clothes and all of the features become important again and collecting dolls may become a highly valued activity. Dolls offer girls a lot of opportunities for socializing and talking to their friends. They like to discuss the dolls, their clothes, and accessories. Boys have their own collections too. They like to discuss cars, trucks, and trains. This is a time when differentiating between the sexes becomes important to them.

Girls should be encouraged to go out for sports, to learn to do things that take skill and endurance. Too much sitting around and playing with dolls can weaken their muscles. They need to get outdoors and play. We want our daughters to be real, vital, and strong young women who can also handle bikes, skates, and team games. It is encouraging to see new role models for girls reflected in dolls in jogging clothes and dancing tights who look like they do an hour of aerobics every day.

Dolls are made by Davis-Grabowski, Effanbee, Eugene, Goldberger, Golden Ribbon, Jescoe, Nisbet, and R. Dakin ($10-$35).

4. Electronic Games

Electronic games can be intriguing, educational, and interesting. However, they can also be gimmicky and damaging to children. I prefer to encourage children to interact with other children and not overdo the time they interact with machines (television or computers). Children need hobbies and creative activities, like model building, to enrich their experiences.

Children need places to play. I would like to see play centers that develop learning and creativity in or near their school. The facilities could include computer games which teach skills that children need and also provide fun and stimulation for their minds. The use of the center would have a time limit, like movies, so that the child would go outdoors and play as well. Other activities would vary to include arts and crafts, music, theatre, and reading. This type of after-school activity center would balance supervision after 3 and assist parents who work until 5 or 6 p.m. Knowing that children have safe, supervised play is of concern to parents throughout their growing years.

A perfect electronic game, in addition to being informative and fun, should be a challenge to the mind, thus providing opportunities to learn.

The following list of available games can assist you in your choice. I advise you to examine each game carefully for its value to your child before buying. Shop around for the ones that offer the most potential and flexibility. Don't be swayed by your child's ploys or by current advertising. Packaging and promotion can make anything look good.

SUGGESTED ELECTRONIC GAMES*

Activision:

Barnstorming	Attractive grahics
Boxing	Hard-hitting action
Bridge	True-to-life play
Checkers	Three levels of difficulty
Dragster	The quarter-mile in under six seconds
Fishing Derby	Catch a fish off a dock
Grand Prix	Auto-racing game
Ice Hockey	Fast action
Skiing	Easily controlled skiers
Stampede	Wild graphics with mounted cowboy and cattle
Tennis	Challenging, basic hand-eye sport

Astrovision:

Amazing Maze/Tic Tac Toe	A maze game
Bally Pin	Best video pinball game
Bingo Math/Speed Math	Fill out bingo cards and race the clock
Football	A good simulation
Galactic Invasion	One of the best space games
Letter Match/Spell 'n' Score/ Crosswords	Well-conceived word games
Music Maker	Allows you to write music in three-part harmony. Since the game console outputs video and audio, you can combine Scribbling & Music Maker for video art.
Scribbling	This game lets you doodle in brightly colored graphics

Atari:

Adventure	Interesting puzzle-action game
Asteroids	The arcade favorite
Basic Programming	Computer programming introduction

*Acknowledgment to *Games* and *Electronic Games* Magazines.

Basketball	Fast action
Brain Games	Repeat sequences
Breakout	Video handball with many variations
Code Breaker	Develop your cryptographic skills
Concentration	Like the old TV show, match numbers with hidden symbols
Flag Capture	Hidden-clue puzzle game
Fun With Numbers	The third "r"
Golf	A double-bogey
Hangman	Nice version of the spelling game
Indy 500	Racing action
Miniature Golf	Fun with moving obstacles
Sky Diver	Parachutes onto a target
Street Racer	Six types of basic car games
Superman	Man of steel battles enemies
Video Chess	A fine challenge
Video Olympics	Eight bouncy hand-eye games

Intellivision:

Backgammon	Good training
Auto Racing	First-rate
Checkers	Challenging
Electric Company Math Fun	Charming graphics to teach math
Electric Company Word Fun	Anagrammatic games
Major League Baseball	A near-perfect video game
NASL Soccer	A winner with lots of details
NBA Basketball	Well executed
NFL Football	Plenty of complicated plays
NHA Hockey	Players glide handsomely
PGA Golf	A real achievement
Tennis	Tough to play
U.S. Ski Team Skiing	Downhill and slalom

Odyssey:

Computer Intro	The basics of BASIC
Crypto-Logic	Good practice for Scrabble
Electronic Table Soccer	A fast version
Football	Plenty of possible formations
I've Got Your Number	Games and math for the younger set
K.C. Munchkin	Odyssey's most popular game
Matchmaker/ Buzzword/Logix	Three-in-one combination
Monkeyshines	Little ape figures cavort
Pocket Billiards	Like a real pool table
Quest for The Rings	Excellent fantasy game

Take the Money and Run	Enjoyable maze/puzzle game
Thunderbird	Good video pinball

Suggestions from the experienced reviewers of *Family Computing*

Rocky's Boots from The Learning Company, a game of Boolean logic;

Snooper Troops series from Spinnaker, a painless way to learn computer concepts;

Microzine, volumes 1-12 from Scholastic Software, each disk provides a nice sampling, consistently interesting and well-done;

Print Shop and Print Shop Graphics Library, volumes 1-3 from Broderbund Software, an instant gratification program for the entire family.

5. Games

When the power goes out we go back to basics. Why not pull the plug yourself and bring out the Monopoly or Parcheesi games? Remember when you were a kid, eating popcorn and playing board games with your parents? Those same games are good for your ten-year-old. Games continue to be a way families can have fun together at home, on picnics and outings, travel and vacations. Buy games that fit you and your pocket book. Games come in two flavors: challenging and silly. Take your choice.

Astro Ray	Educational games, music and art
Avalon Industries	Hexagony, Feudal Diplomacy, Acquire

Game Designers	
Workshop	Imperium
House of Game	4000 AD
Ideal	Electronic Detective
Kadon Enterprises	Quintillions
Milton-Bradley	Chess, checkers
Parker Brothers	Monopoly, Parcheesi, Clue, Careers
Pressman	Master Mind
Selchow and Righter	Scrabble, Trivial Pursuit word games
SPI	Stargate
TSR	Dungeons and Dragons
($10-$30)	

6. Miniatures

As children grow they find they like to save certain things. For some it is models, for others it's insects, cards, or miniatures. Miniatures can include figures, animals, soldiers or other objects. They are formed from molded plastic, cast metal, or carved wood and can be very detailed. The miniatures area is a collector's paradise. The world of miniatures used to be limited to doll house furnishings, but now includes just about any environment in miniature form. Many small collectibles are action oriented. You will want to make a careful selection depending on your available funds and space and what your child needs and will enjoy.

Miniatures are made by dozens of manufacturers. Some of these are Britains, Dee's Delights, Dollhouse Shoppe, Ertl, Garcia and Velez, Lauri, and Zee ($5-$12).

7. Musical Instruments

Children find enjoyment in their musical expression. By this age they are either interested in playing an instru-

ment or not. If they are encouraged to practice for some time every day, it will help them develop much faster. Children find a lot of enjoyment in playing in a band at their school. They will continue if the teacher is inspiring and the experience enjoyable. Don't be surprised if your child turns out to be quite talented. Playing music at home will also give them opportunities to extend their experiences.

Bambino makes a fine electric organ: musical instruments are also made by Douglas, Magnus Organ Company, Reeves International, and Yamaha ($10-$55).

8. Puzzles

You can now choose more complicated puzzles with many more pieces. Children will enjoy them if they can do the puzzle when they want to and have it laid out on some flat surface where it will not be disturbed.

Puzzles are made by American Publishing Company, Milton-Bradley, and Marlon Creations ($5-$15).

9. Scientific Materials

If children show an interest in chemistry or other aspects of science, encourage them, find materials that supplement what they get in school. They will like chemistry sets and other experiment kits. The Nature Company, Edmund Scientific, and other suppliers offer a wide range of scientific products. You can talk to your child's science teacher if you want to find more.

Materials are available from Capsella (Play-Jour), Fischer-America, Nasco, Natural Science Industries, and Tasco ($5-$25).

10. Transportation Toys

Transportation toys retain the child's interest for a long time. They may want remote-controlled cars, boats to float outside, or train sets. They like to create realistic scenes for the trains and play with them endlessly. If your children are interested in transportation, get them a cap, the cars or trucks they want, and let them act out the Indy 500 in the play room. They will be talking, imagining, and interacting around the live events they see on television. Children have amazing imaginations and fantasies that are an integral part of their growing experience.

A SAMPLING OF TRANSPORTATION TOYS ($3-$15)

Britain's	Model farmyard and tractor
Ertl	Farm, service station
Euro-Imports	Replicas of cars and boats
LGB	Train sets

Lionel	Train sets
Mattel	Hot Wheels
Marklin	Train sets
Matchbox	Varied models of cars
Model Rectifier	Model kits, Transformers
Tonka	Cars and Trucks

Additional Selections for Nine to Twelve Year Olds

Aerobie
Baton
Binoculars
Camera
Camping equipment
Chemistry sets
Construction sets
Craft sets
Easy Writer Typewriter (Buddy L)
Flower Press (John Adams)
Hobby sets
Juggling sets
Kites
Oil painting sets (Craft Master)
Pets
Records and tapes
Sewing machine
Sports equipment
Stuffed animals
Tape recorder
Telescope
Travel Game (Innoland)
Typewriter
Work bench and tools
Yo-yo's

CHAPTER NINE

Toys for Children with Special Needs

CAROLYN FOAT

All children learn as they play. Play is children's work. Toys and games are essential ingredients in the intellectual and social-emotional growth of all children. Particularly for the child with special needs, toys may also offer unique opportunities for mastery and success, role-playing, decision making, and trial and error learning. For both children with handicaps and their parents, properly selected toys and games allow opportunities for enjoyable learning with less pressure for achievement or fear of failure.

Parent Involvement Young handicapped children vary in their ability to play independently with toys. Because some play tasks are more challenging for a handicapped child, he/she may not be motivated to play alone with the toy or game. Some handicapped children lack sufficient attention span to focus on any one toy or game more than a few seconds. By playing along with the child, at the child's level, parents can add much enjoyment to the child's activity. It is important not to impose rigid play/activity rules or both child and parent may quickly become frustrated. For example, one parent lamented: "I don't enjoy reading to my child. He doesn't like it either. He keeps stopping me to tell what he sees in the pictures and wants to tell the story himself." The child's interest and focus in playing corresponds with his stage of development and should serve as a guide for adult participation. Observe and follow the child cues as to what he can discover or appreciate from the toy or activity at that moment.

Selection of Toys for Handicapped Children Depending on the type and degree of the child's handicapping conditions, toys considered appropriate for a child's chronological age may or may not be suitable. The reaction of a young handicapped child to a new toy could be positive and enjoyable or negative and discouraging. Close observation of a child's skills levels and play interests will guide one in making selections for the handicapped child. A child will typically demonstrate his enjoyment with overt responsiveness but will silently avoid or ignore a toy she does not find meaningful. A child with special needs should have a variety of toys including some which offer a moderate degree of learning challenge.

Questions to ponder when selecting toys for the handicapped are the same as those for any other child. However, it is especially important to keep in mind the handicapped child's
a. physical strength, coordination and abilities
b. mental ability and developmental levels
c. attention span and concentration skills
d. ability to play with the toys alone or with others
e. enjoyment of the toy

Toys for Making Learning Fun for Handicapped Children Learning proceeds faster when there is an element of fun and excitement. Through play and games children discover and practice many important skills. Since toys and games are fun, children want to play them and therefore practice of important skills is automatic. This is particularly important for the handicapped child who finds some types of learning and skill development frustrating and uninteresting.

A toy or game that maintains the interest of and provides enjoyment for a handicapped child can be a valuable learning tool having multiple uses. For example, a Barnyard (Fisher-Price) offers opportunities for developing:

Visual Skills
1. color matching
2. matching pairs of animals
3. discriminating between objects and animals

Concept Development
1. color recognition and labeling
2. number concepts
3. associative concepts—animals and their young

Fine Motor
1. manipulating doors, moving animals, vehicles
2. constructing fences

Auditory Skills
1. matching animals to their sounds (made by adult)
2. making sounds of tractor and animals

Language Development
1. recognizing animals, barnyard parts, equipment by name
2. naming things in barnyard
3. learning rhymes/songs associated with farm and farmer
4. describing actions taking place on farm

Children with Learning Handicaps The following toys and play activities are recommended for developing specific skill areas in young children with learning handicaps:

Language	**Auditory**
Puppets	Storytelling
Feely bag	Music
Cooking	Fingerplay
Rhymes	Talking Toys
Fingerplay	Sound cans
Stories	Drums and tambourines
Miniatures of common objects	
Playsets (dollhouses, farm, garage or circus)	

Fine Motor	**Visual**
Playdough	Matching objects
Play Tools	Form-board puzzles
Legos	Multi-colored toys
Bristle blocks	Parquetry blocks
Beads and string	Peg boards
Lacing toys	
Finger paint	
Feely (tactile) toys	
Peg Boards	

Gross Motor	**Concept Development**
Large blocks	Graduated cylinders and cubes
Rocking horse	Real-life toys
Scooter boards	Small objects to be counted
Mini trampoline	Sequence games
Bean bags	Attribute logic blocks
Jungle gym	

Blind children Large-muscle play equipment is important to discharge tension normally released through running. Bouncers and swings for babies and slides and gym bars for older children are helpful. Because of their tactile and kinesthetic value, fingerpaint, playdough, and paste are important creative art materials for blind children. Materials with varying textures and tactile attributes (texture-matching puzzles and texture matching boards) are recommended. Sound making and musical toys are enjoyable to blind children, but a homemade collection of sound makers (metal measuring spoons, wooden spoons, rice filled cans, etc.) is not only educational but enjoyable.

Hearing-Impaired Children The encouragement of speech is a primary goal for a hearing-impaired child. Toys and games that develop receptive and expressive language are important. For example, singing, sharing in nursery rhymes, and fingerplays should be encouraged. Materials that are self-correcting, such as Montessori, are appropriate because they allow the hearing-impaired child to monitor his own performance, master cognitive skills and concept formation, and develop a feeling of competence. Visual materials (puzzles, matching games, parquetry, etc.) are also very useful to these children.

Physically Handicapped Because their movement may be restricted, equipment and toys that allow mobility are popular. A rocking horse, scooter board, tricycle, swing, wagon, or cart would be recommended for children with motor disabilities. For playing ball, a soft cloth ball or Nerf ball is preferable, since these children may have impaired abilities to use their hands.

The size of manipulatives such as pegs, puzzle pieces, and blocks should also be taken into consideration. Equipment for sand or water play is especially helpful and enjoyable to the group.

Toy Library for the Disabled A network of toy libraries is growing which feature special adaptations of toys for disabled children. Toy libraries exist now in Rye, New York; Rochester and Rockville, Maryland; Sacramento, California; Bloomfield, Connecticut; Evanston, Illinois; Youngstown, Ohio; and in 18 library sites in Nebraska. Toys are lent out which emphasize play and developmental benefits. Toys are carefully adapted and given with special instruction on how to play with them to the child's best advantage. A network is being established with the help of a Joseph P. Kennedy Foundation grant. For further information contact the National Lekotek Center at 2100 Ridge Avenue, Evanston, IL 60201. Lekotek provides self-help resources for the special child.

Sick or Hospitalized Child When a child is homesick, a number of quiet activities will keep them amused. Keep in mind books, crayons and coloring books, hobby kits, construction toys, games, paper dolls, audio or video cassettes, and puppets. If a child is in the hospital, talk with the play activities coordinator, who will assist in providing pleasant activities that will amuse, educate, and entertain the child. Role playing as emotional support is very important to any hospitalized child. Use puppets, dolls, and stuffed animals to make the transition easier and nurturing. Remember, the presence of a child's favorite stuffed toy will be very supportive in an otherwise unfamiliar environment.

See the Resource section for mail order catalogs from The Able Child and The Kids on the Block, and for books see authors Karnes (*Arts and Crafts for Children*), Grasselli and Hegner (*Child Development*), Honig (*Games for Adults*), Caplan and Frost (*Play*), Haas (*Teacher Resources*), Sinker (*Toys for Children with Special Needs*), and Burtt (*Toys, How to Make*).

Select toys by Adica-Pongo, Artsana of America, Binney and Smith, Child Life Play Specialties, Colorforms, Country Wood Shop, Developmental Learning Materials, Edumate, Fisher-Price, Johnson and Johnson Baby Products, Korver-Thorpe, Learning Materials Workshop, Lego Systems, Mattel, and Shield.

Write to these organizations for more information:

Lets Play to Grow
Joseph P. Kennedy Foundation
1701 K Street NW
Washington, DC 20006

Closer Look
PO Box 1492
Washington, DC 20013

Council for Exceptional Children
1920 Association Drive
Reston, VA 22091

CHAPTER TEN

Outside Play-Home, Park, School and Travel

Children play outdoors easily and enjoy trips to playgrounds and parks. When a child starts using playground equipment, skates, bikes, or other outdoor toys, he should be old enough to know the dangers of such equipment and be taught to follow certain rules.

Bicycles, tricycles, skates or sleds should not be used where there is traffic and should be carefully used in areas where other children play.

Make certain that swings and the other playground constructions are firmly placed in the ground away from walls, fences, and automobile or pedestrian traffic. The equipment should be the right size for the child and assembled according to the directions of the manufacturer. You may want to build your own playground equipment in your yard. Parents, working together, can build a sturdy playground in a park or empty lot near their homes. A good reference for this type of project can be found in a book by Joan Jeremy and Jay Beckwith called *Build Your Own Playground* (Houghton Mifflin Company, 1975, 219 pp. $7.95.)

The authors contend that a playground need not be a sterile layout of asphalt, slides, and swings. They show how to create a play area which reflects children's ideal play spaces. Among the topics covered are building materials, division of labor during construction, and playing areas for children with special needs: They write:

...getting access to a site, finding money for the playground takes persistence and imagination, but it can certainly be done. This kind of fund-raising benefits from the clear image that the group can present simply by saying, "we're building our own playground and we need some help." Among the sources that community groups have tapped are federal, state, and local funds, as well as private donations from foundations or individuals. One group of parents at a co-op nursery school got a promise of funds if it could come up with a matching amount. The parents had very little cash, but they figured the value of their donated labor at $2.50/hr. and used that sum to satisfy the matching requirement...

Scrounging materials can likewise be developed into an art. A playground has the great potential for creative use of surplus materials. Some likely sources of interesting and inexpensive materials are government surplus, salvage stores, scrap metal dealers, state and federal surplus outlets (which often have catalogs), and utility companies. Items that are often available for free include trees from park or highway departments or builders who are clearing sites: tires of all sizes from tire dealers, telephone poles or the short end pieces from the power and phone companies, wooden wire reels, and railroad ties from railroad yards.

Children need to have a balance in their play. From the time they are babies they should play both inside and out of doors. The benefits of play outdoors are great for fresh air, sunshine, and the stimulation of the outer world which broadens the child's experience and curiosity.

The space that is created for the child should offer safety, security, a variety of playthings, and be easily accessible to a bathroom. You will want to obtain or create a place for toys to be stored, a place for water, sand, and digging, and a safe place for the use of a tricycle.

Creating A Playground

You can create a play area for children from materials you can get free or very inexpensively. Playgrounds do not have to look the same. What children do is what counts, running, jumping, swinging, whatever helps them to develop their arm and leg muscles.

Straw and hay: From local fields in the fall or from a feed store. For jumping in or using for a thatched roof.

Railroad ties: From railroad companies and crews. For an imbedded balance beam, the sides of a sandbox, or a make-believe car with a mounted steering wheel.

Large rocks: From road construction sites, gravel pits, or the woods. For damming up a stream to make a pool or stepping stones.

Bricks: Use seconds from a brickyard or construction company. For building forts and constructing a climbing wall with concrete.

Concrete pipes: From concrete companies or the telephone company. For making tunnels and bridges. Be sure they are well embedded in the ground.

Tree sections and tree trunks with limbs: From the city electric company, neighbors, or a lumber mill. For climbing and practicing hammering, sawing, and other woodworking skills.

Sand: From the beach, a construction company, or a sand and gravel pit. For making a sandbox. Should have drainage bricks underneath and a cover to keep cats and dogs out.

Wooden blocks and pieces of lumber: Discards from lumber companies and the city utility company. For building structures with hammers and nails, for stacking and other structures.

Ropes, rope ladders, and cargo nets: From hardware stores and shipyards. For climbing and swinging.

Barrels: From a hardware store or a distillery. For rolling in, making houses and tunnels. Be sure to sand away splinters.

Large, wooden electric wire spools: From the electric company. For making tables, stools.

Discarded rowboat: Ask around piers and docks. Use for imaginary voyages, or drill holes for drainage and use as a sandbox.

Automobile tires: From auto junkyards and service stations. Clean them up and paint them bright colors with paint made especially for rubber. Use to roll, to stack, to climb on, and as swings.

Some Outdoor Play Equipment

balls
bicycles
boats
bricks
garden supplies
hammock (low-slung)
homemade blocks and lumber for building
homemade wooden boxes
pail and shovel
skates
sleds
swings
tricycles
tubs for water, sand, or dirt and flowers
wheelbarrows
wooden ladder for an obstacle course

School: Your Child Plays Outside the Home

When you go visit your child's nursery school, child care center or home, or school, be sure to look at the condition, supply, and quality of playthings and equipment.

1. Are the toys in good working order?
2. Are there enough toys?
3. Is there a good variety of toys appropriate for the child's age and interest?
4. Are the toys easy to get hold of and play with?
5. Are there adequate indoor and outdoor play areas with sufficient equipment?
6. Do teachers find appropriate, interesting, and challenging activities for the children's playtime?

7. Do the children have time to explore their interests?
8. Can children bring toys from home to school?
9. Are the toys available to both boys and girls?
10. Do the toys reflect the educational, creative, and active needs of the child.

Possible Materials Available in School
(Child Care Center, Home, or Nursery School)

If the classroom does not have these items, you or a group of parents may want to provide them:
animals
art supplies
balls
blocks
books
boxes
climbing equipment
craft materials
dolls
dirt, sand
dramatic play items (hats, fabric, shoes, bags)
hoops
magazines
old tires
plants, gardens
punching bag
record player, tapes and records
ring toss
rocker
steps
trains, cars, boats
tricycles

In addition the preschool should have areas that allow for specific activities that encourage play, such as:
cooking area
dress-up clothes and props
housecleaning area
jumping areas, i.e., mattresses, bouncers, carpet
library
music area and instruments
pets
quiet places for rest and relaxation, looking at books, and listening to music.

Travel Play

Children easily become restless during long trips. They need to have activities to enjoy and keep them busy. A good idea is to gather items into a Trip Pak.

A container that will fit under a seat or in an overhead carrier is recommended if travelling by bus, plane, or train. Include place art materials (pads of paper, crayons, pens, scotch tape, children's safety scissors, glue stick, and magazine pictures), games (see list of suggestions), cassette tape recorder and cassettes (stories, mu-

sic, and blank tapes), books, plus a few selected toys from the suggested list of travel toys:

ARC	Pocket Games Great 8
	chess, checkers
Salchow & Righter	Tic Tac Toe
Binney & Smith	Game Time (reusable
	games attached)
Cadaco	MagneSpell
Child Guidance	Pack'n'Go Chalkboard
Colorforms	Various sets
Ohio Art	Etch A Sketch
Innoland	Globe Master game
John Adams Toys	posters to color
	coloring cards
	origami
	paper doll pad
	make mosaics
	Puffin Book of Car
	Games
Leisure Dynamics	Travel Aggravation
International Playthings	Magnetic Games
Milton Bradley	Pocket Simon
Placo	fun art in sets
Pressman Toy Co.	MAD LIBS coloring and
	joke books
Tomy	Drive Yourself Crazy
Western	Match A Shape
Wolverine	Tic-Tac-Toe

You can create games for your children to play:

1. One-of-a-kind pictures—Cut out pictures from magazines for them to arrange and paste down into a new picture on collage.
2. Hidden newspaper words—Each player has the same newspaper to find words that identify subjects, such as people, money, jobs, seasons or other topics.
3. Object hunt—Make a list of objects children can locate on the trip. As they see them they can check them off.
4. Make a puzzle—Have children draw a picture. Cut it into 4 or 5 parts, then have the children exchange pictures, puzzles and reassemble them.

Creative Play

The rest of this chapter incudes helpful information for you to expand the play potential for your child at home or at school. A variety of lists are included for an inventory of possible materials to obtain for creative pursuits. Each item will stimulate your own imagination. Many good activities and crafts books to assist you in selecting the right materials for different projects. Found and scrounge materials are used by creative teachers every day in classrooms to stimulate projects that are fun for children to make themselves.

In addition to the lists of free and inexpensive materials the locations of places where you will be able to get materials, ideas on selecting materials for dramatic play, sand and water art, and crafts are also included. Suggested props to help your child get experience in role-playing are given for a number of situations including automobile repairman, forest ranger, beautician, plumber and others. Role-playing is important for the young child as he gets many ideas about the community and other people through acting out in free-form play, the different people he observes.

As I discussed in Chapter One, play is how children learn about life. Toys are a way for them to have fun. The possibilities discussed in this chapter serve to increase the new options for fun and learning.

List of Scrap Materials for Making Toys at Home

Acetate	Bricks	Clock parts	Packing material
Acorns	Buckles	Clothespins	Paint
Aluminum foil	Burlap	Confetti	Paper, wrapping
Aluminum pie pans	Buttons	Containers	Paper boxes, bags
Bags	Canvas	Corks	Paper cups
Beads	Cardboard (corrugated)	Cord	Paper doilies
Beans	Cardboard rollers	Corn	Paper napkins
Belts	Cardbboard spools	Corn husks	Paper plate
Bobby pins	Carpet scraps	Corn Starch	Paper towels
Bottles (non-breakable)	Cartons	Costume jewelry	Paper tubes
Bottle caps	Cellophane	Cotton	Picture frames
Boxes (varied sizes)	Chains	Drapery swatches	Pine cones
Brads	Clay	Driftwood	Pins
		Eggshells	Pipe cleaners
		Egg cartons	Pie plates
		Excelsior	Plastic bags
		Eyelets	Plastic bottles, baskets
		Fabric scraps	Pocketbooks
		Feathers	Popsickle sticks
		Felt	Pot scrubbers
		Flash bulbs	Ribbon
		Floor coverings	Rocks
		Flour	Rope
		Foam	Rubber bands
		Fruits	Rug yarn
		Fur	Salt
		Gourds	Sand
		Greeting cards	Sandpaper
		Grocery bags	Seeds
		Hangers	Sewing notions
		Hatboxes	Sea shells
		Hats	Sheets, old
		Ice cream containers	Shelf paper
		Inner tubes	Shoe laces
		Jars	Shoe boxes
		Jewelry	Snaps
		Kraft paper	Socks
		Lacing	Spaghetti
		Lamp shades	Sponges
		Leather	Spools
		Linoleum	Stockings
		Liquid starch	Stones
		Macaroni	Straws
		Magazines	String
		Marbles	Styrofoam
		Masonite	Sweaters
		Milk cartons	Tacks
		Mirrors	Tape
		Mittens	Thread
		Nails	Tiles
		Neckties	Tires
		Newspapers	Tissue paper
		Nuts	Toilet tissue
		Oilcloth	Tongue depressors
		Old clothes	Toothpicks
		Orange sticks	Twine
		Ornaments	Vegetables

Wallpaper samples
Wallboard
Wax
Wigs
Window shades
Wire (insulated)
Wire mesh
Wooden crates

Wooden dowels
Wooden spools
Wooden blocks
Wood scraps
Wool
Wrapping paper
Yarn

Free and Inexpensive Materials—Sources

Contractors Lumber, tiles, linoleum, wallpaper, pipes, wire.

Department Stores Fabric swatches, rug swatches, corrugated packing cardboard.

Electric Power Company-PR Dept. Wire, large spools for tables, assorted packing material.

Garment Factories Yarns, buttons, decorative tape, fabric.

Hardware Stores Sample wallpaper books, sample tile charts, linoleum samples.

Junk Yards Unlimited possibilities, clocks, radios, fans, irons, toasters, hinges, handles and fittings.

Metal Spinning or Fabrication Companies scrap pieces.

Paper Companies For unusual kinds of paper, samples, cut ends, damaged sheets, and cardboard.

Phone Company Excess colored wire, spools.

Plumbers Wires, pipes, tile scraps, linoleum.

Rug Companies Sample swatches, end pieces from rugs cut to size.

Supermarkets Cartons, packing materials, fruit crates, materials from displays, cardboard display racks.

Tile and Ceramic Companies Tiles by the pound (inexpensive) and broken pieces.

Free and Inexpensive Materials—Uses

Playground Large cartons, fruit crates, barrels, concrete blocks, bricks, large stones, spools, ladders, sewage pipe, ropes, bicycle tires, sawhorses, tree trunks, planks, wooden clubhouse, and targets.

Dramatic Play Old clothes, hats, shoes, shawls, beads, jewelry, material to be used as saris, capes and togas, pans, glasses, gloves, handbags, wallets, aprons, white coats for professionals (doctors), hand mirror, compacts, long mirrors, old televisions, radios, record players, telephones, irons and toasters; brooms, dustpans, brushes, tubs, fruit and vegetables crates, saw horses, baskets, grocery carts, shopping bags, and play money.

Sand and Water Play Plastic jugs, bottles, cups, old teapots, coffee pots, watering cans, garden hoses, bottles, jugs, jars with lids, tin cans, wood, cork, shells, sponges, styrofoam, marbles, rubber balls, balloons, bubble pipes, hand towels, mops, aprons, food coloring, soap, flour, wire, string, rubber bands.

Construction, Sewing, Woodworking Boxes of all kinds, egg cartons, milk cartons, cookie trays, vegetable cartons, match boxes: plastic bottles, boxes and jugs, cardboard tubing from paper towels and toilet tissue, broom handles, spools, bottle caps, lids, pipe cleaners, white glue, paste, Scotch tape, masking tape, paper clips, staples, string, rope, wire, brass paper fasteners; wheels and gears from clocks, fans, cars; handles, knobs, and hinges; scrap wood, nuts, bolts, nails, washers, screws; cloth of various textures and colors, silk, lace, nylon, net, corduroy, wood velvet, burlap, felt, cotton, yarn, ribbon, rick-rack, lace, thread, buttons, beads, snaps, buckles, zippers, needles, pins, knitting needles.

Collage Tray Yarn, thread, ribbon, lace, stones, shells, bottle caps, broom straws, straws, toothpicks, pipe cleaners, twigs, fabric, scrap paper, wood chips, feathers, sawdust, sand, macaroni, rice, packing paper, beads, sequins, buttons, foam rubber, cork, scrap rubber, cake paints, seaweed, leaves, pine needles, seeds, chalk, wire, string, white glue, rubber cement.

Painting Muffin tins, empty plastic squeeze bottles, jars with lids, tin cans, sheets of plastic, newspaper, aprons, sponges, string, straws, sticks, twigs, toothpicks to be used as brushes, wax, liquid starch and rope clothesline and pins for hanging art work.

Graphics Tin cans, cardboard tubing, rolling pins, pencils, hair curlers, candles to be used as rollers in printing, forks, spoons, knives, potato mashers, buttons, corks, jar lids, blocks, clay, corrugated board, vegetables, rubber bands, paper clips, string, and fabric.

Clay Work Plastic bags and covered tins for storage, plastic material, tools for modeling—pencils, feathers, twigs, forks, knives, spoons, rolling pins, pebbles, shells, leaves, and toothpicks.

Sculpture Scrap wood and cardboard, string, wire, nails, toothpicks, pipe cleaners, straws, sticks, tin foil, assorted paper, and white Glue.

Look for Props

For the Automobile Repairman

Used motor parts, spark plugs, filters, carburetors, cable sets, gears, etc. Tools: hammers, pliers, screw driver, Oil funnel, Empty oil cans, Flashlight, Wiring, Air pump, Windshield Wipers, Key carrier and keys, Rags, old shirts, gloves, Automobile supply catalogs, cap or visor

For the Forest Ranger

Canteen	Nature books
Flashlight	Small logs
Rope	Binoculars
Mosquito netting	Hat
Canvas for tent	Compass
Knapsack	Sleeping bag
Food supplies	Mess kit

For the Beautician

Mirror
Curlers
Hairpins
Hairnets
Dryer
Aprons or large bibs
Brushes
Combs
Towels
Magazines
Empty shampoo bottles (plastic)
Plastic bins
Emery boards
Pencil and paper
Money

For the Plumber

Pipes
Spigots
Plungers
Tools
Hose and nozzles
Spade
Old shirt, cap
Hardware supply catalog
Measuring devices

Other Occupations Your Child May Want to Play

Astronaut	Peace Corps Worker
Bus Driver	Pilot
Doctor	Police Officer
Electrician	Post Office Worker
Fireman	Railway Engineer
Fisherman	Reporter
Flight Attendant	Scientist
Frogman	Seamstress
Grocer	Secretary
Magician	Ship Captain
Martian	Shoe Salesperson
Nurse	Teacher
Officer Worker	Telephone Repairman
Painter	Veterinarian

Use your imagination to locate "props" and costumes that work well with each role. This role playing is very important to the children's social development. Never laugh at the child, but join in with his or her laughter. Remember that play is serious fun for children. Join with them when the occasion arises and they will enjoy and accept your participation. Dollhouses, playsets, dress up clothing, and other playhouse equipment encourages role playing.

See books by Dorsett, Farrell, and Hershoff (*Arts and Crafts*), and Piers and Landau (*Play*) in the Resourse section.

CHAPTER ELEVEN

Views on Toys By Parents and Children

A child needs to be presented with many choices. The decision of what is their favorite toy is determined by what is actually available to them, which in turn depends on what parents find in the stores, their own choices, and financial considerations. If the child enjoys the toy for a long time the item is said to have "high play value." This is not always possible to predict before the child actually plays with a toy. The real play value depends on the toy's suitability, or what I like to call "play potential." Anything can be a toy if it has potential or possibilities for enjoyment, instruction, or a combination of both.

While doing research for this book I interviewed parents in many places throughout the United States. I talked to parents in toy stores, child care centers, and parks. I listened to what parents liked and disliked about the toys their children played with and the toys available for sale. Parents made many comments individually, in groups, and by letter. Some of these comments are included. I would like to thank all of the parents who took the time to talk with me about their experiences and share their child's preferences in toys.

The parents who responded to the queries received four booklets on toy selection prepared by the Toy Manufacturers of America. I would like to thank the TMA for their generosity.

TOY SURVEYS

PARENTS HAVE A LOT TO SAY ABOUT THE TOYS THEIR CHILD PLAYS WITH. PLEASE SHARE YOUR COMMENTS. PHOTOCOPY AND RETURN THE PARENT'S AND CHILDREN'S SURVEYS TO US AS SOON AS POSSIBLE. FEEL FREE TO WRITE WHENEVER YOU HAVE AN IDEA OR COMMENT TO SHARE.

WRITE TO:
INSTITUTE FOR CHILDHOOD RESOURCES
1169 HOWARD STREET
SAN FRANCISCO, CA 94103

PARENT'S SURVEY ON TOYS

My child(ren) are:
a) Age _____, M _____, F _____
b) Age _____, M _____, F _____
c) Age _____, M _____, F _____
d) Age _____, M _____, F _____

Child A enjoys playing with (name three specific toys; include brand names, if known):

1. _____

2. _____

3. _____

Child B enjoys playing with (name three specific toys):

1. _____

2. _____

3. _____

Child C enjoys playing with (name three specific toys):

1. _____

2. _____

3. _____

Child D enjoys playing with (name three specific toys):

1. _____

2. _____

3. _____

My favorite toys are:

1. _____

2. _____

3. _____

What I would improve on the toys my child plays with:
Child A

_____

_____

_____

Child B

_____

_____

_____

Child C

_____

_____

_____

Child D

_____

_____

_____

Comments on Toys from Parents

- I want my money's worth when I buy toys. I pick out what will last, not fads.
- Puzzles help my child with a challenge and help him feel a sense of accomplishment and completion when he puts it all together.
- Books help me teach him language and are great for calming him down after hard play.
- I want sturdier toys. Too many are cheap and don't hold up.
- I want more educational toys at home, not just for teachers at school.
- Children have special needs and so do parents. I want them to have fun when they play.
- I don't know what to get at the right age and I need help when I make selections.
- I want more learning games to help her with numbers and letters.
- Toys should be for learning and life.
- Toys should not be flashy. Even if a child does not take to it right away, if it has possibilities and is imaginative he will learn and have fun. It could become a favorite.
- I am so tired of buying things that look good in ads and on television and then fall apart after one or two days. My child is not that hard on things. The toys are just not built to take a child's activity. Look at this game. So many pieces and they all get lost. It is hopeless and ready for the trash can.
- I want boxes not to be labeled as girls only and only for boys.
- I don't want my children pressured on TV by ads. It's just too much to keep pushing them to buy and they push me. Sometimes I get really angry at advertisers and toy people.
- When I complain about a toy, sometimes they just say they are sorry and there is nothing they can do. Why can't stores return your money or give an exchange within a reasonable time, say 30 days? My child gets shortchanged. I usually don't buy from that company again.
- When I go to the big store to shop no one is there to help or answer questions. It is like an impersonal supermarket. I am not sure if it is worth the price to not have personal service.
- The prices for toys have gotten way out of line. I have to make fewer purchases.
- I wish I could exchange toys with neighbors and friends more often because my child gets tired of the toy after a while and is ready for something else...
- When I was a child things seemed to last longer. Kids get bored too easily now and products don't hold up like they used to.
- I want anything that inspires the imagination of my child.
- We like blocks as they are good for building together.
- Why are violent toys so popular? I don't want them for my child.

PARENTS REPORT ON CHILD'S PREFERENCES

Under One Year
Bathroom mirror
Rattles
Face of baby on diaper box
Chatter Telephone
Musical Busy Box
Musical mobile and rattles
Plastic bowls (small bright-colored)
Rubber doll
Teddy bear
Small telephone
Turn and Learn Toy
Yellow melon baller

One to Three Years
Anything with noise and parts (preferably removable)
Balloons
Ball
Blocks
Bristle blocks
Broom
Books
Cars
Cash register
Dolls
Horses on wheels
Miniature people with assortment of props
Mr. Potato Head
Plastic tool set
Play telephone
Playhouse
Pounding bench and mallets
Pull toy
Puzzles
Raggedy Ann and Andy dolls
Ride-ons
Rocking horse
Sesame Street puzzles
Soft plastic toys
Trucks
Word blocks

Three to Five Years
Airport play set
Bicycles
Blocks
Cars
Coloring book and crayons
Dolls with clothes to change, washable hair
Dominoes
Finger paints
Legos
Playhouse or tipi
Props for playing house, school, work
Puzzles
Snoopy clothing and dolls
Speak'n'Spell

Eight to Twelve Years
Adventure People
Books
Camera
Cars
Checkers
Colorforms
Dollhouses
Dolls
Electronic games
Latch hook kit
Legos
Radio
Roller skates
Skateboard
Sports equipment

Children's Toy Preference

When children were asked: What is your favorite toy?, the answers rapidly poured in, often complete with brand names and manufacturers. The children who responded were well versed in why the toy was "special" for them. Children do know what they like, what they don't like, and why. They discuss toys and games with their friends. They observe others playing. They watch television. They are often astutely critical about specific items.

The toys and games children seemed to like were entertaining for a long time, had novelty, and held their interest.

If you would like to help us keep up-to-date on children's preferences please photocopy the following survey and send it to us for the on-going review of information about toys and playthings. If your child is under five, talk with him or her and fill in the information. If they are older they might want to fill it in themselves. Pictures, drawings, and any additional comments are most welcome.

A Child Comments on Toy Preferences: Age 12

There's so many I just...
The only two that I can think of, that I have right now are the 2XL. I don't know who it is by. I think it's Mattel. It's like a talking robot and it has cassettes you put in it and he asks you questions and you say "true" or "false" or "yes" or "no" and stuff like that and it's kinda cute. There are a whole bunch of different tapes like movies and it's neat.

My second one is Speak and Spell by Texas Instruments and I love it. One of my friends has it and I played with it. It's really great. It plays games and you can spell words and the games are like...sorta like Hangman. You know they have Hangman and you try to find the right letters and first you say whatever appears...the word that appears...there's another game and there's a word that is on the screen and it

CHILDREN'S SURVEY

My Age _____ Grade _____ My initials are _____

I live in_____ Zipcode _____
(Name of city or town and street)

My favorite toy is:

_____

Made by:

_____
(Company that makes it, if you know)

It cost $ _____

I like this toy because:

1. _____

2. _____

3. _____

What I would do to make this toy even better:

1. _____

2. _____

3. _____

The toy I want for my next birthday:

_____

Parents, you are welcome to make a copy of this survey and send the information to us more than once. I would also like to collect information on the changes in children's preferences as they get older.

says "Welcome," "Say it," and it does like 10 words and then it says, "Spell 'welcome'" and it's really neat because each time you push like "w," it goes "w"; "e," it goes "e", you know, it kind of says whatever you push. And it has spelling quizzes and it does different things and it's really neat. It is kind of expensive. The 2XL I like, but I can really do without, but I'd rather have a Speak 'n' Spell.

Selected Results of the Toy Survey

One Year Old
a turtle rattle
a telephone rattle
all kinds of plastic containers
loves to eat and rip up paper
cat (imitates the cat)
plastic cylinders and foam balls (she puts them into the cylinder and removes them with a lot of concentration)
check book cover (she holds on to it)
tambourine
cigar box
rocker holder with post for different colored and sized rings
spoons (holds it, bangs it on table, puts it in her mouth)
fuzzy puppet
clocks
paperweight with snow scene in it (I turn it over for her)

Two Year Old Boys
ball
jack-in-the-box
tricycle
musical pull toy
books
blocks
stuffed animals
kitchen set
dolls
cars
tricycles
pail
small boat
crayons and pens
circus train

Two Year Old Girls
ball
teddy bear
dolls
Raggedy Ann
blocks
stethoscope
Fisher-Price people
pull-apart car
clay
picture books
See N Say
Fisher-Price book with
  pockets
telephone
Play-Doh
balloon
teddy bear
puppet
tricycle

Three Year Old Boys
dolls
rocking horse
dinosaur book
balls and bats
cars and trucks
tools and machines
boxing gloves
stuffed animals

Three Year Old Girls
Play-Doh
finger paints
blocks
Play Family Village
Lego sets
books
play iron
paints and crayons
dolls

stuffed animals
magnet board
Bert and Ernie puppets
tricycle
plastic nuts and bolts
tea set

Four Year Old Boys
fire truck
hammer and nails
bicycle
Lego set

Four Year Old Girls
swing set
tricycle
scissors
kitchen equipment
stuffed animals
pottery making set
craft set

Five Year Old Boys
carpenter set
planes
truck and car
blocks
marionettes
hand puppets
Matchbox cars
rope
bicycle
game of the Presidents
game of the States

Five Year Old Girls
doll with moving eyes
box of treasures
brush and comb set
Fisher-Price merry-
  go-round
stuffed animals
Christie doll
music box
telephone
pocketbook doll and buggy
cards
felt tip pens and paper
Play-Doh
small cars

Six Year Old Boys
Enterprise from Star Trek
Match Box cars
Scrabble
glider
trucks
tool sets

paper planes

Six Year Old Girls
camera
paper
jump rope
Monopoly
bicycle
photo album
dress up doll
tiny dolls
Viewmaster
tiles (for mosaics)
teddy bears
dishes
paper dolls
stuffed animals
swing set
crayons
paints
doll house
large building blocks

Seven Year Old Boys
bicycle
crayons
giant Tinkertoys
hockey sticks
blocks
Erector set
Matchbox toys
trains
chalkboard and easel
drawing materials
pen and paper
baseball cards
Lego sets
models
art supplies
chemistry set

Seven Year Old Girls
merry-go-round
bicycle
ice skates
board games
Paddington Bear
Wizard of Oz toys
dolls
blocks
books
sewing basket
record player
Snoopy pencil sharpener
Pick Up Sticks
Animal Lotto
blackboard

doctor kit
loom
jump rope
pasting and painting materials
Colorforms
Play-Doh

Eight Year Old Boys
football
baseball
bicycle
basketball net and ball
toy cars and race car set
Lego sets
Lincoln Logs
working elevator (building toys)
fishing pole

Eight Year Old Girls
horses
Barbie doll
boat and figures
toy cars
books
flute
candle making kit
Monopoly
bicycle
cards
Viewmaster
records
stuffed animals
jump rope
kick ball

Nine Year Old Boys
frisbee
toy cars
board games
baseball bat, ball, and mitt
football
bicycle
telescope
Lego sets

Nine Year Old Girls
tennis
board games
jacks
stuffed animals
magic game

Ten Year Old Boys
tape recorder
dominoes
space toys
racing cars

Ten Year Old Girls
cards
books
stickers
chess
Scrabble
Monopoly
stuffed animals
dolls
jump rope
records

bicycle
ice skates
painting and drawing
  materials

Eleven Year Old Boys
hockey game
bicycle
microscope
sports equipment
remote controlled plane
  or car

Eleven Year Old Girls
dolls in baby clothes
Chess
roller skates
stuffed animals
drawing materials

Twelve Year Old Boys
baseball or football
  equipment
tape recorder
coin collection

Twelve Year Old Girls
Barbie dolls
board games
books
miniatures
plants
paper and art supplies
backpack

PART III

HISTORY

CHAPTER TWELVE

The History of Toys in America

Children in America played with toys before the time of Columbus. Toys actually have existed in every civilization, as they assist children to develop physically and mentally. Archeologists uncovered a toy factory in India dating back 5000 years. Children in Asia played with kites, dominoes, tops, and dolls. Ancient Egyptians, Greeks, and Romans played board games such as chess and backgammon. When settlers came to this country from Europe, they brought with them the toys characteristic of their culture and community. The settlers discovered that Indian children had some games and playthings not unlike their own. Indian children played ball, hit targets with bows and arrows, played with dolls, made toy animals from wood and bone, and tops from acorns. The new settlers brought with them dolls, ice-skating, and games, and devised new toys. They made corncob dolls and carved wooden toys.

Toy shops began appearing in New England in the early 18th century. Ben Franklin and other boys could buy whistles, kites, marbles and toys of pewter, wood, or tin after the American Revolution. The first manufacturing companies began to create playthings. In 1830, the Tower Toy Company became one of the first manufacturing businesses by creating an association of craftsmen. They produced dolls, doll furniture, toys, and wooden boats. At the same time the Crandall family in Rhode Island began producing toys and obtained a number of patents. These items included nesting blocks, building blocks, a spring horse, and puzzles.

At first wood was used exclusively but other materials began to be used in the mid-19th century. Tin was used, plus rubber from India, and paper.

At the time of the Civil War, the patenting of toys was drastically reduced. Toy guns and weapons were created, along with steam engines. Toy stores did very well until the war began and imports went down. Production after the war saw a rapid growth in the toy industry.

In the 1870's, some toys had wheels and could act as transportation toys. The hobby horse was created. Children had a variety of sleds and wooden toys. Wagons were made by 1880. Novelty work began in 1899, with baby dolls and wooden carriages. Examples of these toys can be seen in special collections. Other products included Lincoln Logs from which play log houses could be built. This was also a time of popular mechanical toys. Dolls that walked, toy pianos, tin toys run by friction "motors" or wind-up springs were popular, as were steam vehicles and the first electric train.

The Milton Bradley Company made toys out of paper and cardboard in the beginning. They created a very realistic game for buying and selling, which was called "Money." They also made a toy clock, safety banks, homes for paper dolls, and a Buffalo Bill gun.

Windup toys were popular in the 1860's. Roller skates were made by J. L. Plimpton, in Boston, 1863. Tricycles became popular in the 1880's. Toys with bells, toy figures, and toy pianos and musical instruments were popular. Knapp Electric Company in the 1890's, made magnetic toys, motors, dynamos and trains. Carlisle and Finch Company of Cincinnati made the first electric train. Although steam electrical toys may have been too dangerous to play with, there was a high demand.

R. V. Ives was the most popular toy company. His son Harry, who became the founder of the Toy Manufac-

turers of America in 1916, was one of the most influential men in the industry. He created electrical toys, steamboats and trains, and a rowboat whose oars worked via a spring. He added iron toys to the collection and was a very successful businessman until the Depression hit.

The Schlesinger Company in 1875 made hundreds of varieties of tin toys, including many kinds of beach pails. Harry T. Kingsbury constructed exact machine prototypes and, after visiting racing car tracks, obtained permission to make models of the automobile in which British Major Seagrave won his international land speed records. He made several models of the race car. In the 1930's the first automobile model made to scale was produced. It sold 300,000 the first year. The deluxe model

carried a music box inside the car. Kingsbury made the first model airplane, the "Lindbergh," and later converted his plant to war production in World War II.

Toy pistols and shooters became popular during the Civil War. Their sales are often correlated to the war occurring at the time. However, during the Vietnam War, toy gun sales were down. The sales of guns increased after the war, along with growing controversy about them.

Water pistols have been a favorite since they were first manufactured. The Daisy Company made the first plunger-type water pistol and an airgun that shot BB's. The Hyatt Company, in the 1870's, made alphabet blocks, checkers, dominoes, and other wooden games. Morton Converse, from 1870's, made dolls and doll furniture for his daughter. He later made a wooden puzzle which sold very well. He also made Noah's Ark and a hobby horse. Within a short time he was making 15,000 rocking horses a year.

The first American board game was the "Mansion of Happiness," invented in 1843 and produced by W. & S. B. Ives Company. The goal of the game was to reach "eternal happiness." Parker Brothers bought the game in 1880.

When George Parker was going to school in Salem, Massachusetts, he began a game company with his brother. In 1888, they produced over 300 games. The first game was called "Banking," and was followed by "Speculation." Later the biggest selling game, "Monopoly," was created. An educational element was found in all the games. The game, "Camelot," came out of the original game called "Chivalry." Another game, "Rook," became a popular card game. In 1937, there appeared a crossword lexicon, in which letter cards, each with the scoring value printed on it, were used to build up words in a crossword puzzle form. It did well, but in ten years another company came out with the game "Scrabble." Companies understood the high competition between them for new products.

With more toys, more companies became involved in selling them in stores and by catalog sales, such as Sears and Montgomery Ward. Companies often offered over a hundred different items. Before the Civil War in the 1880's, there were twelve toy companies. In the 1880's, there were 173 manufacturers of toys, sleds, and carriages, with about 3.5 million dollars worth of business and 1 million dollars worth of imported toys. The population at that time was 50 million. By 1900 the population had risen to 76 million. Toy imports had risen to 3 million. Twenty million dollars worth of toys were bought. By then there were five hundred toy companies with sales of 40 million dollars.

Miniature railroads and novelty items were available in the 1900s. *Playthings* magazine reported that every child in the country received at least two toys. Mechanical toys were popular, as were complete grocery stores with all the packages, and telephone and telegraph sets, zoetropes, animated pictures, stereopticons, and double postcards. Selchow Righter made a moving picture machine. Products for nursery schools and kindergartens were popular, and companies like Milton Bradley produced watercolors and modeling clay for art instruction in school. Toy planes which flew were popular after the Wright Brothers flight. Ferdinand Strauss manufactured windup games and a game called "Diablo," which consisted of two sticks turned by a cord.

Toy cars became popular. Lionel, American Flyer, and later Gilbert Lewis and Marks made electrical trains. Gilbert created the Erector Set before he joined the Lionel Company. During World War I, and later, Gilbert made special additional parts for Erector Sets. He also created chemistry sets, microscopes, and engineering and sound experiment sets.

In 1902, a book, *Christmas Tithe*, written by Elizabeth Harrison was intended as a guide to parents in purchasing toys. She said, "Let the toys be simple, strong, and durable. Base your choice not so much on what the toy is, but what your child can do with it. Children's instinctive delight in putting their own thought into their playthings, instead of accepting the thought of the manufacturer, explains why the simpler toy is often more pleasing to a child than an expensive one."

In 1913, the American Institute of Child Life published a book called *Introduction to Childhood* which expressed "The need for a great number of new toys that fit different psychological ages, stimulating toys that last and can be taken apart with simple mechanisms."

In 1912, the retail toy business increased 50 percent, from 20 million to 30 million in sales. It was felt that the toy industry was the leader in producing simple and salable educational and scientific toys of high quality at a fair price.

Playthings was a magazine founded in 1903 by Robert McGreedy, in which he commented on the absurdity of having the stores filled at Christmas time with toys. Year round sales of toys were beginning to increase.

In 1908, a toy show was set up in Madison Square Garden, with the purpose of being educational, social and commercial. Most of the sales before that toy show took place at the old Broadway Central Hotel. A.C. Gilbert obtained the support of Robert McGreedy of *Playthings* and others and established the Toy Manufacturers of America in 1916, with Gilbert as president and R. Ives as vice-president, Atherton Converse as second vice-president and Leo Schlesinger as treasurer. Offices were established in New York City. Within a short time a credit bureau and a news bulletin was started, along with a collection service and a Washington representative. For more information see the interviews with Tom Arbuckle and Doug Thomson later in this section.

Between 1914 and 1918, toy production doubled due to the disappearance of imports during World War I. A proposal to abolish toy sales during Christmas 1917 caused a furor. The Toy Manufacturers went to the Council of National Defense to plead for continuation of Christmas. Gilbert was quoted at this hearing as saying, "The American boy is a genuine boy and needs genuine toys, he wants guns that can really shoot and that's why we make guns for him since he was big enough to hold them. That's why the American soldier is the best marksman on the fields of France. America is the home of toys that educate as well as entertain and amuse, that help the boy visualize his future occupation, that start him on the road to construction, not destruction, that as surely the public schools and the Boy Scouts, exert an influence that go to solid ideals and solid American character." Then they brought out toys to show the secretary and received a favorable response.

When the war ended the American toy industry decided to be involved in a bigger market than ever

before. But in a short time Germany revitalized its toy industry and imports reached an all time high of 11 million dollars. In general, the prices of the German products were much lower than their American counterparts.

The Depression in 1929 wiped out most toy manufacturers. Tariff bills were introduced as a way of protecting toy manufacturers. Later the tariffs were reduced when the industry was stronger.

Between 1920 and 1950, the population of the United States grew about 45 percent. About that time, parents rediscovered the value of toys and the industry expanded. Many companies were very large and wealthy but many small companies gave them competition. The competition copied ideas, often in a way which would cut their cost. A goal has always been to improve the efficiency and quality of the toys and reduce the price. By 1950, toy manufacturers tested their toys with standard tests, professional testers, and toy buyers before sales.

Preschool toys increased in the varieties available. The use of wooden blocks expanded enormously. In the 1920's and 1930's, nursery school needs were met with a variety of products that were perfect for early childhood education. The Playskool Manufacturing Company produced toys for preschool children. The hammer, nail and peg table was such a product. Interest in early childhood development also resulted in the Cradle Gym and a playpen rail train, a stylized wooden train with cardboard tracks to put over the rails of the playpen.

Creative Playthings expanded the early childhood market and produced or distributed a variety of special new equipment. Human, animal, and natural forms were sculpted in wood for children. The Buddy-L Company was one of the first vehicle toy companies on the market. They made dumptrucks and other copies of big trucks. The Headstrom Company in the 1950's made strollers, baby carriages, and walkers. Lewis Marks, one of the giants in the industry, created many successful toys, including toy trains and windup toys. The Ideal Toy Company which made the first U.S. teddy bear, went on to make other types of stuffed animals and animal reproductions.

Walt Disney Characters became widely distributed and adapted. Mickey Mouse was one of the first licensed characters. A variety of books and materials on these characters were also produced. Book publishing companies expanded their juvenile departments, providing high quality and interesting coloring books and creative books.

Models of ships, planes, and cars have always been popular. The do-it-yourself phase of the 1940s and 1950s brought out more of these products. The Fisher-Price Co., one of the leaders in the toy industry expanded, making creative, imaginative toys of good quality, and improving on market testing. Most companies hold the philosophy that play should be a happy experience for children and that they should be stimulated and educated through specialized products. Most responsible companies make toys that are carefully tested and widely used by children throughout the country.

Many changes have taken place in the industry over the past decade. These include greater use of batteries, the introduction of space-age materials and micro processors, all electronic toys, and new patents. Licensing has had a dramatic effect in the industry in direct relation to the effect of mass media. More characters from television, movies, and comics, improved conditions in mass production techniques, new products, and increased television advertising have kept this an expanding industry. Consumers have demanded products in the space and science fiction area and for computers and electronics.

Toys have almost always reflected the culture, political events, social trends, and advancements in technology. The toy industry, despite criticism, does fulfill a need of children to have fun. A review of the best offerings of toy companies today has been made for THE TOY CHEST. Many specialists have contributed their experience and insight in selected interviews. The toy industry is dynamic and creative in attempting to provide the public with the best it can produce. It is also vulnerable to criticism and responsive to public opinion. We urge consumers to select toys wisely based on their child's needs and interests.

The American Toy Fair 1902–1982

The annual American Toy Fair is one of the largest and best-attended trade shows held in the world. It is spon-

130

sored by Toy Manufacturers of America, Inc (TMA), the industry trade association.

Held in New York City each February, the fair enables close to 850 toy, game, and decorations manufacturers to show their new product lines. Over 12,000 retail and wholesale buyers from every part of the United States and the world participate. More than 3,000 new items are shown to these buyers each year. Approximately 500 permanent showrooms are located in four different buildings: Toy Centers South and North, at 200 Fifth Avenue and 1107 Broadway; New York Merchandise Mart, at 41 Madison Avenue; and 2 Pennsylvania Plaza at Seventh Avenue and 32nd Street. For those companies that do not maintain year round showrooms in Manhattan, exhibit space is available in the Sheraton Center Hotel at Seventh Avenue and 52nd Street, where more than 350 additional manufacturers display their products. Exhibitors from England, Europe, Australia, Canada, and the Far East showcase their products.

The American Toy Fair began prior to World War I when the American toy industry was in its infancy. Early

February was picked for the first Toy Fair in 1902, which enabled American toy makers to show their lines to toy buyers who were passing through New York on their way to European buying trips. Few manufacturers had permanent showrooms in New York then, so many of them remained in the city for eight weeks or so in order to catch buyers again when they returned from abroad.

After World War I, toy manufacturers began opening permanent sales offices in New York, and there was considerable expansion in both permanent and temporary exhibit space. In 1923, the Toy Fair Chamber of Commerce was formed to provide needed coordination between the various exhibits located in the different building and hotels. By 1930, all the temporary exhibits were brought under one management and located in one Manhattan hotel.

Further centralization and efficiency was achieved in 1931 when the Toy Manufacturers of the U.S.A., Inc., as the industry association was then called, assumed management of the American Toy Fair. This included two fairs held in New York: one in February and one in April or May, and a third in Chicago in May.

In 1933, for the first time, a single Toy Fair was held. It was in Chicago in the hope that its later May date would enable manufacturers to complete most, if not all, of their lines. However, a poll of industry members showed that the majority preferred to have the fair in New York. From 1934 until the present, the American Toy Fair has been held each February in New York City. Regional fairs are also held during the year in Pasadena, Dallas, Atlanta, and Chicago. International fairs are held in Nuremberg, Paris, Canada, London, Milan, Hong Kong, and Tokyo.

Changes in Play and Playthings

During much of history children did not have specific playthings created for them, but used whatever was available for play. Unhappily, in tracing history, one also finds abuse, neglect and exploitation of children.

The society we live in today is diverse and values are changing but most parents recognize the value of toys and the importance of play.

Blocks, construction toys, puzzles, and board games are examples of preferred choices. Others include potential playthings parents can select based on their awareness, experience, and interest. Choices are a reflection of our larger society. Children may set trends for new objects to play with but do they also respond to what some adults, designers, and manufacturers think is best for them?

In 1693, John Locke wrote about the value of play and the educational use of special playthings.

In the early 19th century Friedrick Froebel developed a philosophy on the importance of play. He felt play allowed children to learn and develop fully. With the right toys he believed the child would be positively influenced in thinking and expression. He stressed the specific goal that play should allow the child to come closer to his whole being. The early Froebel toys consisted of a ball, sphere, cube, cylinder, wooden blocks and clay. Also included in his educational program were books, music, games, gardening and physical activity. The Milton Bradley Company became the distributor of Froebel's materials in 1869. These materials gained widespread interest and use. Today these blocks can be obtained from Korver-Thorpe. (See the list of manufacturers in the resources section.)

In the early 1900's, John Dewey altered the philosophy of education for young children even further—to encourage motor activity, use of real materials, and expansion of the child's imagination. Teachers and parents began to observe and note the child's view rather than the one which adults imposed on the child's play.

Changes in Play

New materials were developed to reflect these changes: wooden blocks, play equipment, imaginary play areas, sandboxes, puzzles, peg boards, and beads were introduced.

In 1920 Maria Montessori, who had begun her school in Rome, developed many specific learning materials. They were organized into practical life exercises, sense-training devices, and materials for reading and counting. Some of the materials were created to be self-correcting, but also had to be used exactly.

In 1928, Playskool began to distribute the first educational toys and wooden skill toys were made by the Holgate Company in the 1930's. They needed to be explained to adults but were popular with children. In 1930 Fisher-Price began creating toys. In the 1940's small educational toy stores, created by Frank and Theresa Caplan, later became Creative Playthings.

In 1930, there was a greater understanding of the importance of play in helping to develop a healthy person. A major study in play was conducted, by Hartley, Frank and Lawrence, *Understanding Children's Play* (New York: Columbia University Press 1952).

Today, over 700 toy companies exist in the U.S., with over 150,000 toys in manufacture. Many more companies from other countries show their products in New York City each year for consideration in U.S. stores. Toys are made in all price ranges, for all types of activities, and interests. Educational toys are available to assist in learning from many fine companies. This book is organized to assist you in locating toys that focus on active, creative and educational activities. I feel toys should have attributes that stimulate any or as many as possible of these characteristics to have long-lasting benefit.

Some specialists see play as a way for children to express their feelings while others see play as a way to learn. I feel it is a combination of both and dependent on the individual child, his needs and opportunities. Fortunately today children have many choices. I feel children need to be actively interacting with interesting, safe, and stimulating materials from infancy on for maximum emotional and intellectual growth. As a result of the use of proper toys and materials, the child learns many skills and expands his sense of the world and himself.

Children, Toys, and Advertising

Children learn about toys through play with other children, parents and family, and television advertising. "Buy me that one mommy!" is heard over and over from children who have been influenced by television and gain a desire for a specific toy. Sometimes the item is right for the child and is a suitable toy for their age, interests and abilities. Sometimes it is the wrong toy, but the pressure by the child continues regardless, much to the distress of the parent. The parent may finally break down and purchase it to satisfy the child's whim. That toy may have a life of from 1 to 6 hours and never be used again. It will join the rest of the rejects in an already cluttered playroom. Advertising can influence the child, but the parent is ultimately responsible for what the child plays with and how. Especially with the enormous range of selections available today. I feel strongly that parents must sharpen skills of discernment and make observations of their child before purchasing anything.

The purpose of this book is to assist parents and others in wise selection of toys. Please refer to the age categories in the book for basic guidance. If the item you are considering is not included in this book, ask yourself these questions:

1. Can I afford to buy it?
2. How will my child react to the toy?
3. Is it worth the money?
4. Will the toy enhance my child's experiences?
5. Will she/he have fun, learn something, and will the toy have lasting value?

The first TV toy ad was created by the Mattel Company to promote Barbie Dolls on the Mickey Mouse Club Show. Without doubt, the ads started a fad that is pervasive and persistent. Critics of this approach such as Action for Children's Television, conclude that the hard sell of children is inappropriate and influences children in a detrimental way. One way to handle the pressure is to monitor television shows. Short of this it is not easy to shield your child from on-going ads sponsoring products.

Fortunately, the television industry has responded to increased public pressure. They established a code of ethics, guidelines, and other materials for actions in screening ads. They have attempted to respond to public requests. The response by the industry produced a television code that calls for truth in claims, avoidance of misleading phrases, compliance with legal requirements and responsible treatment. Some of these actions, or standards resulted in:

1. stopping demonstrations or dramatizations that are not authentic or exaggerated as to the performance of the toy,
2. stopping unfair glamorization of the product,
3. stopping peer pressure appeals,
4. expanded awareness that children should not be exploited and play value of toys cannot be exaggerated,
5. stopping dramatizations that could scare children,
6. stopping impressions that the toy comes fully assembled at purchase when that is not the case,
7. curtailing the pressure on the child to "ask mommy to buy,"
8. curtailing celebrity endorsements and testimonies, and the use of program hosts, cartoon characters to promote products within or adjacent to the program they appear in,
9. requiring a five-second still shot of the product advertised,
10. Increased cautioning of the advertising industry to be prudent and careful in their selling to young children and parents and to assist in the support of positive aspects in the parent-child relationship.

Since the curtailing of the enforcement staff involved in the monitoring of these guidelines, it is important to monitor the promotions your child is exposed to.

If you feel an ad on TV does not meet these guidelines and is inappropriate for children I suggest you write a letter to the programming director of the network or to:

Director, Children's Television
National Association of Broadcasters
477 Madison Ave.
New York, NY 10022

and send a copy of the letter to:

Action for Children's Television
46 Austin Street
Newtonville, MA 02160

You can obtain useful booklets and other materials on children and television from ACT. Also you may write:

Consumer Information Center
Dept. 515H
Pueblo, CO 81009

About Santa Claus

In 1822, Dr. Clement C. Moore wrote a poem called "The Night Before Christmas." Santa Claus came from the German word Sinter Klaus, the name for Saint Nicholas, who was Bishop of Myra in the 4th century. On feast days starting December 6, three weeks before Christmas, he brought gifts and deposited them in shoes and stockings. The Dutch colonists brought Saint Nicholas with them to New Amsterdam, which would become New York City, thus establishing the custom in the new world. Saint Nicholas and Father Christmas or Papa Noel, from France, all got together to finally become Santa Claus. Gifts were given to children on the basis of good behavior. This is how Santa became a popular image around Christmas time.

Collecting Toys

Many adults are involved in collections of varied kinds of toys from dolls to trains, old wind-ups, paper dolls and other items. Some of the toys are very valuable and highly sought. In some places in the country special antique toys shows are held regularly and many people attend. Some museums in the country offer displays of the special toys such as tin and cast iron vehicles, or precious porcelain dolls. (See list of museums in the resource section.) Special dolls such as Kewpie dolls appeal to some collectors while others prefer imported dolls.

Dorothy Coleman is one of the most distinguished experts in this area. Her comments on collecting dolls are included along with a foremost writer and expert on dollhouses, Flora Jacobs. Other adults collect Teddy Bears, special old vehicles, or metal banks, tin toys, and miniatures. The reasons people collect particular items is interesting. Margaret Woodbury Strong who was the largest stockholder of Eastman Kodak collected 27,000 dolls, 600 dollhouses, and hundreds of circus items. She collected since she was very young and was encouraged to do so by her parents. She traveled throughout the world and even expanded her house to fit the growing collection. She also established a museum in Rochester, New York.

The History of Dolls

Dolls were brought to this country by early settlers. Sir Walter Raleigh, who led an expedition to Virginia, gave a doll to the Indians. Another doll, this one Elizabethan, was given to a Roanoke Indian child. Letitia Penn, named after the daughter of William Penn, was a 20-inch high, wooden jointed, glass-eyed doll painted with a thin glaze of plaster. She was taken to the colonies after 1699. She is currently on display at the Historical Society of Pennsylvania.

Long before this, American Indians had been creating toys for their children out of natural materials. Indian children had dolls made out of corn husks. They played games like La Crosse, and many other active sports. The Kachina dolls of the Southwest American Indians were carved from wood and brightly painted. Used in religious rites, they were believed to contain fierce guardian spirits. Other dolls were made from wood, clay, and other materials.

Often the children of the settlers drew features on their dolls' faces, but Indian children did not, as drawing

of a face on a doll expressed its sorrow. They believed that the doll had a soul.

Most early settlers who came from Europe brought their culture and customs, traditional games, gifts, and dolls. Children in the early days of our country had to work along with their parents, but found time to play jump rope, ball, and hide-and-seek. Dolls were made from corncobs, leather and fabric.

Handmade toys were constructed in the mountains of Virginia, Maryland, the Carolinas, Kentucky, Tennessee, and Alabama. In England dolls made from paper became very popular, particularly dolls made there and in France in the 1840s. Rag dolls were always popular, from Raggedy Ann, first manufactured in 1914. Dolls were available throughout the United States as they were imported from Europe and then began to be manufactured here. Doll houses and doll collecting also became popular.

Some early dolls can still be viewed in museums in this country and all over the world. Disney World has a doll collection. The Museum of the City of New York has many early dolls. Sturbridge, MA., and Williamsburg, VA., have collections from the colonial days.

A demand for dolls increased considerably around the middle of the 19th century. They were made of bisque or unglazed porcelain or wax. Wooden dolls were brought over from France. Articles of clothing were made to go along with the dolls.

In a book dated 1869, there is a statement that a doll is one of the most important playthings. Because of the import restrictions during the Civil War, manufacture was attempted in the U.S. The first rubber doll head was made in 1861 and perfected through many trials. The first composition doll was patented by Ludwig Greiner in 1850. These were very well-constructed doll heads. Dolls were manufactured in Philadelphia, Boston and Hartford, Connecticut. A doll factory was started about 1875 in Covington, Kentucky by Wilt Fletcher. He made doll bodies of cloth, stuffed with sawdust or hair and heads made of flour, glue and cloth. Doll furniture and equipment began to be made in 1860.

During World War I and II, doll making expanded here. Still, bisque doll heads continued to be imported.

The Horseman Company began in other areas of manufacture, but when it began making dolls, it cut out all but dolls. Madame Alexander and Effenbee were among the firms that made only dolls. The Ideal Toy Company, founded by Morris Michtom, made dolls and also the first U.S. teddy bear in 1903.

Raggedy Ann is the oldest licensed product, created by John and Myrtle Gruelle in 1914. She has been the subject of television shows, comics, and movies. She was created when their daughter, Marcella, found a faceless rag doll and asked her father, a political cartoonist, to give it a face. His wife restuffed it and placed a candy heart with the words "I love you" on the newly-created doll. After Marcella died two years later Mr. Gruelle began writing stories as a memorial to his child and created her mate Raggedy Andy. In 1918, the first Raggedy Ann book was published. Since that time, she has been wildly popular. She also precipitated an extensive number of licensed products. Products licensed with Raggedy Ann and Andy illustrate the variety of items that can be created. There are over 100 different companies and hundreds of different forms of licensed products. Others include Garfield, Snoopy, the Care Bears, Mickey Mouse, and Strawberry Shortcake.

The Ideal Company was working on creating a doll head that would be unbreakable. The dolls that Michtom made at first were replicas of comic strip characters, but whose composition heads would crumble if they got wet. He developed rubber substance heads for the Suck-a-Thumb Baby; Flossy Float, which had movable eyes; Twinkletoes, with a warm feeling to the skin; Betsy Wetsy; Shirley Temple doll; Saucy Walker; Magic Skin doll and Baby Coos. The Ideal Company promoted dolls through the Toni Company and created a doll like Betsy Wetsy to aid an older sibling to adjust to a baby in the family. Sara Lee was developed as an authentic black doll.

Dolls became licensed in the second half of the twentieth century with names like the Lone Ranger, Buffalo Bill, Hopalong Cassidy, Dennis the Menace, Howdy Doody, Miss Frances and the Ding Dong School, Bugs Bunny, Roy Rogers and others.

The children of the 1930's played with rubber dolls such as the Dydee baby doll (Effenbee) which wet its diaper after taking a drink from a bottle. Stuffed dolls continued to be popular, along with the bisque and china

dolls. The first Kewpies were registered in 1912 and were also popular. Babydolls became popular. Dolls representing real people have been used for advertising books and plays.

Madame Alexander created her company and named the dolls after literary characters like Little Women, Snow White, Alice, and then famous people such as the Dionne Quintuplets, Raggedy Ann and Andy.

The science of toy making is an extensive one. People like Dorothy Coleman, who are experts, spent their life researching and learning all there is to know about dolls. Mrs. Coleman and her daughter, Emily, spoke to me about dolls and where I could find excellent doll collections. There are several organizations in the United States, among them is the Doll Collectors of America and the United Federation of Doll Clubs. The members of the organization meet for the purpose of purchasing dolls, trading information on dolls as collector's items and special books are published with prices. Hundreds of dolls are made by dozens of companies. Doll collections are magnificent to behold and are often in museums and special shows. (See resources section for a listing.)

Selecting Dolls

Dolls come in all shapes and sizes. In selecting a doll, one wants to find a body that is comfortable for a child and an appropriate size for the child to hold.

Children seem to enjoy playing with realistic baby dolls. They like to play home-type situations, clothe, and communicate with the baby doll. Parents can observe social and emotional development of their children through watching their children with their dolls.

Dolls have universal appeal. Regardless of age, sex, or culture, dolls have high play value for a child. They are good for a child as early as age 2, as a companion, and as a child develops, the doll becomes a special "other" to relate to. Children can spend time with, talk to, and control the "baby" in his own way. The child learns to relate to and feel good in exchanges with people through playing with dolls. He also learns to express feelings by relating to the doll. About the age of three, the play with the doll becomes more specific.

With each doll the child relates a different way. With a collection of dolls, the child can make up a family of different personalities. It is important to relate to the child with sensitivity in expressing care to the "baby." The children care how they are treated.

By the time children are playing with dolls in preschool or day-care situations, they have usually created a variety of imaginary characters with their dolls and puppets. Dolls decorate their rooms and are a form of self-expression, as are their collections.

The child's first doll should be soft. As the child gets older, a reaction doll is appropriate, such as a squeeze toy which makes a sound. Small unbreakable baby dolls are enjoyable. By the time they are 2 or 3 they want a real baby doll, a doll that can drink, wet, change clothes, change positions and which comes with accessories. Over

6 years of age, children are often interested in adult dolls, fashion dolls and accessories. Dolls of all kinds continue to be a very special part of childhood play.

Glamour Dolls

Glamour dolls began with the Barbie Doll collection, by Ruth Handler, who in 1945 founded a company called Mattel. The doll was named after their daughter Barbie. The doll was advertised as a first for TV on the Mickey Mouse Club Show. In 1959 the doll became very popular and later Ken, named after their son, was created. Since 1961, Barbie has had her own magazine and fan club. In 1974 a survey showed 90% of all of the girls between ages 9 and 11 owned one or more Barbie Dolls. More than 92 million dolls have been sold and more than 6 million each year. Her size is 11½ inches with movable arms and legs. A new size and type of Barbie was made later and other aspects have changed over the years. She has earned over ½ billion dollars. Over 20 million costumes are purchased each year. She is sold in over 60 countries. She is still collected by 200 collectors in this country. A variety of books have been done on Barbie, including the *Barbie Doll Encyclopedia and Collectibles.* For more information write The Barbie Doll Fan Club listed in the reference section.

Doll Houses

Doll houses are a popular part of the doll world. Doll houses began in Germany and spread to other countries. They are often beautifully handcrafted. A doll house in the form of a cabinet was made in Sweden and utensils were made to go along with the doll house and furniture. One of the most fabulous doll houses was made for Queen Mary by an architect in the 1920's. The castle cost several million dollars. Several books were produced about this doll house. It is 100 inches long and 62 inches wide and has two elevators. The house is on display at the National Museum of Science and Industry and has been seen by thousands of visitors. The money collected by the display is given to charity.

Doll houses allow a child to play with little characters whom they can dramatize, collect furniture and small objects and enjoy the creative aspects of imagination of play. Doll houses can be simple and basic or more elaborate. They are decorated with a variety of miniatures produced by an entire industry of hundreds of manufacturers and distributors. Prices and products vary greatly so it is worthwhile to decide how much you want to become involved. Many toy stores carry a good selection of items to use in doll houses. You can find accessories or make them. I have included some reference books in this area if you are interested in building your own doll house or making accessories.

Teddy Bears

Teddy bears have been an important item for many generations. In 1902, President Theodore Roosevelt refused to shoot a captured bear and became popular for this act. Later he allowed Morris Michtom, founder of the Ideal Toy Company to use his name in marketing the new toy "teddy" bear. The Steif Toy Company in Germany simultaneously had a stuffed bear that was also popular. Early bears were made of silk plush or mohair cloth and had embroidered features. They are still very popular today and are available with many variations features. A teddy bear could be treasured by a child for many years, so it is best to choose a well-made one. Luckily, there are many wonderfully well-made teddy bears on the market from which you can choose. Listed below are some of the companies which make teddy bears that a child (and adult) will enjoy for a long time.

California Stuffed Toys, R. Dakin and Company, Eden, Gund, Hermann, Ideal, Nesbitt, North American Bear Company, and Steif.

Miniatures

Each year hundreds of manufacturers of the miniatures created for doll houses gather in New York to present their products to prospective buyers. From dollhouses, furniture, and accessories, to everything that it is possible to miniaturize, are gathered on display. The Miniatures Industry Association of America sponsors the event and provides information about this increasingly expanding hobby. Write to them for more information, referral to collectors, sales or other resources, at 319 East 54th Street, Elmwood Park, New Jersey 00707 or call (201) 794-1133.

The choices in toys are almost infinite, with selections from all over the world finding their way to stores, in catalogs or discovered in travelling. One exciting dimen-

sion of toys is the possibility that children have more opportunities to play with toys that are varied and interesting. As long as products meet the standards for toys in the United States you will be safe in your purchases, especially if you buy at a reputable store you know and trust. See resource section for more information on toy organizations, stores, and catalogs.

Toys travel from every part of the world to reach America, and American toys are sent to other parts of the world.

139

Excellent toys have been made in England and Europe for centuries. Collections have been based on prized items from England, France, and Germany. More recently, toys from elsewhere in Europe, Sweden, Denmark, Italy and toys from Asia, Australia, and Canada have been introduced. I have been reviewing toys from all over the world for this book. Toy buyers and sellers meet at shows held in Germany, Hong Kong, Taiwan, Tokyo, Milan, Nuremberg, and Yorkshire. Due to the open market place, buyers have the opportunity to view many choices in every category. To give you some idea of the complexity of the job of a toy buyer, see the classifications listing in the resource section. You can appreciate the complexity of the work when you see so many various types of toys. I looked for the major, most important categories when I organized the TOY CHEST.

You can see what a challenge it is to buy toys for companies the size of FAO Schwarz or Toys R Us. (See the interviews with Meredith Brokaw, Mal Goldman, Harold Goldstein, Scott Goode, Manny Luhn, Ian McDermott, Roy Raymond, or James Skahill).

The history of toys has been brought up-to-date through many interviews with these and other specialists in the toy industry. Experts on design, production, safety, and sales of toys are included as are the specialties in dolls, train collecting, toy lending library, and other topics I felt you would enjoy learning more about. To include all of the contributors I spoke with would require another book, but a selection has been made from all of them for now as a sample representing the diversity in the toy industry.

HISTORIC VIEW OF TOY INDUSTRY

Tom Arbuckle

Manager of Toy Center Building

The center of the toy industry's sales and marketing efforts is appropriately named THE TOY CENTER. Located at 200 Fifth Avenue and joined by a bridge to 1107 Broadway in New York City, THE TOY CENTER comprises almost a million square feet of permanent toy and toy-related showrooms, displaying the products of over three thousand domestic and foreign manufacturers. It is here, in February of each year, the industry first unveils the products that will appear on retailing shelves throughout the world in preparation for the following Christmas.

When, in 1909, The Fifth Avenue Building began renting, the American Toy Industry was virtually nonexistent. Most toys were imported from Europe, predominantly Germany. The industry's growth began during World War I, which prevented most toy importing and gave rise to domestic manufacture. Many of these manufacturers began locating in the area surrounding the building, and by the time World War II had begun, most of the substantial companies, one by one, had moved into the building.

TOY RESEARCH

Carol Blackley

Public Relations Director of Fisher-Price

A fully accredited nursery school is located on the premises of the Fisher-Price toy company in the Research and Development Building. Under the direction of a child psychologist and two professional teachers, children play an important part in helping to determine which toys the company readies for the toy shelves, those which don't make it, and those which will need additional or major revisions.

The nursery is filled with toys, some experimental, some Fisher-Price's and some the competition's. Children are free to share or ignore the toys as observers learn ways a particular model could be modified or improved, and find out which toys are returned to repeatedly. The final products of Fisher-Price reflect the thinking of these children. These young "researchers" helped to select the words that would be inscribed on the Play Desk, the subjects for accompanying art, and even had a hand in the overall design of the portable desk.

The staff notes if the toys are suited to a child's particular stage of development, e.g. can a child play with the toy now and find new ways for play as he or she gains new abilities? Good toys are used simply at first, and as a child's imagination and experience grow, more and more new play situations can be created.

Since it was founded in 1930, Fisher-Price has known the value of observing children and learning from them about their needs and fantasies. The results appear to be worth the years spent in development.

143

TOY STORE INSIDE

Meredith Brokaw

Owner of Pennywhistle, New York, NY

I want parents to know that when they walk into this store and ask me "What can I get that will really benefit my three-year-old, without it being tossed away in a month?" They'll get some solid advice. We made a conscious decision to have toys out for children to play with because I believe a toystore should have that sort of environment. The other reason was that we felt it was important for parents to see how their children interact with certain toys. It's one thing to say "a good set of hardwood blocks is what your three-year-old needs" and it's another thing to have the parents see the children experiment with a lot of toys and see how their child responds to a certain toy. Why should they take our word? A good part of our clientele are parents buying for their children. Some of it is grandparents and friends who may not know the child. Those people have less of the hands-on type of experience with the children.

Tom and I moved from Washington to New York seven years ago. Our children at that point were five, seven, and nine, which are ages of heavy toy use. We moved to the upper west side of New York and I set out to look for a birthday party gift and I had a hard time finding a store that I liked. In fact there were two choices and both of them didn't meet my needs.

I have always been a believer in creative toys. Toys don't have to be bought in a toy shop for children to play with them. My children's favorite things when they were young were called "teacher's boxes"; the boxes had pencils and a pad of paper in them. One thing we have in our shop is a large craft section. We encourage people to put things together rather than to buy a packaged toy with cellophane wrapped around it. Two of my friends in Washington were in the process of opening a toy store when I moved to New York. Subsequently it was sold, but initially we purchased merchandise simultaneously. Toy companies treat you differently when you are a first year business. Now that we are older and have established a track record and a reputation we are treated much differently. The big toy manufacturers that would rather sell to a jobber or a middleman are not the type of people we buy most of our merchandise from. Most of our suppliers are importers whose bread and butter is the small neighborhood store.

We prefer to buy directly. Originally we didn't want to buy from well-known companies because we wanted the reputation of being a store that had unique toys. One thing that anybody in business should know however is that you do learn from your experience and what the market wants. Now we don't try to initiate new products and new markets but rather respond to what our market wants. We know our market wants fine imported toys. But there is a big segment of the population that wants the staples like Fisher-Price.

Fisher-Price is an excellent company and makes very high quality products. Every buyer knows the Milton-Bradley Company [now Hasbro-Bradley] and Parker Brothers. These are very well-known American companies. But we deal with them very minimally. We want to make toys that you can't find anywhere else available, and that is important. There are a lot of people who enjoy unique and unusual things.

We spend a lot of time in showrooms and at toy fairs. They are our cup of tea and we're their cup of tea. We stock beautiful porcelain dolls, German toys and crafts.

We are more than a toystore, we're a service organization. We contribute to the schools around here and are very much a part of the neighborhood. Our prices reflect not just the prices of the toys. We're selling advice, mailing, great gift wrapping, packaging, and delivery.

There has been a great increase in toy sales in the past few years and part of that is due to the great influx of electronic toys. I think definitely that is a demand that was created. The consumer was curious and intrigued and really went after it.

About the electronic toys, I understand the hype in electronics and that it's a new thing that has never been done before, but they're a novelty and people buy it for that.

We try to avoid highly televised items. Take the wind up and battery toys, like the little car that whizzes around and lights up at night; the child who sees it on TV can hardly wait to unwrap it under the Christmas tree, but inevitably is disappointed. The toy breaks or it doesn't look at all like it did on TV or doesn't whiz by at 55 mph like it seemed on TV. They can get away with that on TV because they are showing just the appearance of it. I go and look at those type of toys at the toy fairs and showrooms so that when a parent asks me "Do you carry TRX?" or something like that, I can say no and why I don't.

The first year we opened we couldn't be that pure, so we bought and sold four sets of the TRX. Sure enough, each one came back. We had to send them back to the jobber. It was a lousy toy, but the ads had been so powerful and there were so many requests, you feel obligated to serve your community.

When we have a special request come in, I try to get it from a jobber overnight. If I don't have to buy dozens then it's no problem. It's an easy thing to do and I enjoy being able to provide that service. If it is from a company that requires a large minimum order, I can't do it, it's not good business.

Once you've been in retailing for a while you begin to understand the importance of a freight-free shipment. Freight can be an enormous part of your budget. Most companies will ship it freight-free if you order $750-$1000, so you really need to plan your ordering carefully. It's important to know you're going to do two orders a year. If they are out of an item and I have to reorder, there's still a minimum. That's why I go to a jobber; if a customer wants it and I can get it through that channel, it's worth it to pay more and pay the freight so that the customer can have it. The jobber we use has a big warehouse. We pay a higher price, but the advantage to us is free delivery and freight, and we don't have to warehouse a lot of toys.

The basic toys we carry start with stuffed toys; they are ageless. For babies, musical stuffed animals make the best toys. Dakin makes the best for a reasonable price. The best quality is a German company called Stieff. There's just not a better stuffed animal made as far as I know. The teddy bear comes with the traditional short fur, but also in a fluffier version. They are also collector's items.

For babies, Fisher-Price is an excellent company. Tomy has been growing over the past five years. It has a well-made product, it doesn't break and its play value is very high. They have plastic toys that are very well-made, rattles are good and have a nice range...

...This is a simple mobile. My thing about mobiles is that they should all be musical. It's nice to have something to look at, but you can easily get bored with it. The Fisher-Price company makes a nice mobile with farm animals. Once the child has outgrown the crib, then you can cut the individual pieces off and they have flat bottoms so you can set up a farm scene. Toys can easily have a dual purpose and can be used for a much longer period of time.

Tomy really knows that the child likes to put things in and take things out. Galt makes a wonderful little spring toy; it's a little box with a spring in the bottom. It's wonderful for a one-year-old to put in a block and have it spring a little bit.

I watch kids and the range in their development is truly amazing. The rudimentary push and pull toys are fun for them. There are trucks which have cars that come off the top; they are attached with a magnet. There are cranes, tunnels, dividers and bridges. They all work by propulsion; the child provides all the energy, motion and imagination. Those are the most fun for children.

I like a toy that grows with a child, so that it can be used a certain way at a certain age of development and another way when the child grows older.

I'm not real crazy about makeup kits. The ones we carry are like clown makeup and you can paint your face white and your doll's face and I think that's a lot healthier than the other kits.

The only war toys that we have are from Britain, toy soldiers and things like that. There is quite a demand for those kind of toys. We sell an amazing number of cars, especially by Corgi.

The absolute bestsellers are dolls, particularly Madame Alexander's.

COLLECTING DOLLS

Dorothy Coleman

Antique Doll Specialist

The earliest doll collection began with Lord and Lady Clapham, about 1700. Dolls are a function of civilization. You do not find dolls for play in the outback of Australia and places like that; if you do they are religious figures rather than a play thing.

The first doll that ever came to America was given to a little Virginia Indian girl in 1585 by someone belonging to the expedition of Sir Walter Raleigh, as recorded by John White, the artist. The White picture is in the British Museum and a copy is in the Smithsonian. The doll may have been meant to represent Queen Elizabeth. American Indian children had the European dolls, which were more for religious purposes than play. But you have a doll for religious purposes, and after a few years, maybe a child gets hold of it and . . . it's hard to draw the line between the two functions.

Most dolls were made in Germany and central Europe. England is famous for wooden and wax dolls, Germany is famous for bisque and some wood. We say that 90% of the dolls came from Germany. They were manufactured by families, this is still true in parts of Germany. Individuals made them, not companies.

The early dolls were fairly small. Some of the earliest which collectors have now are the pegged wooden ones from the late 18th century. The Grodnertal Doll is now called the Val Gardena, because in World War I, its place of manufacture was changed from an Austrian valley to an Italian valley. Those were some of the earliest dolls sold in this country and also in England. Most of the dolls were dressed after they arrived.

One of the most beautiful doll collections was Queen Victoria's. This collection was published by George Newnes in 1894 in England. The dolls were dressed by the Queen as theatrical personages and court ladies. It also includes three male dolls, a few babies and creatures made of rags and painted muslim faces. They have tiny ruffles, stitches, pockets. They are delicately finished and very beautiful. The Queen made the costumes herself; she kept a list of her dolls and she named every one. All of this is in the London Museum, the dolls and the information. I have been over there to see it many times.

I would advise parents who are collecting dolls not to buy anything vinyl, which is mostly what you will find. I would also advise parents to get cloth dolls; vinyl isn't durable. If you are going to spend $50-$100 for a doll, you should have something that will be an investment.

A good guide to get is called *Doll Reader: A Collector's Guide to Dolls and Miniatures*, 900 Frederick St., Cumberland, MD 21502, published bimonthly. It is available by subscription. Articles appear on antique collectibles, production of doll heads in France, doll making, paper dolls, doll repair, and doll conventions. (A good reference is *Collectors Encyclopedia of Dolls* by Dorothy Coleman.

CHILDREN AND GAMES

Bernie de Koven

Author and Consultant on Games

Playing games is something that kids can do that doesn't seem to be connected with cause and effect relationships of their reality. They are exploring things. We call them flighty because we don't understand why they are doing it and obviously they are getting some kind of enjoyment out of it. A baby reaches a certain age and starts falling over backward by themselves because it is so much fun to do. He or she plays a game like that. Nobody knows why a child likes that particular game. If you talk to an anthropologist or a psychologist as to why the kid likes the game, you'll get a different answer from each. But it's fun for the kid.

146

It also happens that everything that the kid likes to do is something that seems directly related to his growth. Challenge seems to be universal. The kid does not like to play unless there is some kind of challenge, something unexpected—not too unexpected, but a surprise which could throw you off balance, which is not the same thing as your normal reality, which is different. Play is a very "up" experience for a kid. They are happy and high when they are playing. They make themselves dizzy, and that is a big thing in play. A lot of play is about being dizzy, like on a roller coaster.

Have you ever played a game called Solitaire? Your opponent is not a deck of cards, it is yourself. When you play Solitaire, you are having a little dialogue with yourself, you're talking to yourself, there is an inner voice in you going, "God, I would kill for a red three." The same thing is true with a computer game, only faster, deeper, and more profound. There is a skill involved, the inner dialogue begins. Everytime you make a mistake you have to deal with it. What did I do wrong? What happened? Why did I do that? What did that mean? How many points do you have to score before you have mastered the game? The game will say the maximum possible points is one hundred thousand points. Some kids will go and play it to a thousand points and never play it again. There are other kids who will be determined to get it beyond the hundred thousand points. If the kids like to play computer games, it is alright by me. The games are energizing, exciting, and they provide kids with a way of focusing and measuring themselves. Measuring is a very important part of testing out what they can do.

First of all, the internal dialogue they go through is a psychological balance that has to be structured in order to master a game, and it is a significant one. It seems to me that any kid who is engaged in that kind of dialogue is better for it. There is some kind of psychological integration that is going on; it is a listening to a part of yourself, and at the same time a learning and listening to the whole thing.

How good you feel when you are winning and how bad you feel when you are losing! Think of what you say to yourself when you are winning and what you say to yourself when you are missing. The higher your score, the nastier you are to yourself when you blow it.

When watching a game being played, the first thing I say to myself is, do kids really want to play this? If kids actually want to play this, I'd better figure out why. What are they having fun doing? For sure it is something that is putting them on their way to growth. It is an opportunity for them to utilize skills. It seems to be that the skills called for are skills from the right brain, they are learning to discipline their right-brain through a kind of biofeedback interface with the machine. They are defnitely learning to interpret much more information than if they had to deal with it symbolically.

In the game, Asteroids, targets are moving in all directions. You have to deal with which one is closest to

you, which direction should you turn, your speed, your vector and changing your speed. It's calculus, if you had to deal with it symbolically. But you are dealing with this on another level. Arcade games get progressively harder and harder. If you give the child free rein over games, he will start choosing games that are more and more challenging; it's amazing how hard and complex they become.

The child chooses out of his own free will to do that which is incredibly challenging. To his mind, it is a process of utilizing the mind. He's got to train his mind to interpret data so quickly, some games are pure visual, other games give written data that is changing constantly all over the screen; each game is a different rush. The better you play each game, the wider range you can play. I think the fact that kids now have computers and TV games at home will revolutionize education.

You have to make the games educational now, while they are successful. You have to make educational games for kids to play at home. They've got to be as much fun as Asteroids. You see that's the thing, education's got to compete with the kids like the computer games do. It has to be just as much fun. It's a fantastic challenge, and people are meeting it.

The computer happens to be the very best toy we have ever made in the whole history of the species; we have finally risen to our true beauty as a species. We have found the computer to be a wonderful toy. It is providing all kinds of new ways for us to use our minds. Everybody likes playing them; it's a lot of fun.

SNOOPY AND COMPANY

June Dutton

Determined Productions

Determined Productions began when Connie Bouchet, my sister, went to see Charles Schulz with an idea. She proposed to do merchandising for his comic-strip characters. He felt it was worth a try, so he sent her to United Features Syndicate in New York to get permission to become a licensee. Today everything in the world is licensed.

The license is essential to a manufacturer. It means you are the only one who can legitimately manufacture a certain item. For example, the Snoopy plush; nobody can do a Snoopy plush like we do. If someone makes a Snoopy plush, they are liable to be sued. When that happens the Syndicate lawyers handle it, we don't get involved.

We started in 1961 and now I can't even begin to count the number of toys we produce. Not only do we do a lot ourselves but we have sublicensees. Charles Schulz provides the characters and all the designs are done in our art department from Mr. Schulz's drawings. We can adapt any drawing that he has done, with the background, clothes, and figures. He has to approve any figure, sculpture, or drawing. The artwork first goes to him as a concept; he approves that and then we carry it through.

OVERVIEW OF STUFFED ANIMAL PRODUCTION

Roger Burrill

Executive Vice President of R. Dakin & Co.

The first step in the manufacturing process of stuffed animals is the design. The animals are designed at our headquarters. After a toy is designed and a prototype is made up, it is tested to see what reaction a child may have to the toy. The process has the designers constantly doing research on animals, going to zoos and other places. That is how they get their ideas. Their sketches go to the sample makers. We have some here, some in Korea, and one in South Carolina. They make a prototype and send it back. At that time it is checked for safety, quality, and appearance. We have a checklist we go through. Our safety and quality inspector goes over the whole list. The primary function is just to review these for sharp points, the material the toy is made out of, toxicity, and flammability test.

Let me give you an example of quality and cost—we were having a problem with seams tearing, so we strengthened the thread. Now, instead of the thread breaking the backing, the material started to tear. If we use a more expensive thread, our suppliers are going to put that in their price. Though we increased the strength of the thread that didn't solve the problem because the material started to tear. We went to the material maker in Korea with this problem. He worked on it for a long time and came up with an acrylic and cotton based backing for the material. The acrylic alone was not strong enough. The 50/50 blend brought the pull strength up to 30 lbs. The standard for the industry is 15 lbs. for a seam. We have machines that test for this.

Another example is the metal problem. We used to use metal washers behind the eye so that the eye didn't come out. But in order to get past the metal detectors, you can't have metal anywhere in the stuffed animal. So we had our eye-maker develop a nylon washer to go behind the eye. And that took some time, but now the whole industry is using this nylon washer.

Toy manufacturers really do make efforts to establish high standards. Many of the standards are the Toy Manufacturers requirements, which are more stringent and more comprehensive than government requirements. We've been making stuffed animals for about twenty years.

It's amazing how children react to stuffed animals, and adults too. Stuffed animals are very special toys. I think a stuffed animal for a child is something a child can love and talk to and express their emotions to. It has natural appeal, like pets. It's human nature for humans to have pets.

TRAIN COLLECTING

Bill Clarke

Owner of Bill's Terminal Trainatorium

I first opened my store on January 15, 1947, at the corner of 14th and Market in San Francisco. But my interest in trains began when I got a train with a steel gauge as a kid. At first I sold them, and then about twenty years ago, I started collecting them.

Lionel started making trains in the early 1900's. He had the largest toy company in the world when he retired in the 1950's. All the details are in *The Collector's Guide and History to Lionel's Trains: Vol. I, II, III, & IV* by Tom McComas and James Tuohy, published by TM Productions in Wilmette, IL 60091. Lionel was in business ten years as Ives Corp., which was started by Edward Ives in 1868. In 1910 they decided to go into electric trains. In 1940 they produced the finest scale freight cars.

Lionel Cowen founded the Lionel Manufacturing Company in 1900. He liked to tinker and experiment with electricity. He studied electrical engineering at Columbia University and went to work for Acme Light Company. He developed a magnesium fuse to light the flash bulbs for early photographers, and he opened up a shop to sell dependable mine detonators. He also developed a dry cell battery inserted in a metal tube and attached to a light bulb. He put it in a flower pot and it illuminated the plant. Conrad Hubert was excited about the device and wanted to sell it. Cowen sold the business to Hubert, and Hubert started the Eveready Flashlight Company.

Cowen developed a small electric engine, and he decided to manufacture electric trains. His first model was a crude wooden gondola which ran with a small engine and a battery. The car plus 36 feet of tracks cost $6.00. The electric train was immediately successful, in spite of the fact that many homes lacked electricity. They were trains built to run on two tracks, with a 2⅞" gauge.

In 1906 they came out with a three-rail track built with a 2⅛″ gauge. Tracks with tin plates contributed to the growth of toy trains. Lionel developed an advertising campaign in 1929, and started a radio show called Uncle Don Carny, the chief engineer of the Lionel Engineer's Club.

Collectors look for age and for certain models that are hard to get. Some models were built in great quantities. That one up there, the black one, they made hundreds of thousands of those. But the one right above it, now that one they made in limited quantities. They manufactured that in 1950—57 and in 1964 they quit making them altogether. One recently sold for $1,295. The one below sold for $135 so you can see what they are worth today.

Children usually like the HO. Of course, with HO they can buy an entire set for about half the price of a Lionel set.

One advantage to the HO is that if you put it on a table or a foundation you can fit many more accessories, such as scenery items on it. There are a lot of items you can put on a 4 × 8 with an HO.

You can tell the quality of a model train by just looking at it. If it is not good, if it doesn't meet our standards, then we pack it up and send it back to the manufacturer. For instance, everything we sell is run on a track before a customer ever gets it. You can hear as soon as you put it on a track whether it is good, bad, or indifferent. If it is noisy or what not, then it is not too good. We also check to see if the casting is clean, for safety. Sometimes people buy them anyway because they want a certain model and that is the only manufacturer who makes that model.

If you want to join a train club there is the National Model Railroad Association. (see the resource section for a list of organizations.)

A Conversation With A 10-Year-Old Train Hobbyist

I got the mini-train, then it grew and grew. I sold it. Then my uncle had a train and I asked him for it. It has an engine and a figure-eight track and it's about a seven gauge. Now I have about a half dozen. And I'd get more cars and tracks if I could now. I'd get two cars and fifty pieces of curved and fifty pieces of straight track. I'm building a bridge.

My dad knows a lot about trains. He and I learned by doing it together.

My friends come over to play with my trains. The terminal is 10 years old and pretty complicated to work with. So I don't want to fool around with that.

My friend has the exact same train except it's brand new. But it's more valuable if it is older.

He has final approval of the sample. The Syndicate has to approve the final sample as well. All licensees must get approval from both parties, and everything is carefully copyrighted.

They look at the distribution, packaging, and advertising of the products. We design the packaging. They also look at advertisements in newspapers; they try to see everything.

We hardly ever get complaints. Occasionally Mr. Schulz will say change this or that, but nothing major.

There's always new costumes, new plush toys, and now we have a calendar coming out that has the same format year after year. We tried changing the format, but people would ask, "Where is my Snoopy calendar?" We also have different types of calendars, week by week, month by month, day by day, etc. Interestingly, our products have adult appeal as well. The plush Snoopy, which is the most popular, is bought by everybody—adults and children.

We have a great variety of items. We have the plush toys, outfits, a little carryall for doll's clothes; Snoopy has several little outfits; then there are various accessories, a hammock, piggy banks, Christmas tree ornaments, which we add to every year, a toiletry line; in the ceramics line we have several mugs; in the tin line, canisters and wastebaskets; in the gourmet line, cookie jars and salt and pepper shakers.

Not all the ideas originate from the comic strip. For example, the costumes come from production meetings in the office here. We think up what would be appealing. We start with the comic strip and take off from there.

I lay out the idea, perhaps pull out a current picture from a magazine. I can't do this all the time, and I have two wonderful women who do the layouts or draw up a sketch. In our files we have basic patterns, say for a shirt, and if there are changes that need to be made, like looser pants for jogging, then adjustments can be made accordingly. Of course, in the beginning we made the patterns by laying pieces of fabric over Snoopy, then cutting and sewing clothes to fit. Then we had a pattern and we went on from there. The sequence of events is you get the design, then you fit it on the sample model, and then you go into production.

Snoopy has over 50 outfits. There is the jogging, the European, the Spanish, the French; then we have some characters like Sherlock Holmes, we have sleepers, nighties, tennis outfits, basketball outfits, school, graduation, and Santa Claus. There are also Snoopy calendars, diaries, and other items.

LIBRARY SERVICES AND RESOURCES

Nancy Elsmo—Librarian

Racine Wisconsin Public Library

In response to the needs of families, the American Library Association has developed, through its members, committees and services to assist librarians at a local level.

Special bibliographies, demonstrations, lectures, and resource materials have been developed to assist parents on gaining the information they need on their child. For example, at a national meeting of the American Library Association, the Games and Realia Committee developed a resource list of materials suggested as useful to the members of the ALA. The design, format, packaging, content, use, and versatility were criteria used by the group to decide on what would be included.

Many libraries have adopted the idea of a toy lending library and have this service available. By asking the children's librarian at your own library you will be able to locate the books listed in the bibliography of this book and will find out more about the specific services made available.

SUGGESTED ACTIVITIES FOR PRESCHOOL CHILDREN

Nancy Everhart—Librarian

The definition of toy for a developing baby is a very broad one. Cupboard doors, light switches, garbage cans, and telephones, along with dolls, trucks, and blocks would all be applicable, since the young mind explores each with equal vigor. During the first years of the child's life, the parents do not need to spend enormous sums in traditional toy stores to give their child an enriched life. There are many excellent toys on the market today, as this book points out. The wise parent will purchase the basics and

change a diaper, tell the child the name of the picture. Change the picture every few days. After the child knows the names of body parts, draw a picture of a person with a body part missing and ask the child what it is or have him point to it on his own body.

Multiple games can be played with blocks. Give the child three blocks and tell him to make a tower. Tell him to make a bridge. Add more blocks of different colors and have the child make a tower using only red blocks, a bridge of blue blocks. Use small cars and tell the child to put the car under the bridge, on the bridge, and so on. These kinds of games can be started at two years. Take several different-sized blocks and have the child arrange them from smallest to largest.

In the child's later toddlerhood, purchase a set of magnetic letters for him or her. Use the refrigerator as a learning center to teach the letters when you are in the kitchen. The child's dexterity can be practiced by giving him a shoelace with a knot tied at one end for the child to string Cheerios and macaroni on. Household chores are the most fun "games," and a child of three can sort laundry by separating whites from colors. Dusting and setting of the table may also be done.

There are many simple games you can play with a very young child. Remember, your child would rather have some of your time than the most elaborate of toys.

PUBLIC ACTION COALITION ON TOYS

De Fischler

Coordinator

Public Action Coalition of Toys (PACT) is a tax-exempt, non-profit consumer advocacy and research organization dedicated to preventing our nation's children from suffering blinding, crippling, and other permanently disabling injuries from toys, playground equipment, and other recreational products. PACT is equally concerned about the social implications of violent, sexist, exploitive toys and the lack of ethnic and racial diversity in toys.

Toys, it is widely agreed, play an important role in a child's development. But while one toy may help promote, another might hinder a child's physical, social, emotional, or intellectual maturation. Toys also transmit values, even some steeped in controversy, such as the use of guns. Although no parent really wants his or her child to use violence and aggression to solve conflicts, such toys directly affect how a child deals with frustration.

For our money, we consumers want and expect safe, durable, and fun toys. Not infrequently, however, we end up with a product that soon breaks, or causes injury, or neglects the minority child by illustrating only white children, or discriminates against one sex by showing only girls or boys playing with it, or hampers a child's creativity when it runs on batteries that do all the work.

The toy chest, as this book's title suggests, usually conjures up happy memories or favored childhood play-

ignore the junk. However, no matter how many toys a small child has, there will be times when he or she will be bored. Toys will lay by the wayside and the child will whine or ask, "What will I do now?"

In my days of parenting two children, I searched in desperation for new and varied activities to pass the days. My efforts culminated in the publication of a booklet for parents of children from birth to three years of age called, "100 Ways to Entertain Your Baby," a survival manual to use in times of need. The following are some of the ideas from that booklet.

During the first six months, the infant is being bombarded with stimuli that were not present in the womb. The focusing of eyes and movement of limbs, along with hearing, are all new. Some simple toys at this age could be wrapping paper tied to the side of the crib to look at, different textures of material to feel, soap bubbles blown to let the child watch, and a small amount of water to allow vigorous kicking in the nude, while on a blanket on the floor.

When the baby can sit up, a raw egg on a high chair tray can serve as fingerpaint, a box with ends cut off can be a tunnel, and a card table and sheet can be turned into a playhouse/hideout. Developing skills can be challenged by having the baby place small pieces of cereal into a plastic milk jug, and by placing clothespins around the edge of a cardboard box and letting the baby take them off.

As language develops, place pictures cut from magazines at eye level near the dressing table. Each time you

things. But for 50 families and their friends, the toy chest has meant tragedy. Since 1973, at least 50 children have died because the lids on their toy chest have fallen on their necks or heads.

The federal government proposed standards for toy chests in 1973. These standards have never been implemented. Nine years later, the newspapers reported that the Consumer Product Safety Commission (CPSC) is considering imposing strict rules to prohibit toy chests with lids that can cause strangulation. Stuart Statler, member of the CPSC, is quoted by the *Sarasota Herald Tribune* (4/8/82) as saying, "The message we want to get out is that the kind of toy chests that children are playing with should not be turned into coffins."

In 1982, a lawyer in Philadelphia prepared a lawsuit involving the deaths of two young boys; the electrical light-up toy they were playing with caught fire and they both perished. In the same year, three children died from strangulation associated with a ladder on Creative Playthings Indoor Gym House manufactured prior to 1980. Each victim's head had become entrapped between the top rung and the platform. The manufacturer redesigned the ladders and urged owners of the gym to replace the faulty ladders, at no cost. In 1980, CPSC did not impose a recall. After the third death, CPSC got involved by publicizing its toll-free number to provide information about Creative Playthings' second ladder replacement program.

These unfortunate incidents may sound isolated, but government statistics prove otherwise. According to the National Electronic Injury Surveillance System (NEISS) 1980 data, for children aged from birth through 14 years, at least 58 deaths and an estimated 264,000 injuries requiring emergency room treatment occurred in accidents involving toys and playground equipment. In addition, bicycle-related accidents in that age group accounted for 317 deaths and an estimated 350,000 emergency room visits.

The following statement on war toys by Dr. Jerome D. Frank of The Johns Hopkins University School of Medicine is worth pondering:

What can be done about these problems? Child care and other parent groups cannot be an effective voice, by themselves, for positive change in the toy industry. And while the CPSC, Federal Trade Commission (FTC) have jurisdiction over children's play items in limited ways, the governmental protective apparatus has not been effective

Research has shown that the mere sight of a gun will increase violent behavior. Adults permitted to shock someone who has angered them, delivered more shocks if guns or pistols were used than if badminton racquets and shuttlecocks were used. Children who played with toy guns were more likely to destroy the work of a friendly playmate than children who did not.

Real life confirms the laboratory. The gun murder rate is two to three times higher in states with weak gun control laws than in states with strong ones. The more readily available guns are, the more they are used.

Obviously then, one way to discourage violence is to keep guns out of the environment from childhood on. Children learn mainly from their parents and attitudes formed in childhood last throughout life. By giving our children toys of peace instead of war we show them that we disapprove of violence. This discourages them from resorting to it and may lead them as adults to search for new non-violent ways of resolving conflicts that do not endanger human survival in the nuclear age.

enough. Industries operated for profit often do not adequately police themselves. But they do respond to organized consumer opinion.

Since its founding in 1973, PACT has been dedicated to both encouraging the development of safe, sturdy, and enjoyable toys for children and discouraging the production of toys that injure, exploit, or limit a child's growth, safety, or welfare. PACT's concerns include the toy industry's shortcomings regarding safety, deceptive advertising and/or packaging, sexual and racial stereotyping, flimsy construction, and exploitive marketing practices. Equally addressed are children's needs for appropriate design and play-worthiness, i.e. toys that encourage constructive, non-violent play.

COLLECTING TOYS

Robert Forbes

Vice President, Forbes, Inc.

Like many things in life, one gets inculcated into habits at an early age; I happened to pick up my dad's love for boats and the sea.

As a kid I can remember a group of toy boats that my father had, and because of my nautical bent I was lucky to have them on shelves in my bedroom. Sadly, none of these survived to be part of our present fleet, but the seeds had been sown.

The collecting urge surged at about 10 when I discovered the thrills of Lincoln head pennies. Later, it was photography that caught my eye—here was an area with very little written about it that also had terrific growth potentials. But above all, the material available was stunning. Being in a family of collectors I was encouraged to pursue these interests.

The present collection of boats began about 15 years ago. Dad walked into FAO Schwarz, New York's premiere toy store, and found that they had an antique toy department. A toy boat there reminded him of ones he had had as a kid, and now, at last, he felt he could get the ones he always wanted.

So he did. As with any field of collecting, there is usually somebody else out there who is interested. Dad found a whole network of toy people, but discovered they collected only trains, dolls, or cars.

Old toy boats are relatively rare these days because fewer survived than other toys. The reason for this is simple—by definition, toys were manufactured in large numbers and meant to be played with. So most toys, when play was over, went back into their box or into a trunk for later. But for toy boats, being played with often spelled disaster, because water (especially salt water) is metal's enemy.

In the tub, recovering a sunken boat was easy, though the resulting rust eventually took its toll. While the most fun for a child was to sail the boats on lakes and at

seashores, a mechanical breakdown or a clockwork motor that ran out meant recovery was more difficult and very frequently impossible. And sometimes, the steam powered boats even blew up!

As with real ones, the more toy boats did their thing, the less likely they were to survive.

The difference between a toy boat and a model boat is that a model is unique, hand-built, fashioned after an existing ship, and *not* meant to be played with. But that's not to say there's no detailing on toy boats. In the early years of manufacturing, great attention was paid to the paint jobs, railings, lifeboats, and guns. What added to the "fun-ness" of them was that these details were exaggerated and emphasized rather than just being made to scale. As years went on, this playability was lost and scale became more precise. The two world wars, of course, took their toll on German toy production, but it was the introduction of plastic that changed the toy world forever; the phasing out of ocean liners in favor of the airplane also helped bring about a halt to the manufacturing of toy boats.

Our collection pretty much draws to a close at the year of 1955. The great firms featured in it are Marklin, Bing, Fleishmann, Carette, Arnold, and Falk from Germany; Ives, Orkin, George Brown, and Fallows from the United States; Maltete and Radiguet from France; and various examples from other countries.

Not all the boats float, as not all children had ponds to play on. So our collection has many pulltoys made out of cast iron or wood with lithographed paper on it, and even includes a boat which serves as a child's bank.

Here is my advice for starting a collection:

1. You have to find an area that interests you, otherwise if you're just collecting for investment you'll never have any fun.
2. Within that area, a little bit of research may turn up an aspect of it that is undercollected or unappreciated.
3. Stick to the aspect you've focused on and read as much about it as possible.
4. Now, armed with an interest and a passion, you can start collecting. Among the many things you'll collect, the thing you collect most of along the way is enjoyment.

from *Toy Boats 1870-1955: A Pictorial History*
by Jacques Milet and Robert Forbes.

MAKING TOYS

Linda Gold and Jeff Winokur

Cape Cod Children's Resource Center

Think back to the last time your preschool child was given a new toy, with tissue paper around it, set in a cardboard box, store-wrapped in shiny red paper, decorated with a ribbon and a bow. The child pulls at the bow with excitement and enthusiasm, tears through the paper, maybe stopping to feel the paper and put it on his head,

and listens to the crinkling of the tissue paper. The child is playing with the wrapping while you are wondering if you shouldn't have gotten the box and wrapping paper and skipped the expense of the toy inside.

Though the adult tends to see all this wrapping material purely as a temporary cover for the central object (the recently purchased manufactured toy), the young child sees the package she has just received as a collection of many toys. Certainly there is one brand new Toy. But on the way to finding the Toy, all sorts of ideas are going through the child's head. The cardboard box could be a hat, a dollhouse, a building in a model city, or a puppet theatre. The shiny red paper could be a wall covering in the dollhouse, or an exterior covering for the city building. The string and ribbon could be everything from hair ribbons to a way of defining doors and windows on a house. The cardboard box could even be cut and strung with ribbon and string to make a small loom.

What is so appealing to children about materials adults often see as "junk" or "scraps"? What children choose to use as toys are objects or materials that lend themselves to being incorporated into all sorts of imaginative play scenes. Children enjoy toys whose function is at the start undefined; such a toy has unlimited possibilities for a child. A hard cardboard tube could be a pillar on a bridge, the body of a telescope, the torso of a doll or animal, or part of a mobile, any of which can be called into being any time the child wants.

Children like to use their imagination to create their own brand of toy. They like to use raw materials which do not themselves have constraints imposed on how one uses them. Children like to be able to push, pull, look at, listen to, glue, paint, stack, knock down, cuddle, nail, or otherwise act on these materials. They do it solely for the fun of doing it. As they get older, they like to make their own custom-made, finished product.

Recycled scraps, industrial discards, extra things collected from around the house are ideal for home toy making. The scraps are free or certainly very inexpensive, and are extremely versatile—a winning combination.

A small toy-making workshop can be set up easily and inexpensively at home. The most important ingredient is a collection of scrap materials. We recommend that the materials be sorted and stored in easily accessible containers. (Film canisters the size and shape of metal cookie containers, or 3 to 5 gallon ice cream cylinders are possibilities.) Also important to have available are the proper tools and accessories, many of which need to be bought. They include: white glue, tape, tempera paint and paint brushes, scissors, a ruler, a hammer and nails, some sort of saw and drill, a utility knife, needle and thread. Other hardware items may come in handy: screws, a screwdriver, nuts and bolts.

With the materials around, children will have a million ideas of how they would like to construct, or have constructed, their personal town of toys. A parent's role at first can be just to discover, through observation or direct

questioning, what sorts of toys a child would like to make. Parents can then help the child, first by making sure the raw materials are available, then by providing encouragement and praise for the child's own creations. Parents can also enter into the toy-making process through helping a child who cannot complete a toy because of a lack of skills, as in cutting, using a saw, or drawing a circle. Parents can also help the child make his/her own creation more durable. Children often do not know about reinforcing corners, how much glue is really needed, and other such details.

As well as providing back-up support for the child's toy-making, adults can also decide to create toys of their own design. Historically, older children and adults have provided the younger ones with home-crafted toys. The Appalachian folk toys are passed down from one generation to another; the southern mountains are the home for many who make apple-faced dolls, gee-haw whimmy diddles, and the like. Just look at your own skills and interests. Would you be interested in making a puppet, a board game, a set of playing cards, a stuffed doll, a child-sized table, a doll house? Though these projects sound sophisticated, they can all be made at home from recycled materials.

We hope that by now you are sold on the idea of collecting and using these scrap materials, and are now wondering where to get them. Of course, many already exist in your home, (or your neighbor's). If you live in an area where there is some kind of resource center (possibly connected with a day care center, a teacher center, or other children's program) you should have no trouble acquiring a selection of materials. Otherwise, ask at preschools and elementary schools; teachers (especially art teachers) may have a source of scroungable items. Local retail establishments may give samples or extras. Manufacturing and packaging plants are the basic source of recycled items; many discard vast quantities of useful items all the time. Go through your local yellow pages and pick out factories, outlet stores, or retail concerns which are likely to have some scrap items of interest. Phone them and ask if they have a supply of inexpensive seconds, or discards which they would give away. If you explain that you will be using the recycled items for children's projects, the response is more likely to be positive. (A center for recycled products to be distributed to schools was established in Baltimore and has been very successful.)

Some recycled materials, some tools, and lots of

imagination and motivation are what is needed for a successful toy-making venture.

EDUCATIONAL TOYS

Mal Goldman

Educational Teaching Aids Store

When I got into the business in 1958, there were not many people making educational materials. Three basic companies existed: Childcraft, Creative Playthings, and Constructive Playthings. It didn't take long to get to know everybody in Special Education. In 1959 I saw materials from England, called Philip Tacey, which they had been making since 1861. I thought they were the greatest materials in the world because they were manipulative, tactile, and educative. I started importing them immediately.

In 1961, I went into the business myself. It was very difficult—there were financial problems, but I kept meeting people who were excited about what I was doing and that kept me going. But after two years, Mr. Woldenberg of the Educational Teaching Aids said, "Why don't you come work for me? You can run my business." I started working for him and have been ever since. In the beginning I was responsible for a lot of the items in the catalog, designing and manufacturing.

About ten years ago, my wife and I decided we couldn't stand another winter in Chicago, and we packed our bags and left everything to move out to the West coast. I represent the ETA out here in 11 states and have people working for me. We not only have math, language skills, and special ed, but we also have an early assessment program, about 4000 items all told.

In 1965, Mr. Woldenberg came back from Europe. His child was in Montessori school and he wanted to start manufacturing their toys over here. We became the only producers of Montessori toys in the United States. Mathematically, educationwise or didatically, Montessori doesn't go as far in the public schools, so we have incorporated Montessori beads into the base 10 block and it makes a mathematical progression. I feel our golden beads are the best in the world. They are made of translucent plastic and each bead is a single unit. We do a lot of business with golden beads.

We do a tremendous amount of retail business with parents who are helping their children with school work. We know when teachers have conferences with the parents, because the parents come in with a sheet of paper and say, "The teacher wanted my child to do this." The beginning of the summer that's when we sell, for the summer drill.

When we first started we soon learned that if you call our products toys, the child will destroy them in a minute. If you call them educational devices, they last three or four minutes. They take on a different connotation. I've been in the business for twenty years and I know this is true.

We do parent workshops all the time, especially with the Montessori material. Educational devices encompass a whole different concept and we are pleased to have the parent come in and learn about them. Part of our store is set aside for children to come in and sit down with these games and materials and experience them. They

manipulate the stuff and the parents are surprised by what they can accomplish. I tell the parent to leave the children alone. They are happy playing by themselves, and if the parent leaves them alone, the children are pleased to play with the materials that are there. We've done quite well with that.

Most of these devices are made of wood and they can be passed from generation to generation. If you buy plastic, chances are it will break, if you buy wood, it may cost ten or twenty dollars, but it'll last. People have told me that the materials they bought from me twenty years ago are still being used. Let's say they spent thirty dollars, but they used it over twenty years: the pro-rated cost is next to nothing. Our philosophy has always been to produce the best, not the least expensive.

For a free catalog, write Educational Teaching Aids (see resource section for address).

SELECTING TOYS

Harold Goldstein

Owner of Young Playways

I feature toys and academic aids from preschool to primary grades only. One of the most important toys for the first year of life is called a "cradle gym," which I suspect is one of America's good contributions to the field of toys. The role America has played in toys during the 1880's to the early 1900's has never been duly acknowledged. We compare favorably in the field of toys. The "cradle gym" was a trade name until a year or two ago, then the original manufacturer sold out. Since that time, almost all companies have entered the market with a form of cradle gym.

I look for simplicity; there is an elegance to that. An expensive cradle gym does not do any more for the child than the original simple cradle gym. A complete system is a rod which extends across the crib. You hang from the rod some pieces of equipment for the child, depending on the age. Plastic toys can be grasped for hand coordination. You have to make sure there are no sharp points. There can't be toxic paint or roughness. And you need to make sure the child can't put it in his mouth and swallow it. Safety standards are helpful.

During the early years the child needs toys for hand coordination. I recommend color cones, cylinders in wood or plastic that go on a spindle in graduated sizes for the child to take off. At the age of one, we expect the child to take them off and put them into his mouth. It is an exception if the child puts them back on the spindle. There is a snap and lock piece, it's a large piece, made of plastic, about 1 to 1½ inch in size, that a child can snap together.

No one can really define a toy that educates. At the age of two, real block play begins; you start with cloth blocks, and then the traditional cube, one inch or slightly larger. These have sometimes been called the alphabet cubes, which have been used in the past to test children's

development. The child takes a cube and piles on onto the other; this comes under the heading of "construction," which carries through from early childhood, until an individual decides he doesn't want to be a builder or architect.

Toys should be simple, durable, adaptable to the child's ability to cope with the toy, and should be within the physical development of the child. If a child goes to nursery school, or some form of pre-school activity, the parent can visit the playroom and the environment and become educated as to the kinds of toys that are necessary in the minds of educators.

Children come in and are free to wander around the store. We do direct them to certain items we know will attract their attention and maintain their interest over a period of time.

SELECTING TOYS

Scott Goode

Owner of Lowen's Toy Store

If a parent approaches me and she wants a toy for a two-year-old, I seldom ask "boy or girl" because now everything is for boys or girls. They all want constructive toys. I like Fischertechnik very much. I also like Lego, Playskool, and Fisher-Price.

We look to see that the value is there before we buy the toys. Most games don't last more than three or four months. At first there were only a few board games: Monopoly, Sorry, Clue, Battleship, Parcheesi, and Connect. Now we have "Run Yourself Ragged," which is good; it's a dexterity game.

I worked in this store as a high school student when it was one-tenth the size it is now. I watched the store grow. I finally heard two years ago that the old owners, husband and wife, were going to retire. I approached them and made them an offer. I particularly wanted this store because it's the best store of its kind in the Washington area. It's different from Toys R' Us. They are the leading toy chain in the country, if not the world, but they are heavily involved with promotional things and advertising and I felt I didn't want to be part of that. I want to deal one-on-one with customers and know them by name, and this particular store is now in its second, almost third generation in this community, the same families keep coming back. People I grew up with have children now. They come in to me now and say, "My parents shopped here when I was five and six years old." It's your basic mom and pop store.

The biggest decision is play value. If I'm convinced that a certain doll house has play value, then I want that. If I can tell a customer in all honesty that a particular item has good play value, then I am pretty happy with it. Play value is the single biggest deciding factor in buying a toy.

One of the things I worry about in this business is finding good manufacturers that make quality toys. It is

difficult to explain to a customer that a manufacturer went out of business. I am more concerned about having good manufacturers for my toys than going out of business.

MAKING YOUR OWN PUPPET MAGIC

Sally Grauer

Author and Designer

Puppetry, a folk art for thousands of years, has provided entertainment and education for children and adults around the world. Remember Pinocchio, the little wooden boy whose nose gave him away when he lied? Or Punch and Judy, the 17th century English versions of the quarrelsome couple? Or today's parade of television role models, including Lamb Chop, Howdy Doody, Kukla, and the cast of Muppet superstars led by Kermit the Frog?

Puppets can take a variety of forms, many of them easy enough for you and your children to make and use right at home. Among specific categories, the hand puppet is an unusually simple design, often made just of cloth or felt with features glued or drawn on. A separate head can be made, with a cloth body. Clay or papier-mache can be molded. A humble brown paper bag can become a happy hand puppet. Or you can stuff the toe of a sock with cotton. Anything from Styrofoam balls to potatoes can create the puppet's head.

Start collecting a box of puppet makings. Put in scraps of fabric or yarn, fancy buttons, sequins, and bits of lace. Old gloves, hats, and mittens are useful; so are small, empty boxes and old jewelry.

Use your imagination. An old ball could become a puppet head, with a bandana or handkerchief for the body. Or cut open a sock, sew fabric in the slit, and you have a puppet with a wide-opening mouth.

Probably the easiest hand puppet of all is made of felt. Simply trace the outline of your hand with the thumb and little finger separated. Cut two identical pieces of felt and sew them together with contrasting thread or yarn. Glue on eyes, nose and mouth of another color.

Practice with the puppet until its movements seem natural. Let it hold a pencil and write your name, or pick up a coin from the table. Let your puppet clap its hands, whisper in your ear, hide its eyes.

Your stage can be a cardboard box with one side removed. Leave one top flap on and cut it down to three or four inches for a little shelf for the puppets. A table turned on its side with the puppeteer behind it works well. Even a doorway with a curtain or cloth covering the lower half can create a puppet stage.

Keep props few and simple. Let the puppets tell the story and your family use its imagination.

Puppetry lends itself well to fantasy and to simple comedy, with fairy tales offering an endless supply of material for family sketches. Or check your local library for books with puppet plays. Some will even have improvisation exercises you can build a show around.

And, of course, you may write your own plays to produce. Use holidays. Maybe a Christmas puppet show will become a tradition at your house. Or create a special birthday show, adaptable for every member of the family.

Write for information about the festival or Puppeteers of America, at 5 Cricklewood Path, Pasadena, CA 91107. copyright © 1981. Reprinted by permission of *Friendly Exchange* Magazine.

TOY TESTING FOR QUALITY

Elizabeth Grotz

Product Safety Testing, R. Dakin and Co.

The first thing we look for is safety. Is it sewn well? Are the eyes on right? We do an overall check on that. Then we check against a control. Is the head shape right, does the muzzle look the way it should? Color, plush, everything like that. We look at a lot of things to do with safety and aesthetics. The inspector also oversees the aesthetics as well. It's a combination of things we look for. We take the item as a whole.

The original sample becomes our control. And our branch office has a control that is used to match against the item we have here. So when we visit the manufacturer and talk about the head shape and other points, we make sure the product is consistent with the original design.

In a week I might, along with two other people, inspect two hundred and fifty items. Some of the tests we conduct are: tension, metal detection, flexion for items containing arms or legs that bend, and sharp points. There is a flammability tester for the United States Testing Company. For the tension testing we use a shadow line tension gauge. There is also a bite tester which looks like false teeth. That's to simulate children biting into a toy. We want to make sure we don't have any brittle plastics which can shatter and cause sharp points.

We have specific items that we check on for each piece. If we find a problem, then we quarantine the whole batch to pick out the bad ones. We may have to go back to the original design to get it right.

MEDIA CLONES AND CORPORATE TOYS

Sheila Harty

Author, Center for Study of Responsive Law

I entered my first toy store free of cajoling from the target audience, a child. Instead I brought an adult along to add more objectivity. As we conducted our three-hour tour of one of America's largest supermarket of toys, we both grew horrified at what we observed.

Two things are predominant among the toys available: the influence of mass media and that of corporate America. The paraphernalia from popular film and television series range from the hero figure as a doll to the hero's head as a radio; other toys, labeled with brand

159

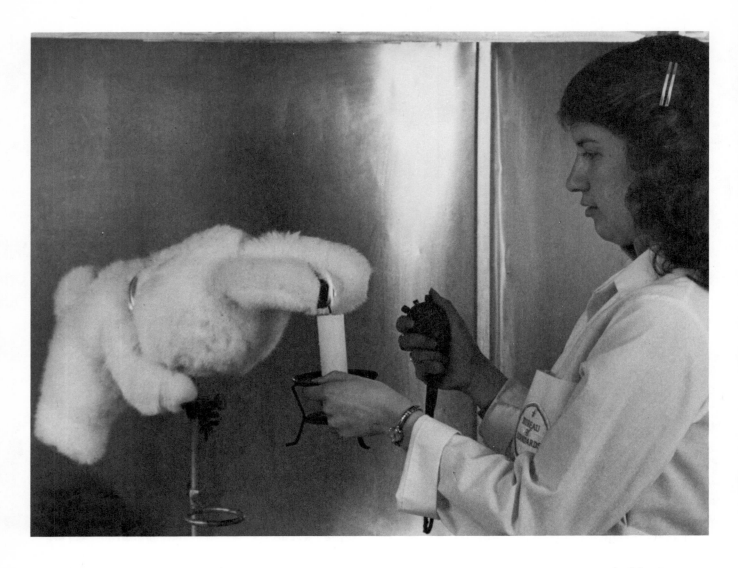

names unrelated to the manufacturer, imitate adult commerce and acquisitions.

Although one can still find the traditional red fire truck, the trend is toward the corporate freight. Gas tankers are labeled with the familiar corporate logos of Mobil, Amoco, and Shell. Trucks are identified by their cargo's trademark, such as Pepsi Cola, Coca Cola and Budweiser. There is a telephone truck labeled Bell Systems, a long haul rig identified as B.F. Goodrich and even a Goodyear Blimp.

Is this merely bringing realism into play? Or is this advertising aimed at imprinting brands on in the minds of future consumers?

Admittedly, it is not surprising in a toy car collection to see Mustangs, Mazdas, Pontiacs, Chevys, or Corvettes. But we saw no Hondas or Toyotas. American manufacturers also know that if you attach a TV image to the car, you can outsell the others, such as Starsky & Hutch radio-controlled Ford Torino. To service these cars, the Mattel Company makes a "Hot Wheels Service Center Foldaway Garage" which offers servicing by Champion, Penzoil, Goodyear, and Shell to the playing customers.

In the domestic department, we find kitchen toys labeled with all kinds of brand name promotion. There are toy Pepsi Cola and Kool Aid drink dispensers, both suggested for three-year-olds and up. These companies seem only to recognize it as improper to encourage the consumption of caffeine and sugar to babies and toddlers. In one "Play Food" kit, you get Kellog's Sugar Smacks, Bran Flakes, Raisin Bran, Ritz Crackers and Pep Cereal. In another kit, you get Morton Salt, Jolly Green Giant Corn, Del Monte Pineapple Slices, Franco-American Spaghetti-O's, Campbell's Chunky and Chicken Noodle Soup, and V-8. A lot of salt and sugar is being promoted in these "meals."

Certainly children are eager to emulate adults. But the usual patterning of toys on adult products perpetuates some habits society may need to alter. Toy kitchen appliances, for example, give the impression that energy conservation is nothing to practice. We see children being sold a "Lil Homemaker Blender Set and Super Mixer," a "Kiddy Mactic Action Appliance Mixer," and a toy "Juicer Blender." There's also a "Pop-up Play Toaster" and even Barbie has her own "Play Food Processor."

160

What are the American manufacturer's arrangements or the toy industry's guidelines behind brand name use on children's toys? Such "licensed" toys are the dominant category in toys today, and the most popular with our TV-bred children. But initial queries to some toy companies uncovered no guidelines or marketing restrictions. It seems to be left solely to "gentlemen's agreements."

One might conjecture that someone must be paying someone for the advertising or the trademark loan. However, the use of registered trademarks must be with permission, but not necessarily for money. The agreement for usage seems to be arranged case-by-case between the toy manufacturer and the corporation whose trademark is desired. As in the case of the "Union 76" toy gas tank truck, the corporation may be pleased enough with the promotional opportunity that it gives consent without charge. Corporations which need such billing sometimes solicit the usage of their trademark.

These encroachments by mass media and corporate America leave one feeling cornered, force fed, and without choices. Indeed, the effects are subtle. Values are displaced by commodities. Our will is surrendered to media manipulation. It's another intrusion in the quality of our lives. Our children are being given advertising in the form of toys.

One objection to many Saturday morning television commercials is that young children cannot distinguish between what is "real" and what is a broadcast advertising image. When TV personalities such as The Incredible Hulk are found in toy stores, on lunch boxes, T-shirts, or coloring books, they appear to verify TV's reality. We are reproducing and perpetuating images as if they deserve to be real. These media clones exacerbate the dominance and the effect of TV in our children's lives. The media images have become their primary reference group, their shared associations. From this, TV has the power to manipulate and program the environment of their imaginations. Yet objections still persist in society against perpetuating the "myths" of Santa Claus, the Tooth Fairy, and angels because, despite their benevolence, they are not "real."

The TV tells children too many things. Other sources of information begin to lose credibility. The child may even defer his or her own creativity to be attentive to the programming. Yet TV is only a one-way communication. This makes all "learning" from the medium slightly propagandistic. If only we could measure mental or spiritual harm to the child as easily as sales of the toy manufacturer or corporate sponsor. Like the health hazards of radiation, the effects of such imprinting may be twenty years down the line, and too late to warn us now.

What makes a good toy? My friend defined it as "one that gives a child options." A toy should be flexible in its uses, less specific in its form, and open to meaning in order to involve the child. A useless toy is one you merely look at, or turn on and look at. Replicated images ask

children to be observers of the corporation's creativity and hence passive consumers of the corporation's values. As a result, the child is not an active participant in play, using his or her critical faculties or physical energies.

CULTURAL RESPONSE OF TOYS

Karen Hewitt

Toy Historian and Author

Owner of Learning Materials Workshop

The toy is a common object in our lives. It is found everywhere: on the floors and shelves of most homes, at the checkout counter in the supermarket, in the ads-punctuated Saturday morning television shows, in nursery schools, early childhood centers, and schoolroom cubbies. The toy is an artifact of universal interest and appeal. It is an object that almost any adult has had experience with but has seldom examined in the light of how it has shaped skills, values, and concepts. This ordinary object that has enriched the fantasy life of childhood has been examined by scholars in the fields of history, literature, psychology, archeology, art history and criticism, education, and cultural anthropology. They have considered its historical development, its interpretation as an object in our popular culture, its use as a source of literary images, and its design components.

Scholarly studies of the toy have shown that, although toys have existed throughout history, the function of the toy and the intention of the designer, the maker, the giver, and the player have changed. These changes reflect a transformation in society, particularly in society's attitudes and actions towards children and their education. In 17th and 18th century America, particularly in New England, the Puritan view of the child as a depraved

creature, born into sin, gave way gradually in the 19th century to a more benevolent and enlightened view. This radical change brought with it a shift in ideas about play and playthings. The toy, tool of the devil in Puritan America, was slowly recast into a beneficial, even necessary part of the educational paraphernalia of the developing child. The concept of the toy as an object with educational potential blossomed during the 19th century, a time of educational reform and an increasingly humanitarian outlook towards children.

An example of a very ancient and basic toy is the rattle. The first rattles were designed to ward off evil spirits, but also served well to distract a cranky infant. The earliest American rattles were made of natural materials such as gourds with dried seeds. In the early 19th century, rattles were first made with wood, willow, and stamped tin. By 1860, India rubber was introduced, then celluloid, followed by plastic in 1890. Many of the early rattles would not be approved by Consumer Products today, because they all contained small detachable pieces. But the main design feature of the rattle was the sound. The newest rattles, such as Johnson & Johnson's Tracking Tube, are more than just sound makers; they exploit the child's visual curiosity by having a slowly moving red liquid into the rattle's handle.

The 19th century cast iron "Queen" stove and Elite Tool Chest for Boys, the Barbie doll, and the Telephone Line Person in the Judy puzzle can be regarded as a statement about changing archetypal images of men and women; the abstract Vitali play people made of smooth polished wood, the meticulously detailed paper dolls from a Bennington collection and the molded plastic Starwars figures can be considered as design statements and comments on varying aesthetic tastes; the S. L. Hill

Spelling Blocks, the Froebel Gifts, the Speak and Spell toy by Texas Instruments can be compared in terms of educational philosophy. Every toy should be looked at as a complex artifact and examined with all these factors in mind. (Addresses listed in the resource section.)

THE WASHINGTON DOLLS' HOUSE TOY
MUSEUM

Flora Gill Jacobs

Founder and Historian

The museum is filled with doll houses on display behind glass. Some of the houses include: The Quaker Oats House, fashioned from Quaker Oats crates and filled with furniture and dolls; The Schoenhut Circus (1903), with acrobats and horses, clowns and dolls; The Wedding Cake house with fireplaces and piano; The Victorian house has an attic, with lights, little trunks, dishes, carpeting, candles, hat stand, chairs, and pictures; The Providence house (1920) has little animals, dresser, roll-top desk, clocks, trunks, sewing machine, table with cards, flowers, and a switchboard operator; The Baltimore is actually a series of six houses in a row. There are many kinds of miniatures, a tin kitchen, and dolls. Another house contains a sewing basket, scissors, baby bath, screens, mirrors, dog, magazine rack, little carriages, a kitchen filled with utensils and a little spice rack.

The museum also contains a miniature general store, gazebo, and a house from Pueblo, Mexico. There are replica of a Public School as well as a fire station, a New York brownstone, and a hat shop.

The museum was founded in February, 1975, and contains a carefully researched collection of antique doll houses, toys, and games, most of them Victorian, and all of them antique.

The museum is dedicated to the proposition that the doll houses of the past comprise a study of architecture and decorative arts in miniature and that toys of the past reflect social history.

In addition to various doll houses, there is a wide variety of toys made of wood, lithographed paper-on-wood, and tin, with such American toy makers as Bliss, Reed, Crandall and McLoughlin well represented. Because the collection is a sizable one, only a portion is on display at the museum at any one time.

Apart from the museum proper, there are two other popular attractions, an "Edwardian Tea Room," where birthday parties take place, and two museum shops, one for doll house collectors and one for doll house builders. The collectors' museum contains a supply of miniature furniture, accessories, and dolls. It is said to be one of the most complete in the United States. The doll house builders museum is supplied with a wide assortment of building and wiring supplies, kits, and books. There are also doll houses for sale, and a consignment corner containing old miniatures, dolls, and toys.

IDEAS FOR BABY PLAY

Sandy Jones

Author of *Good Things for Babies*

I think that toys for babies are vastly overrated. Parents spend thousands of dollars on bright "play-pretties," as my mother calls them, in hopes that the toys will have some intrinsic value to their babies.

In an industrialized society like ours, we always think the answer lies in objects. So we surround our babies with objects. We hold them in objects (cribs, playpens, jumpers), we quiet them with an object (pacifier), and we think that out there somewhere is the perfect toy, an object with just the right sound and color for our beloved baby.

Just to set the record straight: babies should be held on human bodies, sleep nestled close to their treasured mothers and dads, fed with the human breast (preferably attached to someone who loves him or her dearly), and pacified with all the sucking time that Baby seems to want. What is the perfect toy? Your hair, hands, body, and motions!

OK, so you're still on a treasure hunt, and haven't recognized that YOU'RE the treasure. I can give a few suggestions, but recommend them only as supplements to "the real thing."

Babies like bright colors. Their favorites are red and yellow. They also like light from the window or lamps. Suggestion: a brightly colored mobile and crib near an uncurtained window so that baby can peer out at the fluttering leaves. You can make your own mobiles (placed out of baby's reach!) of crumpled aluminum foil or other bright paper.

For a baby's clutching interests, a washable, extra-soft lambskin may be just the thing that baby likes to nap on. (If you are allergic to wool, baby might be too.) Some mothers in primitive tribes wear intriguing necklaces just for baby's mouthing. Perhaps some simple, large wooden beads (unpainted) on a rawhide string would be fun for the baby.

For teething, a cold, wet washcloth is easy enough to hold onto.

For the older baby who is beginning to sit up (six months old), you should select toys that are absolutely safe. No sharp edges, nothing to trap fingers in, mouthable, no toxic paints or small parts that could be broken off and swallowed. In the dangerous category are marbles, balloons (because they deflate and may get caught in the baby's windpipe), and small rattles or pacifiers that could get lodged in a baby's throat. I might add a warning about the strangulation danger from any hanging strings or around-the-neck items.

Look for toys that do something in response to baby's action. A toy that makes noise, or pops open, or makes music when it's pulled are good examples of this kind of toy. Psychologists call this kind of action "con-tingent feedback" and, in essence, because the baby can make something happen, it teaches him that he has some power.

TOY STORE TRENDS

Manny Luhn

Jeffrey's Toys

My parents operated a small variety store prior to the toy stores. At that time toys were sold in department stores, furniture stores, and hardware stores. We opened what was the first toys-only store in a shopping center; no clothing, no furniture, just toys. The toy industry at my level is going to become extinct. Today, toy stores in a downtown area cannot compete with the price structures of other industries. The toy industry is changing because rent has been made the top priority. A lot of this is due to the influence of Toys R Us.

Most people in the toy industry say that Toys R Us is not a factor because we can merchandise around them. Well, whenever you merchandise around Toys R Us, what you do is take out the top 90 percent of the salable toys and try to make a living on the remaining ten. They only take a toy off the shelves for two reasons: 1) it is not profitable, or 2) it is hard to housekeep.

If you're doing volume, your marginal profits can be nice. The computer has changed all industries. The computer has allowed a person to open a chain store out of New York City or wherever they want. The toy industry is not a good concept to run as a chain.

The manufacturers give us an indication of what they want us to do, as far as marketing, before the year

163

starts (not what the customer wants). My son was buying robots ten years ago out of Japan. We sold them very well then, but not in the quantities we sell them in now.

There is a difference in the way that things are bought for each of our three stores. 90 percent of people we wait on at Ghiradelli are tourists who buy lower end items or smaller expensive items they can travel with. At the Sutter store because 40 percent are tourists and 50 percent local we have a different mix of toys. At the Embarcadero we have maybe 10 percent tourist and 90 percent local where our whole day is done between twelve noon and two p.m. In terms of all three stores, we do business with about 500 companies.

My favorite toy is the plush and a very good category. Going back years ago, we used to buy from 14 major plush companies. Now we buy from four, all on the west coast: Russ Berrie, Charm, R. Dakin, and Kamar. We bring in items from California Stuffed Toys in the latter part of the year.

Non-allergenic toys made for children are usually our worst sellers. Our best sellers cater to the adults such as cuddly teddy bears and teddy bears in tuxedos, etc. Most of the major dolls we have are Madam Alexanders or Paulines. These quality dolls are for adults and not for children at all. The few that parents buy for children are put into a glass case for the child to look at—it's really for the adult's collection.

Over the years, out of the top ten toys, Barbie has to be number one and Plush number two. There are Fisher-Price toys that have had tremendous longevity. In the old days we used to use the word "staple." Staple items, which we used to carry, were Lincoln Logs, Tinker Toys, and American Bricks—they're not even on our shelves anymore. Lego has dominated that whole field. I'm talking about dollar sales, something that has continuing sales, that is "profitable" to the store. One time going way back, there were three major companies which dominated the toy field: Louie Marks, Lionel, and American Flyer. They really were the movers and shakers until a little woman from Denver, Colorado came along and upset the whole toy industry with Barbie.

TOY BUYING FOR FAO SCHWARZ

Ian McDermott

Chief Buyer

My first consideration in toy purchasing is quality and closely tied to that is value. I mean value not only from our standpoint, whether it has the right kind of marketing terms, but also whether it has value for the child. Also, would the parent, the purchaser, feel that he was getting value for his money.

We pay much more attention to the safety of toys for infants than we do for a construction set like Fischer Technik, because we know that there's years and years of research went into its development. But if we happen to come across a toy from a cottage industry and we think it has merit, then we would give it a little more consideration from the safety standpoint. But for the most part, American manufacturers do have R & D departments where this is supposedly done before the product ever hits production.

I buy for about thirty two stores now, we go from the east to the west coast and as far north as Boston and south to Florida. We have a central buying team; there are three of us. We buy not only from the American market, 50 percent of what we offer is imported, we go to Europe as well. In the winter there is a big fair in Nuremburg, Germany, plus an Italian show in Milan, and the French fair in Paris, and the British toy show in London. And in the fall, one of our buyers, the merchandise manager, visits the Far Eastern exhibits.

As far as safety is concerned, we've had a rash of problems in recent years with plush toys. In one instance a manufacturer, certainly this was unintentional, put in a filling that contained tiny, tiny particles of metal. It really was quite accidental. The agents from Consumer Products Safety Commission caught it. They were doing spot checks in the stores around the country. I think we have some regulatory agency that has the power to enforce what the toy manufacturers already try to adhere to. But it is this type of problem we have to face.

We shy away from television toys. It was sort of a standard joke in the American toy industry that if you had a toy that was going to be heavily promoted on television, then don't even bother to show it at FAO Schwarz. That's not so today because the increased budgets that these toy companies put into television advertising is really for our benefit also. I would hazard a guess that we lost thousands of dollars in the past because we didn't carry TV toys. Now we do, but we don't feature them in the store. And ironically enough, it seems that there's a self-regulating system in the toy industry now, where most of your popular toys are almost rationed.

One of the big changes in the American toy industry is the introduction of these long-term projections where you have to make a commitment. If you know that it's going to be a heavily promoted line or range, then you have to be in at the very beginning.

One of the most interesting developments in the industry today is a sharper awareness of the profit picture in business. There's absolutely no point today in producing a toy unless you're going to support it and promote it and sell through. Much too often in the past, companies made big runs on certain toys and found themselves left with three-quarters inventory at Christmas.

The key, I think, in the store is the nature of the display. By sectionalizing the toys, all the way from washable plush toys for an infant through preschool toys, children's games, family games, hobbies, all the way down the line; helps buyers. The display and presentation is

even more important than it used to be. It is really essential if you're not only to reach, but get your message across to the public; it's vital, it's the key to selling, which is why we're here.

The backbone of toy selection is really comprised of staples, the basics. It varies from year to year, but the staple things are teddy bears, Raggedy Ann dolls, Snoopy dolls, which have been with us now for over twenty years, wooden toys... that's not to say that we're still selling today something that was originally produced fifty years ago, but each year turns up in a new disguise. It is a new look. The basic toys are the most popular and remain the most popular.

Up to the first year of the Vietnam War, FAO Schwarz carried only a few guns, a small range of BB guns, rifles, and toy pistols, in addition to holster sets, cowboy and western memorabilia. We withdrew from that area due to the public outcry about war toys, not necessarily our consumers, but the general public, and we have only western guns and holster sets today.

We feel play cosmetics for youngsters are simple, innocuous, even though the newer teenage range of cosmetics is all the rage, and several major American companies are raking in big profits from it. We felt it was an area that doesn't really belong in a toy shop.

We are leaders. We set an image that other people will follow. We've been in the business for 119 years. We have a reputation to uphold. We know we're creative, we are usually the first with the newest craze or game. We like excitement and we enjoy what we are doing.

EDUCATIONAL TOYS

Glen Nimnicht and Marta Arango

Creators of the Toy Lending Library

There is no magical way to help your child become a genius or even to have superior intellectual ability. Children differ in their ability to learn, some learn rapidly and with ease, others learn slowly and with difficulty. There are differences that parents must accept and respect. Your challenge as a parent is to help your child develop the intellectual ability he has as fully as possible. Playing games is a way to do this that can be fun for both of you as well as good for your child.

Before we discuss how to play games with your child, let us briefly consider child development in general, since there is a connection between overall development and the ability to learn and play games. There is a relationship between growth and development and the ability to do physical things, such as walking. But this relationship is not nearly as clear and direct as some psychologists have thought.

165

The first rule to remember is that a child's parents and family are the most important people in his development. It is a mistake to think that a child's intellectual development is the responsibility of the school: it is a family responsibility that starts when the child is born. Even after a child starts school the family remains the one continuing influence in the child's intellectual development. The school can only assist you, it cannot replace you.

You should remember, however, that educational toys and games are only tools, they are not ends in themselves. They will enable you to help your child meet the expectations of our society by teaching him some of the skills and concepts society expects a child to know by the time he is six or seven. But the real value of these toys and games is that they can help establish a relationship between you and your child that can extend far beyond the simple skills and concepts he will learn. We believe that you will find that you can encourage your child to develop the mental set of a problem-solver while you are helping him to learn things that you think are important.

We can never guarantee just how much playing with your child will contribute to his development as a problem-solver. It depends partly on the kind of education he receives in school. Nevertheless, if you have accepted our reasoning, it follows that each time you help your child discover a rule, answer his question, see a relationship, take a mental leap, see a pattern, learn to think in different ways or see a general rule from a number of examples, you are contributing to his development as a problem-solver. Since this development consists of thou-

sands of learning episodes and takes place over several years, you cannot do it all at once. But you can take pleasure in each episode that moves your child in the right direction.

After each of these learning episodes, your own feeling of importance in the education of your child will probably increase, and you will feel better about yourself as a parent. As your own self-concept as a parent improves, your child's self-concept will also improve, because the way you feel about yourself will be reflected in the way you feel about your child.

By learning simple skills and concepts, your child will be meeting the expectations of society, which will undoubtedly be reflected in the school he will attend. If he arrives in school able to meet its expectations of him, he will be rewarded with praise. This too will have a positive effect on his self-concept as a learner and he will probably do better in school.

To make certain that the playing remains fun for your child:

1. Ask him only once a day to play; if he says no, wait until he asks you. Pick a time to ask when the child is not involved in something that is obviously a lot of pleasure for him.
2. Let your child stop playing as soon as he wants to and do not press him to tell you why he wants to stop.
3. Let the child change the rules of the game and play by his rules. It is equally important for you to protect yourself and keep the playing fun.
4. Play the games with your child when you want to play.

Don't stop something you really enjoy when playing with him.

5. Stop when you are tired or have something else to do. If the child is really interested, he can play longer than you can. If you know in the beginning that you can only play for ten minutes, tell your child that you have to stop when the bell rings and set an oven timer or an alarm clock so that the child will know when you have to stop. Otherwise, simply say "I want to stop now."

It is important for you to see your child learning. You are more likely to continue playing with your child if you see the immediate benefits than when they are not obvious to you. As you begin to play the different games with your child, you may want to keep a record of the new things he learns each month.

PARENT TOY LENDING LIBRARY

The Parent Toy Lending Library, one of the programs developed by Head Start, was created as a project to exemplify the responsive environment. The chief purpose of the library is to allow parents to recycle toys that their children have gotten tired of. The toys are borrowed and returned much like books in a library. It was used in conjunction with Head Start and other early childhood programs. The idea of a responsive environment is to provide a place where a child can explore his surroundings and master skills. It involves the child's language, background, and social situation. In the past the library program offered a joint parent education program, an

eight-week course once a week for two hours a session. It was designed to introduce parents to the principles of childhood growth and development. To start one in your community, you will need an overall outlay of $2000-$3000 and could be housed in a closet and an available room. The cost should not exceed $100 per parent. It can be developed in conjunction with a child care center, nursery school, or other community organizations.

One of the basic objectives of the toy lending library is to support children in learning about themselves. Children have a healthy self-concept when they:

1. Like themselves, their family and friends.
2. Believe they can be successful.
3. Believe that they can solve a variety of problems.
4. Believe that what they think, say and do will make a difference.
5. Have realistic estimates of their abilities and limitations.
6. Express feelings of pleasure and enjoyment.

Parents can help children gain the skills they need to learn if they believe they can have a positive effect on the child. The child will become more expressive and gain in self-confidence as he or she learns with the help of the parent.

The toys of the original toy library were designed to help the child learn cognitive skills and concepts. Toys which teach other skills can be used, though the stress is on learning to learn rather than the specific concept or specific skills learned in the process. The ground rules for the child are: letting him explore the materials, play when

167

he wants to, can change the rules, and discover the answer rather than be told; the parent helps by describing what it is they are doing, and lets the child set the pace and focus of interest. Criteria for the toys are that they must be appropriate for the age, have non-toxic paint, no small pieces, no sharp points, are durable, and are oriented toward a specific concept. The concepts and skills designed for the original library include:

1. color matching
2. color naming
3. color identification
4. shape naming
5. shape identification
6. letter recognition
7. numerical concepts
8. relational concepts
9. sensory concepts
10. problem solving
11. verbal communication
12. verbal comprehension
13. auditory discrimination

The toy library should have a variety of toys: games, books, records, and educational materials in addition to the basic toys. The basic toys are:

sound cans—metal cans filled with beans or beads

Color Lotto—a square wooden board, divided into nine squares each set of color squares fits the squares on the Loto Board

feely bag—a small drawstring bag with two sets of cut out shapes, say squares and triangles

stacking squares—wooden squares that fit together on a wooden post, red, blue, yellow, green, orange from bottom to the top

wooden blocks—ten sizes of blocks in unit sizes one to ten, the largest block ten times as tall as the smallest block

number puzzle—ten piece masonite puzzle, each piece represents a number one to ten, with pegholes to fit them on

color blocks—sixteen blocks, four each of each color

flannel board—36 small felt shapes, circles, squares, triangles; two sizes; three different colors, red, yellow, blue; eighteen combinations available

Some additional items: nesting boxes, pots and pans, shakers, nuts and bolts, and other items.

alphabet board

beginning matrix game—different colors to be placed on different squares

coordination game—eight cut-out shapes, squares, rectangles, triangles

property blocks—different colors, sizes, shapes, and thickness

hundred pegboard—10 × 10 rows

inset shapes boards—board and twelve matching pieces

pattern box—a long rectangular box and three sets of pattern cards

spinner board—removable pointer that is spun

Formal education should start before the child is five or six, it does not need to take place in the classroom. Formal education can happen in home with the child, with a small group of two to five children, in a day care home with groups of five or more children, in a Head Start or day care classroom, or in a public school in contrast to informal education. The rule of any educational institution is to aid in the family in carrying out their responsibility, that is, the responsibility for the education of their own children. There should be a variety of alternatives to meet the needs of parents and their children. The educational programs should be responsive to the learner's background, culture, and lifestyle.

When children enter a classroom they are free to choose from a variety of activities, such as painting, working puzzles, playing with a variety of manipulative toys, looking at books, listening to records or tapes, using the language master, and building with blocks. They can stay with an activity as long as they like and can move on to something else whenever or often as they like. Small groups may play games, learning episodes with the teacher or assistants, others ask to be read to. Teachers can read to the children, play games, or respond to the spontaneous activities which build the experience that precedes instruction in some skill or concept. Children have large blocks of time for individual activities.

There is a basic theory in all of this: that there is a relationship between maturation and learning, that a child has to mature to a certain point before he can walk and make certain sounds. It is necessary for the parent to think in terms of reinforcing learning and of feedback to the learner. Although a learning sequence is developed for the children, they do not have to adhere to the sequence. For this activity, toys are very carefully evaluated. They were selected based on:

1. their basic purpose
2. their freedom from cultural bias
3. the degree to which they allow a child to interact with them
4. whether the child would want to play with it or continue after five sessions of ten to twenty minutes each or remained interested until he could play the game without error
5. the child selected the toy on his own

In the library there are the following activities: puzzles; different kinds of sequences; building—connector sets, Tinkertoys, logs, tubes; manipulations—lacing beads, cards, pegboards, ladder games; play materials—viewmasters, flannel boards, games, chalkboards, magnetic boards, books and records; music—records and musical instruments; creative play: headphones, puppets, rubber animals, art materials, carpentry packets; outdoor play—jump ropes, sandboxes.

Cabinets and shelves should be available for the display of toys along with a table for checking them out, a box for returned toys, and a box for toys that need repair.

Some important points to remember:

1. Understand your children at each stage and do not push them beyond their own capability.
2. Consider what facilitates their learning at each stage.
3. Consider the kinds of toys and playthings that supplement and expand or reinforce what they have learned in school.
4. Consider toys that allow them to have greater interaction with other children and adults.
5. Consider toys that provide stimulation, challenge, and opportunity to develop self-confidence in their abilities.
6. See if the toy fits the family budget, lifestyle, and has relevance for the child.
7. Consider toys that are durable and can be passed on to other children.
8. Consider a variety of toys which allow children to learn many different types of skills.

This parent toy library has been tried in many places around the country. It may be that your own community has started a toy library already or a group of parents or others may be ready to start one. For more information write the Toy Library Association. (See resource section for the address.)

Toy Libraries in the United States

Children can check out toys at the toy library as they do books in the public libraries. The service is available at many public libraries and by different organizations. The fees vary depending on who is the sponsor. Some toy libraries are created as a business, some as part of other services, and still others are voluntary. In some communities, vans filled with playthings visit schools, nursery schools, and child care programs, and often provide special toys for children with special developmental problems, special needs, or provide toys for children in hospitals. The USA Toy Library Association is made up of educators, doctors, librarians, psychologists, and others. The newsletter, *Child Play*, contains a lot of helpful information and can be obtained by writing: USA Toy Library Association, 5940 West Touchy Avenue, Chicago, IL 60648

TOYS FOR FREE CHILDREN

Letty Cottin Pogrebin

Editor, Ms. Magazine and author of *Growing Up Free*

Once there were two parents who decided to liberate their children from rigid male and female sex roles. They recognized that whatever they brought into their kids'

environment would carry some suggestion of "correct" behavior or sex-typed expectations.

"No more domestic, passive toys for our daughter," said the mother. "That's the end of tough guy toys for our son," said the father.

So on Christmas morning, these enlightened parents gave their daughter a shiny new truck. Under the tree was a soft cuddly doll for their little boy. The parents beamed as their children took the toys up to their playroom.

"This will be the beginning of a new lifestyle," said the father. "Down with sexism in the nursery," said the mother.

A little while later, the parents tiptoed upstairs to observe their emancipated children at play. Through the doorway they saw the little girl cradling the truck in her arms and singing, "aah, aah, Baby," while their son was pushing his doll across the floor and was bellowing, "vroom, vroom, vroom."

That is the gist of the comedy sketch written for television by Rennee Taylor and Joe Bologna. It has never been produced, because the writers themselves withdrew it from the skit.

"We were afraid it would be misinterpreted," explains Ms. Taylor. "People don't realize that it takes more than one toy to undo society's conditioning of sex roles. The audience could have construed it to mean boys will be boys and girls will be mothers, and we didn't want the sketch to end up boosting the biology-is-destiny crowd."

They were wise to worry about the moral that would emerge from the skit. But it should also be said that they were devastatingly accurate about the final scene in the playroom.

Whatever our good intentions, children will not be miraculously transformed by the nonsexist toys we may give them this Christmas. A toy is not a magic talisman. It can't dispel the spirit of sexism in society that is obsessed with notions of "manliness" and "femininity." Studies have shown that, by the age of three, children show a distinct preference for sex-typed activities which reflect what they have absorbed from the culture. Unless the adults in the home are committed to role flexibility, a child will ignore even the most inviting toys if they seem inappropriate. So there's not much to be gained by giving a set of toy dishes to a little boy whose father wouldn't be caught dead in the kitchen.

Understanding the effects of the larger environment upon the child's play interests can spare gift-givers a lot of grief and disillusionment. But having said that, we can still resolve to take toy buying very seriously. After all, healthy children spend over 10,000 hours at play before they enter first grade. Toys and games make a vital contribution to a growing character, personality, and temperament.

Toys are vehicles for brave experimentation. They can be raw materials of childhood fantasy and the practice

pieces for real life. Toys can help a child reason, create, express, manipulate, differentiate, count, spell, read, analyze, construct, categorize, and dismantle. They can teach children to compete or to cooperate. The right sort of toy can be a ready recipient for the child's love or an available outlet for frustration and rage.

Should we buy our daughter the "Suzy Homemaker Oven" because all her friends are getting it for Christmas and she's dying to make a 2½″ angel food cake? Or should we explain that we are generally opposed to toys that require use of electrical outlets, toys that trade on the happy-little-housewife, toys that are overpriced, breakable, and poor substitutes for the real thing?

Should we buy an "Action Jackson" or "G.I. Joe" doll with his authentic wardrobe of uniforms and instruments of destruction, simply because the television commercials have convinced our son that no boy's life is complete without them? Or should we carry on about the masculine mystique and the phony glamorization of the military and the "Barbie Doll syndrome" that exploits pint-size consumers?

I have to admit there is a "Suzy Homemaker Oven" and an "Action Jackson" somewhere in the toy closets of this very house. But that's because I used to be weak-willed, misguided, and indulgent. "Aw, Mom, it's the

funnest thing" once could reduce me to compliant mush. But no more. Now I've got standards the way other people got religion. Whether buying a toy for my own children or for friends, I run it through a rigorous checklist: is it safe, made to last, respectful of the child's intellect and creativity, non-racist, moral in terms of the values it engenders, and nonsexist in the way it is packaged, conceived, and planned for play?

Women are no longer interested in good impressions; we want toys that don't insult, offend, or exclude one sex by inference or omission. We're refusing to buy toys "for girls" that teach hypocrisy, narcissism, and limited aspirations. We're avoiding toys "for boys" that promote militaristic values and a must-win attitude. The question now is, what's left? If we have a budget for new toys, what can we buy with confidence and enthusiasm this holiday season?

In general, the best toys are the least structured ones. They're open-ended. Their playability is determined by what the individual child brings to them. And while a high price doesn't guarantee durability or child-interest, certain larger toy investments of this kind keep paying off with years of pleasure.

A UNIQUE TOY STORE

Roy Raymond

My Child's Destiny

A lot of good stores: clothing stores, toy stores, and shoe stores were in San Francisco, but they tended to be small boutiques. They were spread out around the city and as a small boutique were often out of certain sizes. They had to call another branch to see if the item I wanted was in. My wife and I found we were spending a lot of time in the car driving around with our small children just trying to get the items we needed and that was tiring for them. They did not enjoy jumping in and out of the car and going to different stores.

We looked at the needs from a consumer standpoint and have created a shopping environment for both consumers and parents. We start from a newborn up to about a 12-year-old child, cover all the major product categories: clothing, shoes, toys, books, educational computers, and have a hair salon for children. We also have some educational software that might be for an older or high school child. A parent can come in and find products for all of the needs a child might have in one location.

We open any educational software we carry and let parents or children test it out in the store, whether it's Apple, IBM, or whatever they have at home. We have a fairly liberal return policy. If someone chooses, they can test something at home rather than here in the store, because often it can be cumbersome for people to stay here for 20 minutes and play a program.

We have an overall policy in the store, we guarantee everything. This means that they can bring it back in a day or two, or in ten years and say they didn't feel they got their value out of the product and get a full refund. Very few people have used this. It is something that could be abused by the consumer, but 99.9% of the people are really pretty fair and honest. It gives them security to know that we think it is important, particularly with children's items.

Our unique catalog reaches people around the country. We were not happy with the existing catalogs that were out there and in the way merchandise was selected. Sometimes we got good items and sometimes the quality was a little variable. We wanted to do a catalog where someone could buy anything and be assured it was really the same quality. We now publish over two million copies a year since the Fall of 1984. We're putting together our 4th edition right now, and expect it to be a fairly significant portion of our business in the years ahead.

We have a book boutique that carries 500 to 600 titles. We found a lot of people really like the selection we have, but once they left the store, it was hard for them to recall a title, or select a new book over the phone. We started putting together a catalog of the books we carry in our store. It is available to people who come in from out of the area and to people who have bought other products from our main catalog of toys and clothing.

We designed the store with children in mind. We have two bathrooms in the store designed for children with countertops large enough to be able to change a baby's diaper. We were frustrated with shopping with our own infant and not being able to change her diaper if she needed it. We also have complimentary diapers in the bathrooms in case a parent doesn't have a supply. The staircase we have has two handrails, one at child height and one at adult height. In the dressing rooms for the younger child instead of having a seat, has a bench a child can stand on so mother can try something on the child without having to bend over quite so far. We have a fairly elaborate security system, not so much for product security, but for child security.

On Saturdays, we try to do something special that would be of interest to both the children and the parents. It may range from face painting or cooking for children, to fashion shows of the latest fashions. Sometimes it's topical, like having a speaker come in and talk about dinosaurs when a dinosaur exhibit is in town. We also have representatives from manufacturers come in and talk about specific buyings like LGB trains or the stuffed animals we carry and how to choose a good product in a particular category.

To obtain a catalog, send $2.00 with your request. The address is listed under catalogs in the resource section.

MAKING TOYS

Nancy A. Record

Designer

A lot of people are making their own toys these days. The youngest toymaker I know is Edward, who has been doing it ever since he was able to punch a hole through paper to make a pinwheel. When he was learning to count, he made his own deck of 11 cards, including an ace of iceboxes, a three of trees, a queen of chairs, etc. When I asked him why there were 11 instead of the usual 52, he replied that his game was different. Besides, as the numbers get bigger, the pictures have to get smaller, and he couldn't think of anything smaller than 11 ants.

Making your own toys is far different from buying machine-made items. No matter how simple your idea, or what your materials, cloth paper or wood, your toy is your "game."

I rarely plan a new toy. They seem to make themselves. For that reason, I often do not pencil a pattern on either cloth or wood. Some starts do not get finished, yet little is wasted. Small remnants may be used for smaller toys or decorations. The time involved in experimenting contributes to later successes.

My father taught me how to use his professional table model jigsaw when I was six years old. He said the object was to not hurt yourself or the equipment and to make the best of it with the wood. As he is still using his saw I have one of my own. I use a small, portable Dremel saw, a moderately priced tool which can be used for woodworking, gem and stone polishing, and various other crafts.

I make large numbers of acrobats, all the same shape, but designed to balance in an infinite number of ways. When reproducing them, I trace around the original wood model with a soft pencil directly onto the wood. A paper pattern can also be made (see illustration). Make a clear bold line for easy cutting. Hold the wood firmly when you lead it to the blade; if you imagine drawing with the blade, the cutting goes smoothly. After the figures have been cut out they should be sanded. I use an old tooth brush to scrape off the fine wood dust which clings to newly-cut edges. After sanding, apply a thin coat of gesso. Allow the figures to dry and sand again to remove the grain raised by the moisture, then apply another coat of gesso. Enamel paints with an oil base are best used for simply painted surfaces. As I prefer to work in detail, I use acrylic paints which dry quickly. When the final coats of paint have dried completely I apply a surface of matte or gloss medium.

Sewn and stuffed toys can be made simply from two pieces of cloth sewn together edge-to-edge with a small space left to allow for turning the figure inside out and stufffing. Even large dolls or animals can be made from two boldly shaped pieces. I have made dolls 3 feet long from stiff canvas. I filled the arms and legs first, then I sewed across the hip and shoulder joints and stuffed the remainder of the body. When dressed in soft patterned challis with a calico babushka, the doll's arms and legs swing freely. Old nylons cut in small strips make a soft cushiony stuffing. You can also use commercial polyester battings or, if available, old-fashioned cotton kapok. What you use and how you use it depends on the effect you desire to achieve.

More elaborate sculptural stuffed toys are also easy to make. Shapes can be fitted and revised before you fill the figure. When I made a raven from soft brushed black denim, I stuffed the ribbed wings as I stitched so they would be firmly supported near the center and sag toward the tips.

Even after a toy is filled and sewn up, you can alter its form. I made a blue wool worsted alligator 28 inches long from four pieces of cloth. Two identical shapes formed the body which has four tiny legs and a long ungainly tail. The other two pieces were isosceles triangles sewn together to make a folding diamond shape. After stuffing the body, I cut and fitted the diamond shape to make an open mouth. It didn't look finished and the tail drooped, so I took some tight tucks at several intervals, and the tail twisted in a strong swooping S shape.

Though I am tempted to highly decorate the stuffed toys which I made as gifts, the ones for home use are usually plainly dressed. This is because I know that I have to keep them clean, but also because I tend to add to them as time goes by. The blue alligator has acquired calico neck ruffles, and a soft brown seal now has numerous braid collars.

I keep a constantly changing supply of materials for these toys. There are jars of buttons, odd pins, small bottle caps, snaps (especially very large ones which make beautiful eyes), metal paper fasteners which double for clothes fasteners, zippers of every size and color. I have boxes of braid, rick-rack, ribbon, and lace. Some of the finest trims can be cut off old clothes, negligees, slips, and bed jackets. I find it difficult to dismantle doilies, place mats and towels made by my mother, aunts, and grandmother, so I buy them cheaply at second-hand stores and flea markets. Old pillow slips and dish towels found in these places are often covered with bright embroidered patterns of flowers, fruit, and butterflies. I keep jewelry and coins, and I collect metal and plastic toys from penny gum ball machines. Clippings from magazines, gift wrappings, fruit and vegetable cartons, cartoons and cards, gummed labels and package stickers are good sources for both decorations and ideas. Fabrics for stuffed toys can be purchased or scavenged from old clothes.

To make a puzzle, use three-quarter-inch plywood and choose a piece twice the size of the puzzle. Cut the board exactly in half. One side will be the puzzle base; the remaining side will be cut into the puzzle face.

The subjects for the design are infinite. I like the subject of a train because the track, cut from one edge to the other, provides a frame for the puzzle pieces. After drawing the shapes, cut them out and sand the edges very well so that they will be smooth and fit well. With the train design, there are five pieces which have to be cut out; three of them will be puzzle pieces and two will be glued to the base to provide a frame for the puzzle to fit into.

Glue the two frame pieces to the base using white household glue. Apply the glue evenly to both the sides to be adhered. Let the glue dry briefly before setting them in place on the puzzle base. Weight the glued pieces with a clean piece of paper and several heavy books. While this is drying (about 2 hours), you can begin painting the puzzle pieces. When the base is dry, finish by painting the frame. I always use acrylics as finer designs can be achieved with the fast drying paint. The surface can be coated with acrylic gloss or matte (dull) medium. Finally, glue or tack fabric such as felt to the bottom of the puzzle.

ABOUT *GAMES* MAGAZINE

Ronnie Shushan

Editor

It's important to say right off that *Games* is not a magazine for children, which may be why many children like it, from four-year-olds who do the Eyeball Benders each issue, to older kids who enjoy some of the unusual work and number puzzles. There is, however, liquor and cigarette advertising that some parents prefer to isolate their children from, and some puzzles that are humorously inappropriate for kids. We once got a letter from a mother who was outraged by our "Bar Exam," in which readers were asked to match beer labels to their appropriate bottles.

It is, however, much that children enjoy: slick, colorful, surprising, playful, and enthusiastic without the use of exclamation points. Many teachers adapt some of the material for classroom projects. Some examples are:

- Map puzzles—(What's Wrong with this Map? readers identify all the errors we've planted; Execrable Shapes, outlines of various geographical areas, in combination with each other, to be identified).
- Calculatrivia—some 50 trivia questions must be researched to determine the variables in a "simple little equation" that requires nothing beyond a ninth-grade math education, except extreme care and patience.
- Hidden image puzzles.
- Creative contests (design your dream miniature golf course; write a story using only 3-letter words; draw a mental map of any place in the world).

There are also crossword puzzles, cryptograms, mazes, double crostics, photocrimes, word search puzzles, feature articles, reviews of the best new games, beautifully designed board games with complete rules of play, and as I said, lots of surprises.

I can't really recommend that you subscribe for kids under ages ten or twelve, but if you think you'd enjoy it yourself, there will be material you can share with children of all ages.

THE MANUFACTURER'S REPRESENTATIVE ROLE

James Skahill

Sales Representative (Jesco) and Former President of The Western Toy and Hobby Representatives Organization

The Western Toy and Hobby Representatives is a group of two hundred toy representatives and/or factory personnel. Regular memberships are offered to representatives and associate memberships to factory-oriented sales personnel. I would say we have every primary, secondary, even tertiary toy manufacturer represented at the fair today in one form or another.

The West Coast manufacturers are limited. We have, of course, Mattel, Tomy, Revell, which is a hobby kit manufacturer, Dakin. Not all of these are manufactured here, many are processed overseas and brought here to be packaged and distributed.

This regional show is actually a summation of many shows. There used to be a number of caravans that traveled the coast. We discovered that only about 50% of the manufacturers products were being exposed through the caravan method, most of the selling was through sample cases and catalogs. The purpose of the show is to service the customers in the thirteen states we represent who do not go to the New York Toy Show or who come back here to complete their buying.

I got into this business when I found myself needing a job and ended up in a toy department of a Broadway Department Store. I started my own business in 1958.

Sales representatives don't choose their lines, they compete for them. There are top lines in all the categories that cover the entire spectrum. In music, there are three or four major lines, in games, ten manufacturers. Even as an association we are very competitive with each other and are always looking for new lines.

Each manufacturer will break the nation down into eight or eleven territories. Our show covers thirteen states; some manufacturers split that into three territories, the Pacific Northwest, California, and the Mountain States. Some of our reps cover the entire thirteen states, some cover just California, or Washington and Oregon, so it's split many different ways.

The toy industry is for me challenging and interesting. For those people who are willing to make a sincere commitment I think the toy industry is loaded with opportunities: manufacturing, selling and distributing.

There are so many opportunities, at all levels, in the toy industry today. The thing I would like to see today, not so much for the manufacturer as for the consumer, is the parent being much more selective for the child's sake. A three-year-old boy in house A will not have the same abilities as the three-year-old in house B. I wish parents would use more discrimination.

TOY LIBRARIES IN ENGLAND

Joanna Slonecka

Toy Development Specialist

The toy libraries in England were established to respond to a need for materials for handicapped children. The first one opened in 1967, established by Joan Novis. Now they have more than 800 throughout the country. The first international conference on Toy Libraries was held in England in 1978 and more than twenty countries participated. The second was held in Sweden in 1981.

The original purpose of providing physically and mentally handicapped children with toys and equipment, allowed the child to play and at the same time develop a functional ability. The toy libraries exist for daycare groups, community centers, hospitals, public libraries, and clinics. It began with families exchanging toys between their own homes and buying, as a group, toys which would otherwise be too expensive to buy alone. In addition, parents found the informal contact with other parents very useful.

The organization offers assistance in setting up and maintenance of toy libraries. The annual publication, *The Good Toy Guide,* lists toys that children play with, alongside purposes and descriptive information. Other publications include the journal. Another branch of the association is ACTIVE which helps the children learn and improve their communication skills. ACTIVE was founded by Roger Jefcote in 1975, to assist with technical equipment for disabled children. They design and develop practical toys for the learning of communication and other important skills. The association also publishes books on toys and activities for disabled children and directions for making your own toys.

The Toy Libraries Association offers training, courses, publications, and a regular journal. It advises the toy industry in the production of toys and in many ways helps to improve the production of toys on the market. It does not test dolls, plush toys, character toys or sex-discriminated toys.

For more information write the Toy Libraries Association, Seabrook House, Darkes Lane, Potters Bar, Herts EN6-2AB, England.

DANGEROUS TOYS

Edward M. Swartz

Attorney and Author

A 14-month-old child was playing with tiny wooden play figures, that fit into a variety of the nationally known manufacturer's small pull-type vehicular toys, when he put one of the figures in his mouth. The figure slipped into his throat and, because of the design, caught there and could not be removed by the child's parents. The asphyxiating toy had to be extracted surgically at a hospital, but the anoxia the child suffered between ingestion and extraction left him permanently and severely brain-damaged. Had the figure been designed differently, for example, so that it was larger, the child would have been unable to swallow it in such a manner and would have avoided a tragic disabling injury.

- A seven-year-old child was watching another child fly a kite when the kite dove suddenly, striking the child in the eye. He lost the sight in the eye. Experts' reports established that the kite had design defects and that warnings as to its performance were inadequate. Plaintiffs' proof established that the delta-winged kite had a tendency to dive rather than gently float and drift to earth.

- A child accidentally fired a slingshot, sold as a toy in a dimestore, at his teen-age brother. The projectile struck a playmate in the eye, blinding him. The slingshot had been advertised as a hunting weapon capable of bringing down wild game and should never have been sold as a toy.

- A five-year-old child was sitting in a swing which was suspended on a portable metal exercise bar supplied by the manufacturer to be used in connection with the swing. The directions that came with the bar said that it would support a "200 pound man with ease." The bar fell on the child's head, causing him to sustain massive skull injuries and permanent brain damage. The bar, commonly used in doorways as a "chinning" and exercise bar, and swing were sold to be used together as one unit.

- A youngster was playing with a glass-paneled toy designed to enable him to draw with aluminum powder controlled by magnetized dials. When the child leaned on the glass panel, it shattered and the ragged shards slashed his forearm; moreover, some of the aluminum dust became imbedded in the skin, causing blotchy scarring. Negligence in design was in the use of the glass panel and aluminum powder.

As horrifying as these cases are, they are but a sampling of the cases in which toys cause injuries that leave unsuspecting, innocent children scarred and maimed for the rest of their lives. It is estimated that there are as many as 750,000 injuries as a result of toy-related incidents each year.

Nearly half of all the states have no laws governing the manufacture of toys; of the remaining 26 states, the laws are vague and couched in broad terms. For example, some states with laws prohibiting toys which contain or bear a hazardous substance do not identify what is "hazardous"; others, like Florida, define hazardous substances.

The state statutes abound with ironies. In Montana the Misbranded Hazardous Substance Act prohibits the sale of toys improperly labeled, but the statute seems to apply only to children who can read. The laws in a number of states prohibit the manufacture and sale of a toy or article intended for use by children which fails to bear a proper label warning of danger. Does this mean that those with proper warnings (if there is such a thing for a hazardous toy) can be manufactured and sold?

Chemical sets are routinely exempted from the state statutes. Some statutes, like those in North Dakota and Texas, explain that while they are exempt they must be properly labeled, provide adequate directions, and be geared to children who have attained sufficient maturity and may reasonably be expected to read and heed directions and warnings.

While the value and comprehensiveness of the statutes vary from state to state, not one statute approaches what safety advocates consider a model or prototype for this type of legislation. In fact, most of them are woefully inadequate. In those states where there are statutes, violations of these statutes are punishable by fines of as little as $10 and not more than $5000. This is hardly potent punishment for an industry that recorded retail sales of $7.35 billion in fiscal year 1981.

We can begin by advocating safety in the design and manufacture of toys in every forum society offers. We should enlist the support of parents and grandparents, the largest buyers of toys. We must become more critical in the selection of playthings and, when we find unsafe items on toy store shelves, we should make our concerns known to both the retailer and the manufacturer. Organized consumer movements have proven effective in other areas; the definition and boycott have proven effective in other areas; the definition and boycott of hazardous toys could likewise be very effective.

We must persevere in promoting rigid governmental guidelines for the manufacture of toys in this country and insist on standards for toys imported from other countries. Asking the toy industry to indulge in self-regulation has proven as effective as asking the fox to guard the henhouse.

We must not overlook the media. Not only can they be powerful dissemination tools, but they are also vehicles by which toys are advertised. Encourage local media to join the effort to sensitize the toy industry to the senseless injuries and deaths caused by disregard for safety, and enlist their efforts in monitoring advertising to eliminate irresponsible marketing from their pages or airways.

It is the toy maker who has the final responsibility and is in the best position to anticipate and guard the potential creative and unorthodox uses and misuses of toys for the curious child.

HISTORY OF THE TMA

Doug Thomson

Executive Director of Toy Manufacturers of America

Toy Manufacturers of the USA was formed in 1916. Under the leadership of President Alfred C. Gilbert, the association's activities were governed by a board of directors elected from its membership. All officers were affiliated with their own toy companies. Today, the association is known as Toy Manufacturers of America, Inc. (TMA), is located at the Toy Center in New York City. The members are many of the small, medium, and large U.S. producers of toys, games, and holiday decorations. TMA's membership accounts for an estimated 90% of the industry's retail sales.

The association's prime objectives are to strengthen the American toy industry by encouraging association members to create products having maximum play and educational values.

Services provided for members include operation of a credit information exchange, collection service, compilation of industry statistics, counseling in such areas as physical distribution management and export trade, and a full public relations program. Special committees are also concerned with advertising guidelines, marketing, and governmental relations. Annual membership meetings and seminars are held.

The American Toy Fair, one of the largest and best attended trade shows held anywhere in the world, has been sponsored and managed by TMA since 1931. The first toy fair was held in 1902. Each February, in New York City, the fair brings together hundreds of toy, game, and decorations manufacturers and thousands of commercial buyers from every part of the United States and many foreign countries. There are approximately 800 toy companies in the United States, predominantly small businesses, which produce an estimated 150,000 products each year. The fair is open to all these manufacturers, whether they are members of TMA or not. New products number approximately 3,000 to 4,000 items per year. Most of these can be inspected by American and foreign buyers at the toy fair. In recent years, manufacturers from foreign countries have been invited to exhibit their products at the fair, thus expanding the size, scope and importance of this major toy industry event.

Safety is a high priority on TMA's list of major concerns. The association engages in a continuing toy safety assurance program guided by its Safety Standards Committee. Toy Manufacturers of America is proud of its efforts and accomplishments in the cause of toy safety that extend back more than 50 years and include collaborative projects with the National Safety Council and the American National Standards Institute (ANSI). Liaison with the former began in the early 1930's and led to such cooperative ventures between TMA and the Council as a National Accident Reporting Service in 1946 and a National Clearinghouse for Toy Injuries in 1958. The association's work with ANSI is exemplified by the joint move in 1955 to establish a standard for the coating finishes on playthings and other articles used by children.

A detailed comprehensive voluntary Toy Safety Standard was developed by the TMA in 1976 and cost over $1,000,000. Subsequently published by the National Bureau of Standards 72-76 (PS 72-76), it applies to all aspects of toy design, function, engineering, and production. Others participating in its development were the United States Consumer Product Safety Commission, American Academy of Pediatrics, Consumers Union, National Safety Council, several national retail organizations, and toy industry safety experts. PS 72-76 covers all kinds of products commonly defined as "toys" and includes more than 100 separate testing and design specifications to assure that normal use and abuse of toys will not result in a hazard that could cause an injury.

Among the kinds of testing procedures performed under PS 72-76 are those for use-and-abuse, sharp points and edges, small parts, wheel-pull resistance, projections, flammability, toxicity and electrical/thermal and acoustical energy. Products not covered by the standard are bicycles and home playground equipment (both of which have their own safety standards), skateboards, art materials, craft sets, model kits, rockets, sporting goods, air pistols, and rifles.

The association's public relations staff has developed a series of consumer information slide shows on play, and pamphlets on toy selection, safety, and children's play.

Toys have always represented the adult world in miniature for children. It is how they learn about the world around them. Playing and the toys they play with help children develop physical, mental, and social skills.

TOY STORAGE

Tony Torrice

Children's Environmental Designer

There are virtually dozens of publications in bookstores and on newsstands that offer hints and handy checklists for creating attractive rooms for children and young adults. Yet very few of these articles take head-on the task of designing efficient means for storing all the "things" that children are surrounded with, and collect, as they grow. Much careful attention is placed on the proper care and loving of the child, yet often this same attention to practicality is overlooked in order to be charming.

This section will offer you several ways to organize in a safe and efficient manner all the many belongings of children, and still afford them easy access to their tools of learning. When posed with the problem of creating enough adequate storage in a room design, I offer three

easy clues to accomplishing this task S.O.S.—SIMPLE, ORGANIZED, and SAFE.

SIMPLE: Children learn a tremendous amount of new information in their early years, most of which contributes to the patterns they will carry with them throughout the remainder of their life. With all this bombardment of new thoughts and ideas, it is no wonder that children are easily overstimulated, and cannot see the obvious connection between different things around them. This is also true for the way children view their toys and rooms. Consequently, the best way to begin in finding efficient storage is to look for simple containers that offer easy access. Beware of the large toy chests that have bulky tops that are often too heavy for toddlers to lift. Cabinets with tricky latches and locks become more of a frustration than a help. Unless you deliberately want to hide away things such as medications or harmful objects, storage in the early years should be low to the floor, and open, then gradually rise and become enclosed as the child grows. Remember, to a small child, high shelves and out-of-reach places make for a foreign and inaccessible land.

ORGANIZED: Here too it is important to keep in mind that too much information can become counterproductive to our goal of efficient storage. It is no simpler a task for children to keep their rooms organized and neat than it is for them to count, read, or learn to tie their shoes. This ability is learned and discovered. Begin by making some agreements with your child as to where toys, learning tools, supplies, etc., will be kept. This might well be accomplished by first sketching the room on a large piece of paper, then placing in the sketch mutually agreed upon areas for storing personal belongings. Then the act of actually arranging the room to our "blueprints" will become more of a fun activity.

Color can also play an active role in organizing a room's storage. Bins colored red might be assigned the job of housing blocks; blue may take on the storage of doll clothes; or green may be for art materials. This way children can see from afar the proper storage bin, and make the association easily. Peel-off vinyl lettering, which can be purchased at stationery stores, can be used to label each bin with its proper contents, i.e. "paints," "beads," "cars," etc.

The idea of assigning jobs or functions to different parts of the room has been used quite successfully by Montessori teachers. Maria Montessori created what she called "Casa Bambini," quite simply The Children's House. Each part of the schoolroom had a specific function, such as music, math, geography, sensory play, and practical life exercises. All the objects used in each area were assigned a place on the shelves, agreed upon, and sometimes color-coordinated for that area, so the younger children could associate the objects to that area. This format can be used in much the same way for storing childrens' toys and personals, in their bedrooms or play spaces.

SAFE: Now that we have begun to focus on keeping storage simple and organized, let's make a special note on safety needs that are sometimes overlooked until it is too late.

Curiosity is a powerful learning force in a child's life, and everything is a new adventure to explore. Needless to say, glass containers or sharp metal edges should be avoided with toddlers and infants. Careful attention ought to be given to inspecting any furniture or storage units that may be acquired, thus avoiding injury from exposed nails, or unfinished edges. That same top-heavy toy chest, referred to earlier, also poses a serious safety concern if it should slam unexpectedly on a little one's fingers or hand while searching for that favorite truck at the bottom. Check to see that paint finishes on furniture is non-toxic; most furniture manufacturers make note of that in their brochures.

Children who are confined to special equipment, such as wheelchairs or crutches, need particular attention as to safety. For example, drawers should have easy glides with stops, so they will not fall out if pulled too quickly. More importantly, be sure once again to position all storage within easy reach, avoiding unnecessary spills.

With these three basic rules in mind, let's now take a look at the different age levels, and explore some examples.

Infants receive many small and colorful toys upon their arrival: rattles, dolls, mobiles, teething rings and the like. It is not too early to plan on storage that will assist in building your child's room plan down the road. Stackable cubes with clean assorted drawers can be arranged to handle storage of diapers, and lotions as well as toys. A board secured to the top of several stacked cubes could also serve as a changing table, or perhaps arranged underneath a window with foam cushions, could become a comfortable window seat. These cubes are often available in unfinished pressboard or wood, and can be painted easily. Once again, be sure not to "overcolor." Your child is still developing the intricate use of his or her eyes. The simpler the information, the better. You will find that these modular cubes offer you continued versatility and use as your child grows, and can be rearranged or repainted when the need arises.

Toddlers are enjoying, to say the least, the newly discovered pleasure of mobility; new places to explore, and new things to hold. Consequently it will be important to be sure small items such as beads, or crayons don't end up in their mouths. Common plastic food storage containers with snaplock lids, can handle this task neatly. Even coffee cans with plastic lids can be spray painted and serve as storage for crayons and the like. Be sure that any sharp edges are bent back, and that the spraypaint is non-toxic.

As children begin to reach *school age*, there comes with it a tremendous barrage of toys and learning tools. Your skills at organizing will be needed most here. I've found that an open bookcase can be of great help. Plan with your child as to where specific objects will be housed on this bookcase. Plastic washtubs that are found in houseware departments and hardware stores come in various colors and can assist in logically sorting blocks from clay, or crayons from dolls. If possible, try to find tubs that have an ample hand grip so that your child can move the entire tub to the floor and, after having returned all the contents to the tub, place it back on the shelf. Color coordinating and labelling the tubs can begin at this age level as well.

As children learn and grow at school, more and more papers and books will start to find their way home. A corkboard or magnetwall can handle and display artwork or achievements efficiently. The addition of a few more stackable cubes can assist in transforming an infant's room into a living space. Handy plastic milk cartons serve the dual jobs of stackable storage and when flipped over, provide nifty stools for watching a puppet show or listening to storytelling. I've watched many children take these same cartons and build forts and fantasy games for hours. It is also a good time now to focus in on a specific area to designate as a work station for projects.

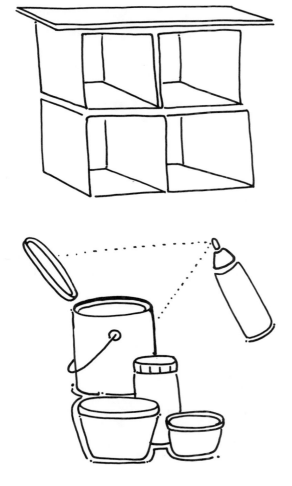

As time goes on this same area can become a study space for books and homework. Children who have limited access need to have this work station high enough to handle the approach of a wheelchair or related equipment and be sure that drawer pulls and handles are large enough to provide for limited hand use.

Most importantly, don't be afraid to ask your children as they grow older just what they feel makes their space and storage work most efficiently. Often what they perceive as their room is quite different. Young adults often like to place their mattresses atop several of our storage cubes and create a platform bed with storage below for records and books. Closets that previously housed low shelving and closet rods now handle taller storage or perhaps a dressing area.

If you follow these steps of simple, organized, and safe storing, the handling of the myriad of toys and equipment that come in to your child's life will be easier and more practical.

For more information or to arrange for a consultation write: Tony Torrice, Just Between Friends, 1240 California Street, San Francisco, CA 94109.

THE CANADIAN TOY LIBRARY ASSOCIATION

Joanna Van Levetzow

Director, Canadian Association of Toy Libraries

A Resource and Information Service for anyone interested in the concepts of TOYS and TOY LENDING. Our members and supporters include:
- Parents and Professionals
- Parent Self-help Groups
- Parent Resource Centers
- Home Day-Care, Nurseries, Schools
- Early Childhood Educators, Teachers, Students
- Physical & Development Health Services, Clinics, Hospitals, Treatment Centers
- Community Health Centers, Infant Stimulation Programs
- Public Libraries, University Library Faculties
- Recreation Departments; Play Environments
- Toy Designers and Makers; Toy Distributors

THE TOY LIBRARY
What is it?
A collection of SAFE
STURDY
STIMULATING
TOYS

of high quality, each for loan to your CHILD for ENJOYMENT and EXPERIENCE according to his DEVELOPMENT.

What does it provide?

- A variety of toys to choose from
- Access to toys otherwise often too expensive or inaccessible to many families
- A chance to try out new toys before buying
- Space for play in an unstructured, non-threatening atmosphere; an early social experience
- Encouragement in concepts of sharing and respect for property of others
- A meeting place for parents with mutual interests in young children, toys, and play materials
- An introduction for the pre-reader to the world of books

Toys for Children with Special Needs

For Children who are:
- handicapped
- confined to hospital or bed
- isolated geographically or by cultural or language differences
- underprivileged

The toy library can provide a service of great value, interest, and stimulation, and an opportunity for parents to help each other.

Toy Safety is the concern of the Canadian Toy Testing Council, Canada Safety Council, and Consumer and Corporate Affairs, Canada. It is also our concern and the concern of everyone who has to do with children.

Our Association encourages member toy libraries to consider carefully the safety aspects to toys provided for loan, and to help people, as consumers, to look for quality in construction and design in toys and play materials. Toys for lending should be selected according to the criteria recommended by our Association.

The Resource Center has been established as a specialized reference library to help existing toy libraries, and people interested in toys, toy lending and the value of play in the healthy development of the young child.

Objectives

- to collect and make available for reference toys and play materials, books and pamphlets, books and pamphlets transcripts, cassettes, photographs and films on play in the broad sense, with a focus on Toy Lending and the special needs of young handicapped children
- to increase awareness of the wide range of toys, their quality, uses and play potential; and to encourage wise choices
- to promote ideas for new toys, and for home-made playthings

The Collection

- Toys and Play Materials: a selection of toys is on permanent display; information about them and other recommended toys is readily available
- Books: a number of books have been acquired which deal with many aspects of play and parenting, toys and toy making, etc.

- Pamphlets: relevant material, Canadian and International. Please send us yours to share
- Articles: files of relevant articles from periodicals, professional journals, newspapers. Photocopies at 15¢ a page may be requested.
- Audi-visual Material and Film: we hope to increase our small collection. A slide-tape introducing the idea of toy lending may be rented for $20.

Staffing

Volunteers donate their time and expertise. The Center is open to the public whenever volunteers are available, or by arrangement with the Director.

You are invited to become a member of the Association by completing the membership form and enclosing the annual fee of $5, for individuals, $10 for organizations, $15 overseas (airmail)

Membership Includes:

- access to the collected skills and knowledge about toy libraries
- a membership list, updated at 6 month intervals
- a newsletter twice a year
- periodic regional newsletters

Other Services by Arrangement

- Workshops offered from time to time for those interested in starting a toy library
- Individual or Group Consultation and Presentations
- Slide tape rental, "An Introduction to Toy Lending"

Publications

- Toy Libraries: How to Start Toy Library in Your Community (1978)
- Toy Libraries 2: The Many Uses of Toy Lending (1980)
- A Toy Lending Proposal (1980)

For more information: Canadian Association of Toys Libraries, Suite 1207, 50 Quebec Avenue, Toronto, Ontario M6P-4B4.

TOY SURVEY
Debbie Wager
Co-chairperson, Consumer Affairs Committee,

Americans for Democratic Action

An important part of the 10-year survey is a Toy Box and a Trash Box. Into the Toy Box will go the toys especially recommended by the Committee. These box recommendations are based on safety, good play value, realistic packaging and advertising, sturdiness, and durability.

The toys relegated to the Trash Box are toys considered bad buys by the Committee. The criteria are danger, both potential and actual, poor construction, lack of play value, high level of frustration, complex instructions, not living up to TV advertising or package illustration, not doing what they are supposed to do, or simply breaking down.

The toys surveyed by the Committee are not your old standards, but are the hot, relatively new "TV" toys. No effort was made to be all-inclusive.

These toys were selected by highly qualified and experienced toy surveyors. The Chairperson of the ADA Consumer Affairs Committee is Ann Brown. The Chairperson of the Toy Survey Committee, Debbie Wager, has been directing the Toy Survey for nine years and is an expert on toys. Her co-chairperson, Charley Malloy, has been working on the Toy Survey for eight years and is equally proficient. All of the members of the seven person committee have children of their own.

INFORMATION ABOUT THE TOY PRICE SURVEY

Debbie Wager

Consumer Affairs Committee of ADA

I. How the toys are chosen:
   A. Pre-survey of local toy stores
   B. Monitoring of TV advertisements
   C. Consultations with important toy merchants in the city, including an independent inner city toy store and a local chain with stores in the city and suburbs. The toys surveyed are not just highly advertised national best sellers; they were predicted to be especially big sellers in the Washington, DC, market.
   D. Consultation with editors of toy magazine in New York City.
II. The number of toys:
   A. There were originally 45 toys surveyed; 35 remain, almost double the number surveyed last year. Ten were unavailable at so many stores that they were later dropped.
III. When the survey is taken:
   A. In November
   B. A total of 26 stores or more are surveyed. All of the new stores in the survey are suburban chain stores.
IV. Object of the Report and Toy Pricing Survey:
   To give the consumer the most necessary tool he needs to make him co-equal to the businessman in the marketplace—price information. Armed with this weapon, the consumer can make intelligent choices. He can decide if he wants to pay extra for the gift wrapping and the charge account services or if it is worth it to use the extra gas to drive to the suburbs.

The aim is not to bring all stores down to one price level; stores can charge what they like, but an intelligent consumer can buy where the prices are the lowest.

Competition is the name of the game in our free enterprise system. And price competition is strongly enhanced by the release of price information. This principle is well illustrated, in microcosm, by the results of the release of the Consumer Affairs Committee's Toy Price Survey.

The survey has been received with enormous interest by consumers each year in the metropolitan Washington, DC, area. The stores know this survey will be repeated each season. In fact, our surveyors were greeted with much interest and much concern by many of the stores they surveyed this year. Toy department managers followed the surveyors around, commenting, advising, and trying to get a peek at the list. Naturally the stores cannot anticipate exactly which toys will be included. The Chairperson of the Toy Committee received anxious calls from several merchants.

We believe the more active price competition is engendered among toy merchants by this small effort each Christmas season; witness that Toys 'R' Us again assumes price leadership.

The Consumer Affairs Committee recommends to the Washington, DC, Office of Consumer Affairs that price surveys be instituted by that Office on many groups of items throughout the year. The dollar value to consumers would be enormous from such an effort.

CHILDREN'S ADVERTISING

Sarah Woodward

Public Information, Better Busines Bureau

When you see advertising directed to children on television, in newspapers, comic books or magazines, it has almost certainly passed a number of evaluations for acceptability. However, from time to time consumers may still have questions about individual advertisements. One group that responds to inquiries about children's advertisements is the Children's Advertising Review Unit of the National Advertising Division, Council of Better Business Bureaus.

The Children's Unit was established in 1974 to assure the truth, accuracy and fairness of advertising directed to children. While supported by business, it is part of a non-profit organization dedicated to the public interest. Its basic activity is the ongoing evaluation of advertising directed to children under twelve years of age. This is accomplished by continually monitoring print, television, and radio advertising, and reviewing advertisements provided voluntarily by advertisers. When advertising is found inaccurate or unfair to children's perceptions, the Children's Unit seeks modification or discontinuance through the voluntary cooperation of advertisers. All case decisions are reported in a monthly press release issued by the National Advertising Division. Prior to production, the Children's unit will comment on proposed advertising copy at the request of the advertiser.

The Children's Advertising Guidelines, published by the Children's Unit and available to the public free upon request, provide the basis for investigating advertising directed to children. They are periodically revised to reflect new insights gained from experience and research. In addition to the truth and accuracy of advertising claims, the guidelines also deal with such matters as social values, product presentation, pressure to purchase, endorsements, safety, and premiums.

Your watchful eyes and attention to advertising are important. Here are some important things to look for:

If the answer to any of the following questions is NO, the advertising may be questionable.
- Is the size of the product made clear?
- Does the ad clearly indicate what is included in the original purchase?
- Are separate purchase requirements clearly indicated?
- If batteries are needed, is that clearly stated?
- If assembly is required, does the ad clearly say so in language that a child will understand?
- Are other essential disclosures clearly voiced or worded, legible, prominent, and in language understandable by the child audience?
- In ads featuring premiums, is the premium offer clearly secondary?
- If fantasy elements are used, are they clearly "just pretend"?

If the answer to any of the following questions is YES, the ad may be questionable.
- Are children shown using a product in a way that the average child couldn't?
- Does the ad show more than the number of toys that might reasonably be expected for a child to own?
- Is the child or adult shown doing something unsafe?
- Is the child or adult shown using a product not intended for children?
- Is a child-directed advertising appeal being used for vitamins or medication?
- Does the ad suggest that a child will be superior to friends or more popular if the child owns a given product?
- Does the ad employ any demeaning or derogatory social stereotype?
- Does the ad suggest that an adult who buys a product for a child is better or more caring than one who does not?
- Does the ad reflect unfavorably on parental judgment and other generally recognized sources of child guidance?
- Does the ad show bad manners or use offensive language?
- Is a food product now shown within the framework of a balanced diet?
- Does the ad imply that one food provides all the nutrients contained in a well-balanced food plan?

- Does the ad suggest overconsumption of a particular food product?
- Does the ad urge children to ask parents or others to buy the product?
- Does the ad use such words as "only" or "just" to describe the price?
- Do program hosts or characters appear in the commercials within their own program?
- In print publications, are the title characters of the publications used in ads within their own publications?
- Is there anything misleading in the ad about the product's benefits.

If you have a complaint about a particular advertisement, or would like a copy of the guidelines, please write to Children's Advertising Review Unit, National Advertising Division, Council of Better Business Bureaus, Inc., 845 Third Avenue, New York, NY 10022. Keep in mind that the Children's Unit concerns itself only with national or broadly regional advertising directed to children and not with programming.

THE TOY THAT COMES BACK

Helane Zeiger
Yo Yo specialist and author, *World On A String*

The yo-yo is the second oldest toy in the world; only the doll is older. Throughout its long and colorful history, dating back to ancient Greek times when the yo-yo was called a "disc," it has been a very popular plaything. In Europe, kings, princes, and noblemen played with yo-yos. In the Philippines, yo-yos were so well liked that playing with them became a national pastime. Today, giant yo-yo companies like Flambeau Plastics in the United States turn out 14 to 20 million yo-yos a year, attesting to the fact that people all over the world still enjoy playing with yo-yos.

One reason for the yo-yo's popularity is that it can be made out of a variety of materials. Down through the ages, the yo-yo has been fashioned by hand (or manufactured) out of rock, ivory, animal horns, precious metals, woods, and, most recently, plastic. The yo-yo is such a basic toy that even today anyone, a child or an adult, can easily put together a wooden one. Simple, step-by-step directions for assembling a homemade yo-yo can be found in the chapter, "Yo-Yos" in *Games of the World* (Ballantine Books, 1977).

In addition, the yo-yo is to this day a very inexpensive toy. Although there are a few exotic yo-yos on the market that sell for as much as twenty dollars, the majority of decent, playable yo-yos fall into the one dollar to five dollar price range. If maintained properly, any yo-yo, regardless of cost, can last a long time. All that is required to keep a yo-yo in top shape is minimal attention to the string and yo-yo axle. When a yo-yo string breaks, wears out or gets a knot in it, it can be changed without having to purchase a new yo-yo. Replacement strings are available where yo-yos are sold and directions for changing the string appear on the package.

Care should be taken when removing an old string not to scratch the axle, which can damage the yo-yo permanently. The slightest cut in the axle will wear out new strings in two or three spins. (For complete instructions on how to keep a yo-yo in good working order, see Zeiger's *World On A String: The How-To Yo-Yo Book*, (see bibliography).

Without question, the main reason generation after generation have fallen in love with the yo-yo is simply because it is a wonderful toy that brings hour after hour of enjoyment to anyone who plays with it. From learning basic techniques to mastering more advanced tricks, the yo-yo is a continual challenge. Once novices get the hang of making a yo-yo "sleep," they can quickly progress to such basic tricks as "Walk-the-Dog," "Buzz Saw," "Land Rover" and "Rock-the-Baby." Once these tricks can be consistently executed, more difficult tricks such as "Brain Twister," "Double or Nothing," and "Skyrocket" await the yo-yo enthusiast.

Since yo-yo play depends largely on eye-hand coordination, parents should be advised that the sleeping yo-yo with the string looped around the axle, is a terrific toy for youngsters nine or older. But in the hands of younger children, or for that matter anyone whose coordination is not sufficiently developed to control the yo-yo, it can become a frustrating plaything as well as a dangerous weapon. For younger children, a beginner's yo-yo, one where the string is knotted to the axle so that the yo-yo can only go up and down and does not "sleep" when hurled downward, is highly recommended.

As children get older, they can more fully appreciate what can be done with a "sleeping" yo-yo. What once appeared to be an impossible trick to execute at nine becomes a "snap" at twelve, thirteen or fourteen. As children grow and muscle coordination increases, so does the pleasure derived from yo-yo play. The yo-yo is, in fact, not just a child's toy. People from nine to ninety can appreciate the ups and downs of this ever-challenging portable toy that can be played with practically anywhere at anytime. Why not give it a whirl!

Shooting Star

Once you have perfected Texas Star, you can turn it into a "Shooting Star"! Here's how. Make a Texas Star. With the remaining string hanging down from the top center point, circle the start one or two times by swinging the yo-yo towards you and over the top of the star. As the yo-yo comes toward you on the last swing, shoot out all the string as if you were doing the Forward Pass. Be ready to catch the yo-yo as it shoots back toward you.

BUYING TOYS

Sy Ziv
Chief Buyer for "Toys R Us"

Our concept is unique, it is a supermarket concept. You go through the entrance with your cart, walk around the store, and go to the checkout. The advantages to a consumer in buying toys this way is there is less labor involved, so that cuts the overhead. Cost matters to the consumer.

In our beginning, if someone was selling things for a dollar we tried to find a way to cut it to 68 cents.

Many stores are taking up this concept; as we grow so do the concepts of the manufacturers. Larger manufacturers can first of all find the necessary resources and can utilize them better than a small company. They can do a better job of packaging and merchandising. Certainly there are certain types of toys better sold in a smaller situation. But we don't generally get into those kind of toys.

That does not mean we sell shoddy goods either. I've tested toys right out there in the middles of the store. If it didn't make it, it went back to the manufacturers. We are really concerned about safety.

Parents must be aware too. Even one of the most common toys, the baseball bat, is one of the most dangerous things to have around. If any toy gets into the hands of a child that is too young, then it is dangerous. The parents are responsible. They need to have support from the industry for preventing injuries. If the package says the toy is for a certain age, the parent still has to make a judgment if that applies to their child.

There is no way in the world that a toy manufacturer would sell any product that hasn't been tested; that's just bad business. Unless there is an extreme example of the cost of production getting too high. I don't want to see toys not being made and kids not having fun. What a toy does for a kid is give him something to play with.

I think the child and the parent should pick out the toy together. I think it should be a good toy initially; don't buy junk. You should know what your child wants first. If you buy a book, you're not going to read it if you are not interested in it. Your child is the same way. Your child knows what he is into. You see what your child is into all about your living room. Or you will try things and learn over a period of time what your child likes. But you can't make rules for all children, because they are all different.

Now if I look at a toy to put in this store, I equate it with a movie I saw a long time ago; it was animated, the sound and voices were great, but it bombed because no one knew the people who made it. The name means something. I guess it's something like a batting average. Sometimes I pick things that aren't great. For instance, I looked at the Barbie doll and thought that was silly; and GI Joe, there was such a controversy about boys playing with dolls, then they boomed. So it's hard to say when something is going to be hot. You can look at something and say that's fair, that's okay, or that looks pretty good. I don't mean anybody can't gauge, just that it's hard.

Movies generally don't sell very well, but then *Star Wars* appeared. The reason that Dungeons and Dragons is such a hit is I think kids have those fantasies; when I was a kid I had fantasies about Frankenstein. Things that really stimulate kids are like their fantasy life. But they can get into their fantasy mode and not enjoy anything else.

Some parents are concerned about sexist toys. I think you'll find sexism wherever you go. But kids play with dolls and blocks whatever sex they are. This is especially true for the younger child.

This is an entreprenurial business, trends change, but you don't just jump into things, you have to give them a lot of consideration. Tigers are selling well, but the factory says, we're not making them anymore. I don't know if you remember tigers, but at one time Exxon was really promoting tigers and they were selling very well. You have to think at least six months in advance.

I like toys that my children will enjoy and are relatively well made, that aren't going to be destroyed in a day or two. My children have Capsella, Star War figures, books, board games, hand-held electronic games, and lots of other things.

In buying, I have very little hang-up with my biases. I don't view it personally; I buy what's good for the store. There are other tastes than mine; I might like one flavor of ice cream, but other people might like something else. I can't construct a store on what buyers like. We've got to have a very diversified group of buyers. After a while you learn what sells and what doesn't sell, and some things sell at times when they won't sell at other times.

As far as cosmetics, they've been around for a million years, we just go through cycles. We used to sell cosmetics, but they went out for awhile and now they are back. It's like everything else, there's nothing new under the sun, it's just a repackaging and an update or something. Cosmetics have really expanded lately though. It used to be you'd have a lipstick and cologne set in a little bag.

What it is really is the child's version of the adult world. We miniaturize the adult world. Most of the things are miniaturized. I've got a little toothbrush over there.

It's whatever is exciting; if fashions are exciting, we have that. There are various ways we go about it: we can make it up and have personal fashion, or we can use mannequins, or dress up the Barbie dolls. We are concerned with what is going on in the adult world.

A license is a license, and our license is to make money, that's all. If you look at it from that viewpoint then it seems very narrow, but the toy business is an adult business.

We do have some of our own characters. We have a giraffe. We have a whole menagerie section with animals; the giraffe is one of our special items. Our giraffe is like Mickey Mouse. A mouse is a four-legged animal, but Mickey Mouse is a two-legged animal with hands. Our giraffe is a two-legged animal with hands.

CONCLUSION

PERSONAL REFLECTIONS ON TOYS

I have found in my research—after listening to both friends and critics of the industry—that toys are like any other business in America or any other country, consumer-oriented and responsive to demands of the marketplace. The toy companies try to respond to an ongoing and intense interest in the well-being and healthy development of children and are also interested in making a profit.

I have learned more about the Toy industry than I could ever cover in one book. It has been frustrating to have to reduce the amount of information I have gathered into only one book. I have gained an enormous respect for most of the industry's commitment, ingenuity, and productivity to serve children. The toys that have been recommended and the companies that make them are dependable and stable. If in the future there is a problem with anything that has been recommended in this book, I would like to know.

Many excellent toys are produced outside the United States. Europe, the Far East, Canada, and Australia are among the many countries competing in the U. S. market. Many of the small companies that have become successful are based on a limited, but very special, product line. I would appreciate knowing about new

products and will continue to inform the public about the well-made and useful ones I find. Whenever possible, I have tried to locate companies that were not large or well-known, but who had good products to offer and to give them equal exposure. Bringing new products to light is not easy in the overcrowded toy market.

If in using this book, parents will make better selections from among all the choices for children, and as a result have happier, healthier and more playful children, then the years of effort that went into this book will have been well worth it.

You have an important function as a parent, to purchase toys that are useful and worthwhile, with your child's healthy development in mind. Certainly everything you purchase does not have to be "significant" but it should be a factor in most of the toys you select. Lots of fun and silly items are in the marketplace and provide good laughs, provide an hour of entertainment, or resolve some desire you or a grandparent wants to indulge. This is fine, however try to keep in mind that most of the time what is ultimately best for the child is not being deluged with an overload of playthings. Selectively locate the

objects that challenge, provoke, stimulate, foster creativity, and exercise the body. Allow for personal exchange with others. Toys are after all a social opportunity.

Please remember that in your own community many children are not as fortunate to have a variety of toys, for many reasons. During your local TOYS FOR TOTS drive give away toys your child has outgrown and help others to be able to play and have a happy childhood. During the year many child care centers, nursery schools and kindergartens would appreciate contributions of toys, puzzles, games, books and other products that can be donated. The social opportunity is not only for receiving and playing, but for giving and sharing.

I recommend that you review the suggested books and interviews to learn more about toys. It is personally worthwhile to have the experience of making at least one hand-made toy in some form for your child. I created an innovative item for my daughter to watch as she sat in the infant seat and it stimulated her attention. One of these days I may find a way to make it again to share with babies. I have had many new ideas for toys and often see ways to improve the existing items I study. You will find that you can make toys from designs and add your own improvements, or find ready made items that need to be assembled and finished. I have included some of these resources. You will find a lot of satisfaction in creating something with your own hands and your child will appreciate it very much. You will also have the thrill of receiving the first craft item he or she makes at nursery school or child care. You may want to make things together that are fun and many good books are available with toy craft suggestions. Parents were the original creators of stuffed or soft dolls. The wooden toys made so famous by Creative Playthings and now carried by many fine importers were often begun in the hands of a creative woodcarver. (Creative Playthings was where I started as a toy consultant many years ago.)

The photographs in this book will give you an idea of the many types of good toys on the market and all the ways children play from crib to their teens. Sports play is an extension of games that began when we were young and playing persists as we grow up. Talent is nurtured while we are young and impressionable. Manual dexterity in whatever form requires practice and is developed by providing the right tools, like blocks, to the developing preschooler. The integration of play and toys is essential to the child's healthy growth. Play is the way the child learns and through play, experiences life. We must try to remember to play, enjoy ourselves, and set a good example for children. Playfulness enhances life. Toys enhance play. Good toys provide safety, security, and stimulation for children.

It is hoped that you have enjoyed the tour of THE TOY CHEST. I hope I have been able to answer most of the questions you have been asking. In addition to the many organizations listed in the next section, please feel welcome to write to us at the Institute for Childhood Resources if you have any further questions. Requests requiring research may be subject to a nominal fee which will help support the Institute. Any fees charged would be agreed upon in advance. My goal for the book is to serve as a spokesperson for the child and to share his or her point of view. It helps to clarify the issues that arise for adults when considering toys for children. I hope by listening to each other: children, parents, manufacturers, designers, and all the others connected with the toy industry, we can assist children to have more quality toys to play with. Children grow, learn, and unleash their imaginations by playing with toys. What more could we want for their future? A peaceful, playful world.

PART IV

RESOURCES

A. WHERE TO TURN FOR FURTHER INFORMATION

To assist readers in following up with more information, resources, problems, or related questions, use the list below to contact the following organization(s) when you wish to:

Register a complaint with the government on toys

> Commissioner
> U.S. Consumer Product Safety Commission
> Washington, DC 20207
> 800 638-8326

Object to deceptive packaging or false advertising

> Director
> Federal Trade Commission
> Bureau of Consumer Protection
> Washington, DC 20580

Register a complaint with the toy industry

> Executive Director
> Toy Manufacturers of America
> 200 Fifth Avenue
> New York City, NY 10010

Register a complaint about toy advertising

> Director
> Childrens Advertising Review
> Council of Better Business Bureaus Inc.
> 845 Third Avenue
> New York City, NY 10022

> Director
> Childrens Advertising
> National Association of Broadcasters
> 477 Madison Avenue
> New York City, NY 10022

> Director
> Action for Children's Television
> 46 Austin Street
> Newtonville, MA 02160

Comment directly to audience information at these TV stations

> American Broadcasting Company
> 1330 Avenue of the Americas
> New York City, NY 10019

> Columbia Broadcasting System
> 51 West 52nd Street
> New York City, NY 10019

> Mutual Broadcasting System
> 135 West 50th Street
> New York City, NY 10019

> National Broadcasting System
> 30 Rockefeller Plaza
> New York City, NY 10020

Write to editors of toy trade publications

> Editor
> Playthings Magazine
> 51 Madison Avenue
> New York City, NY 10010

> Editor
> Toy and Hobby World
> 1107 Broadway
> New York City, NY 10010

> Editor
> Toy Trade News
> 757 Third Avenue
> New York City, NY 10010

Receive consumer information

> Center for Parent Education
> 55 Chapel Street
> Newton, MA 02160

> Consumer Federation of America
> Consumer Product Safety Network
> 1314 14th Street, NW
> Washington, DC 20005

> Public Action Coalition on Toys
> 902 Heron Drive
> Silver Spring, MD 20901

Respond with comments or queries on toys or games

> Institute for Childhood Resources
> 1169 Howard Street
> San Francisco, CA 94103

Information for parents with handicapped children

> Closer Look
> PO Box 1492
> Washington, DC 20013

Booklets on health and a safety first aid chart

> American Academy of Pediatrics
> PO Box 1034
> Evanston, IL 60204

Publications and reference service

> National Safety Council
> 444 North Michigan Avenue
> Chicago, IL 60611

B. BIBLIOGRAPHY OF BOOKS FOR CHILDREN AND ADULTS

ARTS AND CRAFTS FOR ADULTS

Brown, Jerome C
Papercrafts for All Seasons
Belmont, CA, David S Lake Publishers, 1984, ISBN: 0-8224-5189-1, $5.95, 28 pp.

Instructions and diagrams of making seasonal art projects using crayons, stencils, paper, and old materials.

Brown, Osa
Metropolitan Museum of Art Activity Book
New York, Random House, 1983, ISBN: 0-394-85241-9 $6.95, 88 pp.

History, explanations, photographs, and illustrations about crafts, models, toys, games, puzzles, and mazes from the museum's collection. Also includes instructions on making them.

Dorsett, Judy
Handbook of Creativity, A How-To Book
Cincinnati, Standard Publishing Company, 1984, ISBN: 0-87239-729-7, $7.95, 128 pp.

A resource book of simple explanations of the creative process. Includes diagrams and instructions for making puppets, preparing food, and playing games and puzzles.

Haas, Carolyn Buhai
The Big Book of Recipes for Fun
Northfield, IL, CBH Publishing, 1980, $10.95, 279 pp.

Creative learning activities for home and school for children from preschool through grade 6, presented in an easy-to-use recipe format with illustrations.

Hershoff, Evelyn Glontz
It's Fun to Make Things From Scrap Material
New York, Dover Publications, 1980, ISBN: 486-21251-3, $4.50, 373 pp.

399 easy projects to educate and develop latent abilities using inexpensive accessible materials.

Leeming, Joseph
Fun with String
New York, Dover Publications, 1974, ISBN: 0-486-23063-5, $2.95, 161 pp.

A collection of string games, useful braiding, weaving, knot work, and magic with string and rope.

Sunset Books
Children's Clothes and Toys
Menlo Park, CA, Lane Publishing Company, 1983, ISBN: 0-376-04088-2, $4.95, 96 pp.

Includes special sewing techniques, money-saving ideas, and 30 color photos to help you fashion projects such as a folding bed, animal slippers, and bean bag chairs.

Complete Book of Babycrafts
New York, Arco Publishing Company, 1981, ISBN: 0-668-05342-9, $18.95, 184 pp.

Step-by-step instructions, diagrams, and photographs of over 50 projects to make for your child. Includes clothes, toys, crib accessories, baby carriages, and nurseries.

ARTS AND CRAFTS FOR CHILDREN

Amery, Heather; Civardi, Anne
The Funcraft Book of Print and Paint
New York, Scholastic Book Services, Ottenheimer Publishers, 1976, $2.95, 47 pp.

Shows how to print patterns and pictures in various ways on paper, cardboard, and cloth.

Bae, Young
Paper Robots
San Francisco, Troubador Press, 1981, $3.50, 31 pp.

Cutouts of robots to color, cut-out and play with.

Benjamin, Carol, Lea
Cartooning for Kids
New York, Thomas Y Crowell, 1982, $3.95, 71 pp.

How to draw simple cartoon animals and people with various expressions, creative idea suggestions for humor, and the use of cartoons in greeting cards and notes.

Butterworth, Nancy T; Broad, Laura
Kits for Kids, How to Turn Ordinary Objects, Projects, and Events Into Activities and Gifts for Kids
New York, Saint Martin's Press, 1980, ISBN: 0-312-45702-2, $7.95, 208 pp.

For parents, teachers, group leaders, and kids. Over 100 projects to do, gifts to give, and experiences to share with children age 3 and up.

Farrell, Kathy; Sweeney, Mary
What Can We Do Today, Mommy?
Stanford, CA, Growing Together Press, 1980, ISBN: 0-0960-4118-0, $6.95, 127 pp.

A collection of activities to help children from the age of 2-5 years to learn through play.

Fiarotta, Phyllis and Noel
Be What You Want To Be! The Complete Dress-up and Pretend Craft Book
New York, Workman Publishing Company, 1977, $5.95, 304 pp.

More than 200 craft projects to make props for role playing many occupations. Includes instruments for the musician, disguises for the private eye, and equipment for the photographer.

Fiarotta, Phyllis
Confetti: the Kids' Make-It-Yourself, Do-It-Yourself Book
New York, Workman Publishing Company, 1978, ISBN: 0-911104-95-X, $5.95, 224 pp.

Over 150 easy-to-follow imaginative crafts for parties, i.e. decorations, games, invitations, and food.

Frazier, Beverly
Nature Crafts & Projects
San Francisco, Troubador Press, 1971, ISBN: 0-912300-23-X, $2.25, 32 pp.

Ideas and illustrations of projects and crafts related to nature, including feathers, stones, flowers, and plants.

Karnes, Merle B
You and Your Small Wonder Book 1: Activities for Parents and Toddlers on the Go
Circle Pines, MN, American Guidance Service, 1982, ISBN: 0-913476-58-5, $6.95, 161 pp.

More than 150 parent-tested activities to enrich your baby's development and turn everyday routines into learning adventures.

Karnes, Merle B
You and Your Small Wonder Book 2: Activities for Parents and Toddlers on the Go
Circle Pines, MN, American Guidance Service, 1982, ISBN: 0-913416-59-5, $6.95, 157 pp.

More than 150 parent-tested learning activities and adventures to share with your active toddler throughout the day.

Morris, Neil
Toys Through the Ages Activity Book
Cambridge, MA, Cambridge University Press, 1982, ISBN: 0-521-27068-5, $2.50, 16 pp.

A collection of games, puzzles, dolls, and masks with brief histories and drawings to fill in, color, and cut-out.

Swanberg, Nancie
Toys Through the Ages
San Francisco, Troubador Press, 1980, ISBN: 0-89844-016-5, $3.50, 30 pp.

A series of histories of toys through the ages with detailed outline illustrations to be colored in.

Thompson, David
Easy Woodstuff for Kids
Mount Rainier, MD, Gryphon House, 1981, ISBN: 0-87659-101-2, $8.95, 115 pp.

Step-by-step instructions, illustrations, tools, and materials for making projects out of wood for 3 years and older.

Whyte, Malcolm
Troubador Treasury
San Francisco, Troubador Press, 1979, ISBN: 0-912300-86-8, $4.95, 60 pp.

Puzzles and projects representing the best of Troubador Activity books.

Wolfe, Marcia
Easy Crafts for Children—167 Crafts/Full-size patterns
Cincinnati, OH, Standard Publishing Company, 1985, ISBN: 0-87239-844-7, $4.95, 64 pp.

A child's craft and Bible-oriented book with full-sized patterns to cut, color, paste, fold, bake, mold, paint, and eat.

Wolff, Margaret
The Kids' After School Activity Book
Belmont, CA, David S Lake Publishers, 1985, ISBN: 0-8224-4228-0, $6.95, 92 pp.

Contains instructions for more than 79 explorations, creations and other activities, such as growing vegetables, holiday decorations, puzzles, making snacks and making movies.

BOATS

Milet, Jacques; Forbes, Robert; Ehrenclou, John
Toy boats, 1870-1955, A pictorial history
New York, Charles Scribner's Sons, 1979, ISBN: 0-684-15967-8, $24.95, 110 pp.

A wonderful collection of photos and information about boats.

CHILD DEVELOPMENT

Aston, Athina
How to Play with Your Baby
Charlotte, NC, East Woods Press, 1982, ISBN: 0-914788-73-6, $7.95, 119 pp.

Explains how to work with the baby's discovery of the world through play. Identifies the signs and signals of each stage of development and suggests ways of playing for each stage.

Grasselli, Rose N; Hegner, Priscilla A
Playful Parenting
New York, Marek Publishers, 1981, ISBN: 0-399-90117-5, $14.95, 317 pp.

Games to help infants and toddlers grow physically, mentally, and emotionally.

Johnson and Johnson Baby Products Company
First Wondrous Year
New York; Macmillan. 1978. ISBN 0-02-077100-2 $10.95,
410 pp.

Developmental information with many photographs and
excellent section on play and learning.

CHRISTMAS AND BIRTHDAY ACTIVITIES

Gibbons, Gail
Things to Make and Do for Your Birthday
New York, Franklin Watts, 1979, $2.50, 47 pp.

Includes projects, games, jokes, and party foods for
celebrating birthdays.

Johnstone, Anne G
Santa's Toyshop
New York, Playmore Inc., 1980, $2.95, 10 pp.

Pictures and Story of Santa's Toyshop.

Sibbett Jr, Ed
Santa Claus and Other Xmas Jumping Jacks
New York, Dover Publications, 1981, ISBN: 0-486-24184-
0, $2.95, 16 pp.

Twelve easy-to-assemble full-color toys that move. Cut-
out line drawings on firm paper especially designed for
the Christmas season.

DOLL HISTORY

Bradford, Faith
Dolls' House
Washington, DC, Smithsonian Institution Press, 1977,
$1.00, 31 pp.

A private antique collection of dolls and doll furniture
shown in photos which are used as backdrops for a
delightful story about the spirit of the doll characters
themselves in 1905.

Coleman, Dorothy S, Elizabeth A, and Evelyn J
The Collector's Encyclopedia of Dolls
New York, Crown Publishers, 1968, ISBN: 0-517-00598-0,
$27.50, 704 pp.

Covers all dolls, makers, materials, etc., to 1925.

Eaton, Faith
Dolls in Color
New York, Macmillan Publishing Company, 1975, ISBN:
0-02-534710-1, $6.95, 188 pp.

Full color photos of international dolls, the history of
dollmaking since the 15th century and dollmaking
techniques.

Holz, Loretta
**Developing Your Doll Collection For Enjoyment and
Investment**
New York, Crown Publishers, 1981, ISBN: 0-517-54131-9,
$16.95, 243 pp.

Covers dolls, restorations, displaying, storing, pricing,
and selling your collection. Extensive lists of doll books,
periodicals, museums, doll auctioneers, doll-show sponsors, and doll organizations. Has 125 photographs.

Swanberg, Nancie
Dolls Through the Ages
San Francisco, Troubador Press, 1979, ISBN: 0-89844-
005-X, $3.50, 30 pp.

Historic information with color-in illustrations of dolls.

Young, Sheila
**Lettie Lane Paper Dolls: Full-Color Reproductions of 24
Paper Dolls**
New York, Dover Publications, 1981, ISBN: 0-486-
24089-4, $3.00, 16 pp.

Lettie Lane paper dolls and stylish apparel from those
originally published in Ladies' Home Journal 1908.

Ferguson, Barbara Chaney
The Paper Doll, a Collector's Guide With Prices
Des Moines, IA, Wallace-Homestead Book Company,
1982, ISBN: 0-87069-401-4, $14.95, 151 pp.

This guide is packed with pictures and prices of paper
dolls of every type and vintage. The author also shares her
knowledge of how to preserve and protect them.

DOLL MAKING

Better Homes and Gardens
Cherished Dolls to Make for Fun
Des Moines, IA, Meredith Corp, 1984, ISBN: 0-696-
01077-1, $6.95, 80 pp.

Dozens of patterns and tips on making dolls with fabrics,
yarn braids, and other materials.

Great Women Paper Dolls
Santa Barbara, CA, Bellerophon Books, 1979, ISBN:
0-88388-025-3, $2.95, 25 pp.

A collection of famous women paper dolls with costumes
to color and cut-out. Includes short history and personal
philosophy of each.

McCracken, Joann
Dollhouse Dolls
Radnor, PA, Chilton Book Company, 1980, ISBN:
0-8019-6865-8, $8.95, 167 pp.

Discusses and shows how to make, detail and costume
dolls in one inch to one foot scale.

McMurtry, Rosemary; Brem, Charlotte
McCall's Super Book of Dolls, volume 1
New York, McCall Pattern Company, 1979, $2.95, 96 pp.

How-to-make instructions of unique doll collectibles with many actual-size patterns.

Neuschutz, Karin
The Doll Book: Soft Dolls and Creative Free Play
Burdett, NY, Larson Publications, 1982, ISBN: 0-943914-01-9, $8.95, 179 pp.

Discusses child play at different ages and covers social and environmental influences. Gives detailed instructions on how to make a variety of simple soft cloth dolls.

Swanberg, Nancie
Great Ballet Paper Dolls
San Francisco, Troubador Press, 1981, ISBN: 0-89844-027-0, $3.50, 30 pp.

Doll costume paper cutouts from famous ballets.

DOLLHOUSES AND MINIATURES

American Colortype Company; Margaret Woodbury Strong Museum
Cut and Assemble Paper Dollhouse Furniture: A full color antique toy
New York, Dover Publications, 1981, $2.95, 16 pp.

A complete set of miniature furniture for four rooms, easily assembled with scissors and glue.

Johnson, Audrey
How to Make Doll Houses
Newton, MA, Charles T Branford Company, 1977, ISBN: 0-8231-1008-X, $2.50, 112 pp.

Descriptions, instructions, and pictures of making a variety of doll houses including a schoolhouse, a modern house, a 19th century draper's shop, a farmhouse, and a sweet shop.

Millstein, Jeff
Building Cardboard Doll Houses: Five Classic American House Designs You Can Build Yourself
New York, Harper Colophon Books, 1978, ISBN: 0-060-90612-X, $3.95, 78 pp.

Step-by-step instructions and plans for five classic American house styles built between 1700 and 1900.

Noble, John
A Fabulous Dollhouse of the Twenties
New York, Dover Publications, 1975, ISBN: 0-486-23375-8, $2.50, 48 pp.

Detailed captions and 42 photos of the famous Stettheimer Dollhouse, a mansion of the 1920's at the Museum of New York.

Tangerman, E J
Build Your Own Inexpensive Dollhouse With One Sheet of 4 x 8 ft Plywood and Home Tools
New York, Dover Publications, 1977, ISBN: 0-486-23493-2, $1.50, 44 pp.

Clear instructions, diagrams, and photos of how to make a basic two story dollhouse. Includes information on tools and materials needed and suggestions on how to finish.

Weiss, Rita; Fontana, Frank
Miniature Iron-on Transfer Patterns for Dollhouses, Dolls and Small Projects
New York, Dover Publications, 1979, ISBN: 0-486-23741-9, $1.75, 24 pp.

Over 100 designs and instructions for projects and dollhouse furnishing and clothing using transfer patterns.

FOLK TOYS

Kraska, Edie
Toys and Tales From Grandmother's Attic
Boston, MA, Houghton Mifflin Company, 1979, ISBN: 0-395-28582-8, $6.95, 80 pp.

A workbook and history of fifteen folk-art toys, crafts, plays, and stories from the Boston Children's Museum. Includes instructions and cut-outs for making them.

Rogowski, Gini; DeWeese, Gene
Making American Folk Art Dolls
Radnor, PA, Chilton Book Company, 1975, ISBN: 0-80196-123-8, $6.95, 162 pp.

Instructions for making and constructing 24 unusual early American, inexpensive, whimsical dolls. Includes photographs and pattern illustrations.

Schnacke, Dick
American Folk Toys: How to Make Them
Baltimore, MD, Penguin Books, 1973, ISBN: 0-014-04620-9, $3.50, 160 pp.

Instructions, diagrams, and lists of materials needed to make classic American folk toys—from skill and action toys to puzzles, tops, dolls and games.

Temko, Florence
Chinese Papercuts
San Francisco, China Books and Periodicals, 1982, ISBN: 0-8351-0999-2, $10.95, 167 pp.

Comprehensive history and how-to-guide to China's age old handicraft of paper-cutting.

GAMES FOR ADULTS

de Koven, Bernard
The Well-Played Game: A Player's Philosophy
Garden City, NY, Anchor Books, 1978, ISBN: 0-385-13268-9, $3.95, 183 pp.

Tells how we can all enjoy the state of excellence that the well-played game brings—a way of playing that is even more satisfying than winning.

Gregson, Bob
The Incredible Indoor Games Book
Belmont, CA, Pittman Learning Company, 1982, ISBN: 0-8224-0765-5, $10.95, 185 pp.

Instructions and diagrams of 160 games and activities such as theater games, action games, paper crafts, and food sculpture for teachers, group leaders, parents, and kids.

Hagstrom, Julie; Morrill, Joan
Games Babies Play and More Games Babies Play: A Handbook of Games to be Played with Infants
Pocket Books, Simon & Schuster, 1981, ISBN: 0-671-83628-5, $2.95, 255 pp.

Baby's games from 6 weeks old to 12 months, to develop relaxation, understand movements, etc.

Harris, Frank W
Games
Sunnyvale, CA, Frank W Harris, 1982, $6.95, 84 pp.

The philosophy and meaning of games is discussed along with instructions for playing them. Its purpose is to teach recreation and leadership.

Honig, Alice S
Playtime Learning Games for Young Children
Syracuse, NY, Syracuse University Press, 1982, ISBN: 0-8156-0178-6, $9.95, 117 pp.

An easy-to-use handbook of 24 games to help parents and day care/nursery school people teach skills to children from age two through kindergarten.

Mayne, Lynn
Fabric Games
Boston, Houghton Mifflin Company, 1978, $6.95, 125 pp.

Directions and patterns for 15 games to make, play and hang on the wall.

Munger, Evelyn Moats; Bowdon, Susan Jane
Beyond Peek-a-Boo and Pat-a-Cake: Activities for the Babies First Year
Chicago, IL, Follett Publishing Company, 1980, $7.95, 198 pp.

Creative ideas for day-by-day play and care. A rich guide for helping baby grow, experience the world and express personality.

Smith, Evelyne E
Kid's Games
New York City, Dell Publishing Company, 1981, 69 cents, 64 pp.

A parent's guide to over 50 favorite games for kids of all ages for parties, picnics, trips, and rainy days.

Weinstein, Matt; Goodman, Joel
Playfair
San Luis Obispo, CA, Impact Publishers, 1980, ISBN: 0-915166-50-X, $8.95, 249 pp.

A book about games where everyone wins, and the goal is pure fun, recreation and relationship. Through words and pictures it offers skills, games and practical ideas that you can incorporate in your life and work.

Zaslavsky, Claudia
Tic, Tac, Toe
New York, Thomas Y Crowell, 1982, ISBN: 0-690-04316-3, $9.50, 90 pp.

Traces the history and development of the three-in-a-row game for two players, popular all over the world, that is similar to games played in ancient Egypt.

GAMES FOR CHILDREN

Campbell, Kate
100 Ways to Amaze a Kid
San Francisco, Lexikos, 1982, ISBN: 0-938530-08-9, $3.95, 60 pp.

A selection of the world's best tricks, whimsies, games, and pastimes.

Cassidy, John; Rimbeaux, B C
Juggling for the Complete Klutz
Stanford, CA, Klutz Enterprises, 1977, ISBN: 0-932592-00-7, $6.95, 31 pp.

An amazing booklet: how to juggle for the beginner with comical illustrations and 3 cloth bags enclosed in a net attached to the booklet.

Ferretti, Fred
The Great American Book of Sidewalk, Stoop, Dirt, Curb, and Alley Games
New York, Workman Publishing Company, 1977, ISBN: 0-911104-59-3, $1.95, 48 pp.

More than 60 games that matter and how to do them, including marbles, jacks, hopscotch, and leapfrog.

Ferretti, Fred
The Great American Marble Book
New York, Workman Publishing Company, 1973, ISBN: 0-911104-27-5, $2.50, 159 pp.

The complete collection of marble games and marble history.

Hindman, Darwin A
Kick the Can and Over 800 Other Active Games and Sports for All Ages
Englewood Cliffs, NJ: Prentice-Hall, 1956, ISBN: 0-13-515163-5, $3.95, 415 pp.

A comprehensive reference guide of games and recreational activities.

Palmer, Laura
The Big Book of Board Games
San Francisco, Troubador Press, 1979, ISBN: 0-08944-002-5, $3.50, 28 pp.

Fourteen classic games to color and play.

Schindler, George
Basic Balloon Sculptures
Woodside, NY, National Paragon-Reiss, 1983, ISBN: 0-910199-01-9, $5.99, 86 pp.

An illustrated book of easy-to-make Balloon Sculptures for children and adults including animals, hats, and fruit baskets.

Sparling, Joseph; Lewis, Isabelle
Learning Games for the First Three Years
New York, Berkeley Publishing Group, 1979, ISBN: 0-425-04752-0, $2.95, 226 pp.

A guide to parent/child play. How to and why to play. One hundred games arranged to reflect typical patterns of child development.

Weiss, Harvey
Games and Puzzles You Can Make Yourself
New York, Thomas Y Crowell Company, Fitzhenry and Whiteside, 1976, ISBN: 0-690-01111-3, $7.50, 56 pp.

Simple text and illustrations introduce 38 inexpensive easy-to-make games and puzzles.

KITES

Dyson, John and Kate
Fun With Kites
Woodbury, NY, Barron's Educational Service, 1978, ISBN: 0-8120-5139-4, $7.95, 89 pp.

The history, construction, flying and design of kites from caterpillars, fish, faces, and many lands.

Newnham, Jack
Kites to Make and Fly
New York City. Penguin Books, 1977, LCCN: 76-53918, $1.95, 32 pp.

How to make and fly four different kites: a flat kite with a tail, a bowed kite without a tail, a box kite and a lightweight stunt kite.

Thiebault, Andre
Kites and Other Wind Machines
New York, Sterling Publishing Company, 1982, ISBN: 8069-5464-7, $6.95, 96 pp.

MASKS

Grater, Michael
Cut and Color Paper Masks
New York, Dover Publications, 1975, ISBN: 0-486-23171-2, $1.75, 9 pp.

Nine easy-to-do projects of cut and color clowns, animals and funny faces.

Grater, Michael
Monster Masks
New York, Dover Publications, 1978, ISBN: 0-486-23576-9, $2.00, 32 pp.

Colorful face masks to cut-out.

MODELS

Gillon Jr, Edmund V
Cut and Assemble a Western Frontier Town
New York, Dover Publications, 1977, ISBN: 0-486-23736-2, $3.50, 32 pp.

Twelve authentic buildings of a 19th century New England village to cut and assemble.

Gillon Jr, Edmund V
Cut and Assemble Victorian Houses
New York, Dover Publications, 1979, ISBN: 0-486-23849-0, $3.50, 8 pp.

Minutely detailed and authentic group of four Victorian houses to cut and assemble.

MacLaughlin Brothers
The Pretty Village: An easy to assemble antique toy town in full color
New York, Dover Publications, 1980, ISBN: 0-486-23938-1, $4.00, 32 pp.

Authentic full-color reprint to cut and assemble, of all 18 of the structures from the Pretty Village, reproduced directly from an 1897 original

Martin, Dick
Emerald City of Oz
New York, Dover Publications, 1980, ISBN: 0-486-24053-3, $3.95, 40 pp.

Cut and assemble Emerald City with figures.

Price, Brick
Model-Building Handbook
Radnor, PA, Chilton Book Company, 1981, ISBN: 0-8019-6863-1, $8.95, 176 pp.

Professional techniques and illustrations showing how to assemble, detail and paint life-like miniature figures and scratchbuilding models of trains and submarines.

PLANES AND THINGS THAT FLY

Hardy, Marvin
Balloon Magic
Sandy, UT, Randall Book Co., ISBN: 0-9341-2669-0, $1.00, 63 pp.

Simple step-by-step instructions and photographs for making balloon art figures for decorating, teaching aids, magic tricks, party games, and story telling. Includes package of balloons.

Kline, Richard
The Ultimate Paper Airplane
New York, Simon & Schuster, 1985, ISBN: 0-671-55551-0, $6.95, 126 pp.

Step-by-step instructions for making seven different models of the plane that confounded the experts. Featured on "60 Minutes".

Morris, Campbell
The Best Paper Aircraft
New York, Perigee Books, 1985, ISBN: 0-399-51113-X, $4.95, 33 pp.

Easy-to-follow instructions for 14 flyable models including super loopers, jump jets, the concorde, and more.

PLAY

Caplan, Frank and Theresa
The Power of Play
Garden City, NY, Anchor Books, 1973, ISBN: 0-385-09935-5, $3.95, 334 pp.

The importance of play to the child at different ages and stages in development is emphasized in a lucid analytical study by authorities concerned with educational toymaking.

Cherry, Clare
Creative Play for the Developing Child, Early Lifehood Education Through Play
Belmont, CA, Fearon Publishers, Inc., 1976, $11.95, 260 pp.

Illuminates the value of play in relation to child development during the first few years of life, stressing the importance of play/learning attitudes and environments.

Frost, Joe L; Sunderlin, Sylvia
When Children Play
Washington, D.C. Association for Childhood Education International, 1985, ISBN: 0-87173-107-X, $35.00, 355 pp.

Proceedings of the International Conference on Play and Play Environments.

Madaras, Lynda
Child's Play: A Manual for Parents and Teachers
Chicago, Contemporary Books, 1982, $6.95, 152 pp.

A valuable resource book discussing practical and expansive alternatives of child's play.

Mergen, Bernard
Play and Playthings
Westport, CT, Greenwood Press, 1982, ISBN: 0-313-22136-7, $35.00, 281 pp.

A history and reference guide about children's play in America.

Piers, Maria W; Landau, Genevieve Millet
The Gift of Play and Why Young Children Cannot Thrive Without It
New York, Walker and Company, 1980, ISBN: 0-8027-0657-6, $9.95, 123 pp.

Explores the newest psychological insights, with a blend of science and common sense, into the significance of play for children.

Piers, Maria W; Landau, Genevieve Millet
A Guide to Fun and Learning in the Romper Room Years, The Wonderful World of Play
Pawtucket, RI, Hasbro Industries, 1978, free 16 pp.

Discussion of the child's world of play.

Piers, Maria W, editor
Play and Development, A Symposium
New York, W W Norton Inc, 1977, ISBN: 0-393-00871-1, $2.95, 176 pp.

This book contributes substantially to the understanding of the importance of play at successive developmental stages. The six contributors establish play as an essential human-survival function.

Sutton-Smith, Brian and Shirley
How to Play with Your Children (And When Not To)
New York, Hawthorn Books, 1974, ISBN: 0-8015-3685-5,
$4.95, 274 pp.

Places in proper perspective the newest ideas about the
importance of play in developing the personality of the
child from birth to 13 years.

PUPPETS

Engler, Larry; Fijan, Carol
Making Puppets Come Alive
New York, Taplinger Publishing Co, 1980, ISBN:
0-8008-5073-4, $7.95, 192 pp.

A method of learning and teaching puppetry.

Peters, Sharon
A First Start Easy Reader: Puppet Show
Mahwah, NJ, Troll Associates, 1980, $0.95, 28 pp.

A children's story on how to create a puppet show.

Renfro, Nancy
A Puppet Corner in Every Library
Austin, TX, Nancy Renfro Studios, 1978, ISBN: 0-931-
04401-4, $7.95, 110 pp.

Inspirations for librarians to try new ideas with puppets to
a joyful learning experience for children.

SPACES AND PHYSICAL ENVIRONMENTS

Beckwith, Jay
Make Your Backyard More Interesting than TV
New York, McGraw Hill, 1980, ISBN: 0-07-004266-7,
$6.95, 117 pp.

Shows step-by-step how to build a variety of interesting
play structures from sandboxes to complex modular play
areas. Detailed drawings.

Frost, Joe L; Klein, Barry L
Children's Play and Playgrounds
Boston, MA, Allyn and Bacon, Inc., 1979, ISBN: 0-205-
06586-4, $8.95, 273 pp.

Creating play spaces inside and outdoors.

Palmer, Bruce
Making Children's Furniture and Play Structures
New York, Workman Publishing Company, 1974, ISBN:
0-911104-25-9, $3.95, 144 pp.

Shows how a home can be equipped for young children.
Examines the purpose of play and analyzes the design of
toys.

Stoddard, Alexandria
How to Create a Room for Your Child: A Child's Place
Garden City, NJ, Dolphin Books, 1979, ISBN:
0-385-87885-4, $5.95, 168 pp.

Practical approach to designing a child's room and creating an ongoing environment as a place for the child to
grow.

STORIES FOR CHILDREN

Bond, Michael
Paddington's Storybook
New York, Houghton Mifflin Company, 1984, ISBN: 0-
0395-3667-4, $13.95, 159 pp.

Ten favorite Paddington Bear stories. This series of thirty
titles is available in many languages other than English.

Fleming, Denise
Teddy's Best Toys
New York, Random House, 1985, ISBN: 0-394-87111-1,
$3.95, 8 pp.

A soft, nontoxic washable bear and book for preschool
children.

Gruelle, Johnny
Raggedy Ann and Andy Alphabet and Numbers
Indianapolis, IL, Bobbs Merrill Company, Howard Sams
and Company, 1972, $3.95, 64 pp.

A simple, child's book with rhymes and stories with the
alphabet and numbers.

Gruelle, Johnny
**Raggedy Ann and Andy and the Camel With Wrinkled
Knees**
New York, Dell Publishing Company, 1951, $1.95, 125 pp.

A children's story about the adventures of Raggedy Ann
and Andy.

Hofmann, Ginnie
Who Wants An Old Teddy Bear?
New York, Random House, 1978, $1.25, 30 pp.

Simple story with illustrations.

Ketchum Jr, William C.
Collecting Toys For Fun and Profit
Tucson, AZ, HP Books Inc, 1985, ISBN: 0-89586-250-6,
$7.95, 96 pp.

Covers major toy categories with advice on finding,
buying, selling, display, and storage.

There Is a Mouse In My Toy Box: A book about shapes
Los Angeles, CA, Price/Stern/Sloan Publishers, 1984, ISBN: 0-8431-1196-8, $2.50, 6 pp.

A fun book for children.

Wilkin, Eloise
Baby's Toys
New York, Putnam, 1985, ISBN: 0-448-00427-X, $2.95, 12 pp.

Toddlers story-board book with illustrations of boy and toys.

Williams, Margery
The Classic Tale of the Velveteen Rabbit or How Toys Become Real
Philadelphia, PA, Running Press, 1981, ISBN: 0-89471-128-8, $3.95, 46 pp.

A children's story-tale of a little boy's pet toy rabbit coming to life.

Harris, Leon A
The Great Diamond Robbery
New York, Atheneum Publishers, 1985, ISBN: 0-689-31188-5, $10.95, 33 pp.

Maurice the French mouse takes up residence in an American department store and repays their hospitality by foiling a diamond robbery.

Beaumont, Cyril William
The Mysterious Toyshop
New York, Holt, Rinehart and Winston, 1985, ISBN: 0-03-005852-X, $13.50, 32 pp.

A new toyshop, full of wonderful dolls and miniatures for both children and adults, is found to harbor an amazing secret.

TEACHER RESOURCES

Cole, Ann; Haas, Carolyn; Weinberger, Betty
Purple Cow to the Rescue
Boston, Little, Brown and Company, 1982, ISBN: 0-316-15106-8, $8.95, 160 pp.

Suggests a wide variety of activities which help you learn about yourself, become more independent, prepare for school, enjoy traveling and moving, and rest after or during a busy day.

Haas, Carolyn Buhai
The Big Book of Recipes For Fun
Northfield, IL, CBH Publishing, 1980, $10.95, 279 pp.

An easy to use recipe format and abundance of appealing illustrations will captivate children from preschool through grade 6.

Haas, Carolyn B; Berman, Barbara B
Look At Me, Activities for Babies and Toddlers
Glencoe, IL, CBH Publishing, 1985, ISBN: 0-9604538-5-7, $8.95, 221 pp.

This book offers suggestions and ideas to help parents and teachers communicate and share with babies and toddlers through fun, easy-to-do, success-oriented activities.

Hill, Dorothy M
Mud, Sand, and Water
Washington, DC, National Association for the Education of Young Children, 1977, $2.00, 38 pp.

Explores the value of and rediscovers the fascination of working with sand, mud and water in a living-learning environment.

Hirsch, Elizabeth S
The Block Book
Washington, DC, National Association for the Education of Young Children, 1974, $1.98, 108 pp.

Examines the learning/growth process, esthetic, experiential and social interaction that occurs by playing with blocks.

Kamii, Constance; DeVries, Rheta
Group Games in Early Education Implications of Piaget's Theory
Washington, DC, National Association for the Education of Young Children, 1980, $8.50, 256 pp.

Insights and practical information about the importance of group games for children's development and directions for playing them.

Weiss, Rick and Debe
Puppet Plays for New Creatures: Adaptions of the Parables of Jesus
Cincinnati, OH, Standard Publishing Company, 1985, ISBN: 0-87239-830-7, $4.95, 63 pp.

A teaching aid for children, learning about the application of the Bible in everyday life as told through puppet creatures.

TEDDY BEARS

Bialosky, Alan; Tynes, Robert
Making Your Own Teddy Bear
New York, Workman Publishing Company, 1982, ISBN: 0-89480-211-9, $7.95, 111 pp.

Step-by-step illustrated instructions on making a Teddy Bear family. Includes traceable patterns and costumes.

Bialosky, Peggy and Alan
The Teddy Bear Catalog
New York, Workman Publishing Company, 1980, ISBN: 0-89480-133-3, $4.95, 223 pp.

History, care and repair, lore, and prices with hundreds of photos on various types of bears.

Whyte, Malcolm
Hugs and Cuddles Teddy Bear Paper Dolls
Los Angeles, Troubador Press, 1984, $3.95, 30 pp.

Two full-color Teddy Bear Paper Dolls, large full-color foldout backdrop, miniature Teddy Bear Book to make and read. Over 80 costumes and objects to cut out and play with.

Wolf, Jill
Teddy Bears Are Always There
Yellow Springs, OH, Antioch Publishing Company, 1985, ISBN: 0-89954-291-3, $1.95, 12 pp.

An illustrated story book about Teddy Bears including 12 collector stickers of Teddy Bear characters from other Antioch stories.

TOYS FOR CHILDREN WITH SPECIAL NEEDS

Sinker, Mary
The Lekotek Guide to Good Toys
Evanston, IL, North Shore Lekotek, 1983, $12.95, 89 pp.

A resource guide providing support and self help resources to the parents of teachers of handicapped children. Contains a selection of toys and games with descriptions on how to use them.

TOYS, CHILDREN'S BOOKS ABOUT

Boase, Wendy
Toyland
New York, Random House, 1984, ISBN: 0-394-86662-2, $1.95, 26 pp.

An Early Bird "Hide and Seek" Book for preschoolers that makes learning fun with simple words and colorful pictures. Strengthens skills of observation and memory.

Scarry, Richard
Richard Scarry's Toy Book
New York, Random House, 1978, ISBN: 0-394-83962-5, $2.95, 30 pp.

Eight punch-out toys, no scissors, no paste, easy-to-assemble.

TOYS, HISTORY AND COLLECTION

Ayres, William S
The Warner Collector's Guide to American Toys
New York, Warner Books, 1981, ISBN: 0-446-97632-6, $9.95, 255 pp.

A visual collection of over 500 different cast iron, wood, tin, steel and paper toys are classified by maker, age, decoration, dimensions, materials, and mechanisms. Historical information.

Baker, Linda
Modern Toys, American Toys 1930-1980
Paducah, KY, Collector Books, 1985, ISBN: 0-89145-277-X, $19.95, 263 pp.

Color photographs with collectors' information of modern toys from 1930-1980.

Johnson, Peter and Anne
Toy Armies
London, B T Batsford Limited, 1981, ISBN: 0-7134-3901-7, $9.95.

An extensive review of the history of toy soldiers and the collection of the Forbes Museum.

King, Constance E
Antique Toys and Dolls
New York, Rizzoli International Publications, 1979, ISBN: 0-8178-0278-7, $30.00, 256 pp.

Photos of history and background of old and antique toys, dolls, puzzles, and board games.

Kitahara, Teruhisa
Robots: Tin Toy Dreams
San Francisco, Chronicle Books, 1983, ISBN: 0-87701-335-1, $8.95, 111 pp.

A collector's album, featuring 250 photos of madcap Space Age gadgetry, from early Buck Rogers-type rocketships to modern spacemen, monster-robots, and mechanized space vehicles.

O'Brien, Richard
Collecting Toys: A Collector's Identification and Value Guide
Florence, AL, Books Americana, 1985, ISBN: 0-89689-048-1, $14.95, 380 pp.

A collectors identification and value guide on toys such as vehicles, aircraft, soldiers, comic characters and animal-drawn toys.

Lynn, Elizabeth A
The Silver Horse
New York, Bluejay Books, 1984, ISBN: 0-312-94404-7, $9.95, 126 pp.

Eleven-year old Susannah follows her brother and his beautiful silver horse to the Land of Lost Toys, where she finds herself in the middle of a fantastic adventure.

Whitton, Blair
The Knopf Collectors' Guide to American Antiques-Toys
New York, Alfred A Knopf, Chanticleer Press, 1984, ISBN: 0-394-71526-8, $13.95, 478 pp.

Color photographs, descriptions, and prices of 397 representative examples of all types of American toys made from the mid-19th century to the present, as well as European and Japanese toys.

TOYS, HOW TO MAKE

Burtt, Kent G
Smart Toys For Babies From Birth to Two
New York, Harper and Row, 1981, ISBN: 0-0609-1124-7, $8.95, 166 pp.

77 easy-to-make toys to stimulate your baby's mind, plus games to play.

Caney, Steven
Steven Caney's Playbook
New York, Workman Publishing Company, 1975, ISBN: 0-911104-38-0, $4.95, 240 pp.

Projects, construction, games, puzzles, and other activities for children. Organized according to spaces where they play.

Joffke, Freya
Making Soft Toys
Millbrae, CA, Celestial Arts, 1981, ISBN: 0-89742-044-6, $7.00, 59 pp.

Tells how to make simple children's toys (puppets, dolls, and special surprises) with little cost, using natural materials. Detailed but simple instructions and sketches.

Metz
How to Make Soft Toys and Dolls
Menlo Park, CA, Sunset Books, Lane Publishing Company, 1977, ISBN: 0-376-04692-9, $2.95, 80 pp.

Instructions and illustrations on making soft toys and dolls, including animals, finger puppets, ballet dolls, and gingerbread men dolls.

Roth, Charlene Davis
The Art of Making Cloth Toys
Radnor, PA, Chilton Book Company, 1974, ISBN: 0-8019-5871-7, $7.95, 210 pp.

A how-to book that includes complete instructions for making 19 different cloth toys, along with photos and line drawings.

de Sarigny, Rudi
How to Make and Design Stuffed Toys
New York, Dover Publications, Mills & Boon Limited, 1978, ISBN: 0-486-23625-0 $5.95, 235 pp.

How to make soft toys from assortments of patterns and create your own soft toy designs.

Sibbett Jr, Ed
Wooden Puzzle Toys: Patterns and Instructions for 24 Easy-To-Do Projects
New York, Dover Publications, 1978, $2.25, 24 pp.

Patterns and instructions for 24 original wooden toy puzzles.

Stevenson, Peter
The Art of Making Wooden Toys
Radnor, PA, Chilton Book Company, 1971, $9.95, 250 pp.

Descriptions, blueprints, illustrations, and photographs of making wooden toys. Includes puppet theater, dollhouse, barn, castle, plane, truck, and boat, etc.

Williams, Alan
The Kids and Grownups Toy-Making Book
New York, William Morrow and Company, 1979, ISBN: 0-688-08507-5, $7.95, 159 pp.

Homemade toys, including mobiles, boats, aircraft, and a treasure toychest.

TOYS, SELECTION AND SAFETY

Community Playthings
Criteria for Selecting Play Equipment for Early Childhood Education
Rifton, NY, Community Playthings, 1981, free, 40 pp.

Datre, Donna
The ABC's of Toys and Play
New York, Toy Manufacturers of America, 1981, 25 cents, 15 pp.

A consumer information booklet that includes a toy selection guide, toys as learning tools, parental involvement in play and the history and importance of play.

Toy Manufacturers of America
Parents Are the First Playmates
New York, Toy Manufacturers of America, 25 cents, 6 pp.

Guide for parents and teachers.

Toy Manufacturers of America
Playing Safely With Toys
New York, Toy Manufacturers of America, 25 cents, 6 pp.

Guide for parents and teachers.

Toy Manufacturers of America
Toys Are Teaching Tools
New York, Toy Manufacturers of America, 25 cents, 6 pp.

Guide for parents and teachers.

U.S. Consumer Product Safety Commission
The Safe Use of Electrical Toys
Washington, DC, U.S. Consumer Product Safety Commission, free, 8 pp.

Safety guide.

TRAINS

Andreas, Michael
PSL Model Railway Guide Baseboards, Track, and Electrification
Cambridge, England, Patrick Stephens Ltd, 1979, ISBN: 0-85059-385-1, $7.75, 64 pp.

A practical railroad modeling handbook that tells about track layout, baseboards, constructions, electrification, and wiring. Photos included.

Edmonson, Harold A
The ABC's of Model Railroading
Milwaukee, Kalmbach Publishing Company, 1979, ISBN: 0-89024-536-3, $4.95, 72 pp.

A beginner's book of text, photos, and diagrams to help you learn about the basics of model railroading.

TRAVEL ACTIVITIES

Latta, Richard
Games for Travel
Los Angeles, Price/Stern/Sloan Publishers, 1984, ISBN: 0-8431-0406-6, $1.75, 25 pp.

Intriguing puzzles, brain-teasers, counting and code games, etc. to play. Handy tablet form for travel.

McToots, Rudi
The Kid's Book of Games for Cars, Trains & Planes
New York City, Bantam Books, 1980, $4.95, 167 pp.

Over 160 games new and old to entertain and amuse the traveler or stay-at-home, including string, knots, paper and finger play.

C. MAGAZINES ABOUT TOYS FOR CHILDREN AND ADULTS

Barbie
Telepictures Publications
300 Madison Avenue
New York City, NY 10017

Articles and photos about
Barbie and friends. $5/year

Computer Entertainer
Suite 126
12115 Magnolia Boulevard
North Hollywood, CA 91607

Reviews new products for
home computers. $22/year

Doll Reader
Hobby House Press
900 Frederick Street
Cumberland, MD 21502

Information on all aspects of
dolls. $20/year

Dolls: The Collector's Magazine
Acquire Publishing Company
Inc
170 Fifth Avenue
New York City, NY 10010

Colorful photos with excellent
articles. $17.50/year

Dragon
Dragon Publishing
PO Box 110
Lake Geneva, WI 53147

Articles and information on
dungeons and dragons. $24/
year

Enter
Children's Television Workshop
1 Lincoln Plaza
New York City, NY 10023

Articles and photos. $14.95/
year

Family Computing
Scholastic Inc.
740 Broadway
New York City, NY 10003

Articles on computers,
software, and games. $19.97/
year

Games
515 Madison Avenue
New York City, NY 10022

Articles and lots of games to
play. $14.95/year

Model Railroader
Kalmbach Publishing Company
1027 North Seventh Street
Milwaukee, WI 53233

Extensive and useful
information. $14/year

Muppet Magazine
Telepictures Publications Inc
300 Madison Avenue
New York City, NY 10017

Articles, interviews, and
information. $6/year

Nutshell News
Clifton House
Clifton, VA 22024

Monthly magazine for
miniature enthusiasts. $29/year

Sesame Street Magazine
Children's Television Workshop
1 Lincoln Plaza
New York City, NY 10023

Games, articles, and
illustrations. $8.95/year

The Teddy Bear and Friends
Hobby House Press Inc
900 Frederick Street
Cumberland, MD 21502

Articles, photos, and resources.
$9.95/year

D. PUBLISHERS

Allyn and Bacon Inc
    470 Atlantic Avenue, Boston,
    MA 02210
American Guidance
    Publisher's Building, Circle
    Pines, MN 55014
Anchor Books
    Garden City, NY 11547
Antioch Publishing Company
    888 Dayton Street, Yellow
    Springs, OH 54387
Aro Publishing Company
    PO Box 193, Provo, UT 84601
Arco Publishing Inc
    215 Park Avenue South, New
    York City, NY 10003
Association for Childhood Education
International
    3615 Wisconsin Avenue,
    Washington, DC 20016
Atheneum Publishers
    115 Fifth Avenue, New York
    City, NY 10003
Bantam Books
    666 Fifth Avenue, New York
    City, NY 10019
Barron's Educational Series Inc
    113 Crossways Park Drive,
    Woodbury, NY 11797
B I Batsford Limited
    4 Fitzhardinge St, London,
    W1H-0AH England
Bellerphon Books
    36 Anacopa Street, Santa
    Barbara, CA 93101
Bluejay Books
    130 West 42nd Street, New
    York City, NY 10036
Bobbs-Merrill Company Inc
    4300 West 62nd Street,
    Indianapolis, IN 10017
Books Americana
    PO Box 2326, Florence, ALA
    35630
CBH Publishing Inc
    446 Central Avenue,
    Northfield, IL 60093
Carr Publishing
    PO Box 5132, Wheat Ridge,
    CO 80034-5132
Celestial Arts
    231 Adrean Road, Millbrae,CA
    94556
Charles Branford Company
    PO Box 41, Newton Centre,
    MA 02159

Chanticleer Press
    See: Alfred A Knopf
Chilton Book Company
    Chilton Way, Radnor, PA 19089
China Books and Periodicals
    2929 24th Street, San
    Francisco, CA 94110
Chronicle Books
    One Halladie Plaza, San
    Francisco, CA 94102
Collector Books
    PO Box 3009, Paducah, KY
    42001
Community Playthings
    Dept 2, Rifton, NY 12471
Contemporary Books Inc
    180 North Michigan Avenue,
    Chicago, IL 60601
Crown Publishers Inc
    One Park Avenue, New York
    City, NY 10016
Dell Publishing Company Inc
    345 East 47th Street, New York
    City, NY 10017
T S Denison
    9601 Newton Avenue South,
    Minneapolis, MN 55431
Dolphin Books
    Garden City, NY 11547
Dover Publications
    180 Varick Street, New York
    City, NY 10014
East Winds PressBook/Fast &
McMillan Publishers, Inc
    429 East Boulevard, Charlotte,
    NC 28203
Fearon Publishers Inc
    6 Davis Drive, Belmont, CA
    94002
Follett Publishing Company
    1010 West Washington
    Boulevard, Chicago, IL 60607
Greenwood Press
    88 Post Road West, Westport,
    CT 06881
Grossett and Dunlap
    51 Madison Avenue, New York
    City, NY 10010
Growing Together Press
    PO Box 2983, Stanford, CA
    94305
Gryphon House Inc
    3706 Otis Street, PO Box 275,
    Mount Rainier, MD 20712
HPBooks Inc
    PO Box 5367 Tuscon, AZ 85703

Harper Colophon
    10 East 53rd Street, New York
    City, NY 10022
Harper and Row
    10 East 53rd Street, New York
    City, NY 10022
Frank W Harris
    1171 W Iowa Avenue,
    Sunnyvale, CA 94086
Hasbro Industries Inc
    1027 Newport Avenue,
    Pawtucket, RI 02861
Hawthorn Books
    260 Madison Avenue, New
    York City, NY 10016
Hobby House Press Inc
    900 Frederick Street,
    Cumberland, MD 21502
Holt Rhinehart and Winston
    383 Madison Avenue, New
    York City, NY 10017
Houghton Mifflin Company
    Two Park Street, Boston, MA
    02108
Impact Publishers
    PO Box 1094, San Luis Obispo,
    CA 93406
Johnson and Johnson Baby Products
Company
    PO Box 836, Somerville, NJ
    08876
Kalmbach Publishing Company
    1027 North Seventh Street,
    Milwaukee, WI 53233
Klutz Press
    2297 Harvard Street, PO Box
    2992, Stanford, CA 94305
Alfred A Knopf Inc
    201 East 50th Street, New York
    City, NY 10022
David S Lake Publishers
    19 Davis Drive, Belmont, CA
    94002
Land Publishing
    80 Willow Road, Menlo Park,
    CA 94025
Little, Brown and Company
    34 Beacon Street, Boston, MA
    02106
Macmillan Publishing Co.
    866 Third Avenue, New York
    City, NY 10022
Marek Publishers
    200 Madison Avenue, New
    York City, NY 10016

McCall Pattern Company
    230 Park Avenue, New York
    City, NY 10017
McGraw-Hill Book Company
    1221 Avenue of the Americas,
    New York City, NY 10020
William Morrow and Company
    105 Madison Avenue, New
    York City, NY 10016
Nancy Renfro Studios
    1117 West Ninth Street,
    Austin, TX 78703
National Association for the
Education of Young Children
    1834 Connecticut Avenue NW,
    Washington, DC 20009
National Lekotek Center
    2100 Ridge Avenue, Evanston,
    IL 60204
National Paragon-Reiss
    57-07 31st Avenue, Woodside,
    NY 11371
Ottenheimer Publishers Inc
    · 300 Reisterstown Road,
    Baltimore, MD 21208
Patrick Stephens Limited
    Bar Hill, Cambridge,
    CB3-8EL, U.K.
Penguin Books
    625 Madison Avenue, New
    York City, NY 10022
Pitman Publishing See: David S
Lake
Playmore Inc
    1107 Broadway, New York City,
    NY 10010
Pocket Books
    1230 Avenue of the Americas,
    New York City, NY 10020

Prentice-Hall
    Route 9W, Englewood Cliffs,
    NJ 07632
Price/Stern/Sloan Publishers Inc
    410 North La Cienega
    Boulevard, Los Angeles, CA
    90048
Randall Book Company
    Suite 103, 9500 South 500
    West, Sandy, UT 84070
Random House Inc
    201 East 50th Street, New York
    City, NY 10022
Rizzoli International Publications Inc
    712 Fifth Avenue, New York
    City, NY 10019
Running Press
    125 South 22nd Street,
    Philadelphia, PA 19103
Scholastic Book Services
    50 West 44th Street, New York
    City, NY 10036
Charles Scribner's Sons
    115 Fifth Avenue, New York
    City, NY 10003
Simon and Schuster
    1230 Avenue of the Americas,
    New York City, NY 10020
Smithsonian Institution Press
    Suite 2100, 955 L'Enfant Plaza,
    Washington, DC 20560
Standard Publishing
    8121 Hamilton Avenue,
    Cincinnati, OH 45231
Sterling Publishing Company
    2 Park Avenue, New York City,
    NY 10016
Sunset Books
    See: Lane Publishing Company

Taplinger Publishing Company
    132 West 22nd Street, New
    York City, NY 10011
Thomas Y Crowell Company
    10 East 53rd Street, New York
    City, NY 10022
Toy Manufacturer's Association of
    America
    200 Fifth Avenue, New York
    City, NY 10010
Troll Associates
    320 Route 17, Mahwah, NJ
    07430
Troubadour Press
    See Price/Stearn/ Sloan
U.S. Consumer Product Safety
    Commission
Washington, DC 20207
Walker and Company
    720 Fifth Avenue, New York
    City, NY 10019
Wallace-Homestead Book Company
    580 Waters Edge, Lombard, IL
    60148
Warner Books Inc
    75 Rockefeller Plaza, New York
    City, NY 10019
Franklin Watts Inc
    387 Park Avenue South, New
    York City, NY 10016
Workman Publishing Company
    One West 39th Street, New
    York City, NY 10018

E. PARENTING RESOURCES

Building Blocks
3893 Brindlewood
Elgin, IL 60120

Practical information, ideas, and activities to experience with young children. $10/year family, $15/year child care edition

Growing Child and Growing Parent
Dunn & Hargut
22 North Second Street
PO Box 620
Lafayette, IN 47902

Formatted for standard 3-hole punched looseleaf binder. A free trial subscripton to *Growing Child* is available. Information on pregnancy and child development. $15.95/year

Newsletter of Parenting
2300 West Fifth Avenue
PO Box 2505
Columbus, OH 43216

Helpful articles in up-to-date monthly magazine. $14.95/year

Parent's Choice
PO Box 185
Waban, MA 02168

Articles and product reviews in a useful quarterly. $15/year

Practical Parenting
Meadowbrook Press
Deephaven, MN 55391

Useful tips on child rearing in these easy to read and use booklets. Free stuff for parents. Other books, catalog available. $7.50/year (5 issues)

Tot Lines—bimonthly newsletter
Warren Publishing
PO Box 2253
Alderwood Manor, WA 98036

Activities, ideas, and articles for the parent with learning games and lots of useful information. Bimonthly. $12/year (6 issues)

F. A SELECTION OF FILMS ON TOYS

Film information contributed by the Craft and Folk Art Museum in Los Angeles and the San Francisco Unified School District Audio Visual Department.

CAT'S CRADLE

This animated film takes the children's game of cat's cradle and transforms it into a variety of other forms using fantasy and imagination. 11 minutes. color.
International Film Bureau
332 South Michigan Avenue
Chicago, IL 60604

THE AMAZING COLOSSAL MAN

Papier-mache puppets and model soldiers animate this science fiction thriller created by twelve children (ages 5 to 12). It tells the story of an invasion from outer space of a monster from Planet Aros. 6 minutes. Color.
Yellow Ball Workshop
62 Tarbell Avenue
Lexington, MA 02173

TCHOU-TCHOU

Building-block animation tells the story of a peaceful world where two children play until the world is invaded by a nasty dragon. During the night the children change the dragon into a train. 14 minutes. Color.
National Film Board of Canada
CRM/McGraw-Hill
Delmar, CA 92014

CHRISTMAS CRACKER

This animated film tells three Christmas stories: a story about jingle bells in which boy and girl paper cut-outs move to music, a story about a dime-store rodeo in which tin toys perform a ballet, and a story about a Christmas tree trimmer who builds a space vehicle in order to pluck a star from the sky for the top of his tree. 9 minutes. color.

National Film Board of Canada
CRM/McGraw-Hill
Delmar, CA 92014

JUMPROPE

A poetic portrayal of the joy of children jumping rope. 7 minutes. Color.

Viewfinders
PO Box 1665
Evanston, IL 60204

TOPS

A lyric celebration of brightly colored spinning tops, hands, and related toys which shows how many tops are operated. 8 minutes. Color. No sound.

Encyclopedia Britannica
425 North Michigan Avenue
Chicago, IL 60611

CALDER'S CIRCUS

Alexander Calder and his wife mobilize the performers in his famous miniature circus. 19 minutes.
Pathe Cinema Corporation
4 West 58th Street
New York City, NY 10019

TOCCATA FOR TOY TRAINS

Historical toy trains and antique dolls from the Museum of the City of New York are animated in this collector's catalogue. 14 minutes. Color. No sound.

Pyramid
PO Box 1048
Santa Monica, CA 90406

CARNIVAL FANTASY

A collector's catalog of electrically-operated creatures (fortune tellers, mechanical peanuts, etc.) that populated Coney Island's marquees, boardwalk food stands and game rooms. The documentation of the genuine marvels is transformed into fantasy by the superimposition, in-camera, of shots of neon signs and the lights from carnival rides. 7 minutes. Non-verbal.

Sol Rubin Motion Pictures
PO Box 40
New York City, NY 10038

MATRIASKA

Animated Russian wooden dolls move and combine. 5 minute. Color.

National Film Board of Canada
CRM/McGraw-Hill
Delmar, CA 92014

NUTCRACKER

An animated adapted version of the story of the Nutcracker. 26 minutes. Color.

International Film Bureau
332 South Michigan Avenue
Chicago, IL 60604

PIÑATA

Creating a piñata of toys, how to make it, and decorate it. 11 minutes. Color.

Atlantis Productions
850 Thousand Oaks
Thousand Oaks, CA 91360

G. A USEFUL CLASSIFICATION OF TOYS
Selected from the Manufacturer's Product System

activity books
airplane model kits
alphabet sets
animal figures
automobile miniatures
balloons
balls
bath toys
battery-powered boats, cars, trains
bean bags
bicycle and velocipede accessories
blackboards
boat model kits
books
bubble blowers
ceramics
circus toys
coloring books
computers
cooking and kitchen utensils
costumes—masquerade
cowboy accessories
crafts
doctor kits
doll bassinets
doll houses, accessories
doll carriages
dolls—fashion
dolls—foam

dolls—historical
dolls—international
dolls—licensed, fashion
dolls—rubber
dummies-ventriloquist
electronic games
game boards
games
gyroscopes
hobby kits
hoops
house cleaning sets
infant toys
inflatable toys
jacks and ball sets
jigsaw puzzles
juggling sets
jump ropes
jungle gyms
kaleidoscopes
kites
magic sets
magnetic letters
make-up kits
masks
mechanical toys
mechanical wind-up toys
miniatures
mobiles

musical toys
music boxes
paint sets
playhouse sets
pull toys
puppets
puzzles
radio-controlled toys
ride-ons
rocking horses
sand toys
science toys
sewing cards & sets
soft toys
software
squeeze toys
stuffed toys
take-apart toys
tape recorders
telephones
telescopes
trains—HO,I,N,O,S,Z gauge
trampolines
video cassettes
viewers
wagons
wooden toys
yo-yos

H. SELECTED TOY STORES IN THE UNITED STATES

Note: Toys R Us has 300 stores around the country which sell a full line of toys and other equipment. Please look for the local listings under toys in the yellow pages in the area you live. For a complete list write to their home office in Rochelle Park, New Jersey.

ARIZONA

Nogales
Capin Mercantile Corporation
109 Nelson Avenue

Phoenix
Little House Toys
7611 West Thomas Road

Toy Shoppes
Billmore Fashion Park
2564 East Camelback Road

CALIFORNIA

Anaheim
Century Models
1238 South Beach Boulevard

Berkeley
Discovery Corner
Lawrence Hall of Science
University of California
Our Body and making faces puzzle

Colma
Toys R Us
775 Serramonte Boulevard

Costa Mesa
FAO Schwarz
South Coast Plaza Mall
3333 Bristol Street

Fair Oaks
The Ark
4245 Crestline Avenue

Garden Grove
Constructive Play things
12372 Garden Grove

Los Angeles
California Toys
752 South Broadway

Chess and Games Unlimited
7 locations

Educational Toys
647 South La Brea Avenue

Hollywood Toys
6562 Hollywood Boulevard

Mena Toys
1702 Sunset Boulevard

Los Gatos
Wooden Horse
50 University Avenue

Mendocino
Kolor-Phorme
512 Main Street

Menlo Park
Educational Teaching Aids Store
3905 Bohannon Drive

Loco-Boose
3215 Middlefield Road

Mill Valley
Toy Mill
419 Miller Avenue

Novato
Arthurs Toy Town
2033 Novato Boulevard

Sacramento
FAO Schwarz
Historic Boyd-Davis Building
101 K Street

San Francisco
Bill's Terminal Trainatorium
2253 Market Street

Chan's Trains
2450 Van Ness Avenue

Educational Toys
475 19th Avenue

FAO Schwarz
180 Post Street

GET Toys and Hobbies
11 Lake Shore Plaza
34th Avenue and Sloat Boulevard

Hobby Company
5150 Geary Boulevard

Jeffrey's Toys (3 locations)
445 Sutter Street
2 Embarcadero Center
900 North Point Street

James Company
3836 24th Street

Kindel and Graham
539 Mission Street

King Norman's Toys and Hobbies
645 Clement Street

My Child's Destiny
70 Grant Avenue

Play With It
1660 Haight Street

Puzzle People
Pier 39

Thumbelina
2338 Clement Street

The Toy Store
Pier 39

San Mateo
Talbots Toyland
445 South B Street

Trains, Nothing But
Trains
138 West 25th Avenue

Santa Rosa
Toy and Model
711 Coddington Mall

Sunnyvale
Engine House
672 Alberta

Venice
Old Venice Lionel Train
Store
1344 Washington
Boulevard

Westwood
Toyorama
2018 Westwood Boulevard

COLORADO
Colorado Springs
Stuffed Safari
750 Citadel Drive East

Vail
Toymakers' Trail

CONNECTICUT
Milford
Child World

Mystic
Ben Franklin Kite
Shoppe
PO Box 392
½ Pearl Street

Stamford
Enchanted Village
Stamford Town Center
100 Grey Rock Place

FAO Schwarz
Stamford Town Center

DISTRICT OF COLUMBIA
FAO Schwarz (2 locations)
3222 M Street NW
5300 Wisconsin Avenue NW

Smithsonian Institution
Museum Shop
900 Jefferson Drive SW

Washington Dolls House and
Toy Museum
5236 44th Street NW

FLORIDA
Bal Harbour
FAO Schwarz
9700 Collins Avenue

Fort Walton Beach
The Child and Company

Miami
Villa Clara Stores Inc
1951 West Flagler Street

Palm Beach
FAO Schwarz
318 Worth Avenue

GEORGIA
Atlanta
Enchanted Village
1317 Cumberland Mall

FAO Schwarz
1414 Penmeter Mall
4400 Ashford Dunwoody
Road

Valdosta
Playland Toy Stores
1700 Norman Drive

ILLINOIS
Chicago
FAO Schwartz
Water Tower Place
845 North Michigan
Avenue

Toys et Cetera
5206 South Harper
Avenue

Toy Gallery
1640 North Wells

Skokie
Constructive Play Things
5314 West Uncoln
Avenue

IOWA
Des Moines
Younkers Department
Store
Seventh and Walnut

KANSAS
Shawnee Mission
Constructive Play Things
2008 West 103rd

KENTUCKY
Louisville
FAO Schwarz
Stewarts Dept Store

Something To Do Stores
Inc
301 East Market Street

LOUISIANA
New Orleans
FAO Schwarz
333 Canal Street

MAINE
Portland
Child World
Pine Tree Shopping
Center

MARYLAND
Baltimore
Arthur Watsons
Embraceable Zoo
Harborplace
201 East Pratt Street

Great Bears
Harborplace
301 South Light Street

Puppet Show
Harborplace
301 South Light Street

What's Your Game
Harborplace
201 East Pratt Street

Bethesda
FAO Schwarz
Montgomery Mall

Lowens
7227 Wisconsin Avenue

Gaithersburg
Enchanted Village
Lakeforest Mall

Rockville
FAO Schwarz
Game Boutique
White Flint Mall

MASSACHUSETTS
Boston
FAO Schwarz
40 Newbury Street

Springfield
Child World
1570 Boston Road

Whitman
Hide Away Toys Inc
Kings Castleland
Route 18

MICHIGAN
Novi
Enchanted Village
Twelve Oak's Mall

Saint Joseph
Hobby Horse
223 State Street

Grand Rapids
Toys R Us
3445 20th Street

MINNESOTA
Minneapolis
Toys Works
318 West 48th Street

NEW HAMPSHIRE
Meredith
Just For Kids
Main Street

NEW JERSEY
Middlesex
Bea Skydell's Dolls and
Toys
476 Union Avenue
Paramus
Child World
Garden State Plaza

FAO Schwarz
Fashion Center
Rochelle Park
Toys R Us (Home Office)
395 West Passaic
(Write to them for a
complete list of all
locations)

NEW YORK
Copake
Campbell Village Gift
Shop
Chrysler Pond Road
Great Neck
Enchanted Village
310 East Shore Road
New York City
Able Child
325 West Eleventh Street

Mary Arnold Toys
962 Lexington Avenue

FAO Schwarz
745 Fifth Avenue

The Gift Center
United Nations
Headquarters

Gingerbread
9 Christopher Street

Laughing Giraffe
1065 Lexington Avenue

Museum of the City of
New York
Fifth Avenue and 103rd
Street

PennyWhistle Toys (2
locations)
1283 Madison Avenue
448 Columbus Avenue

Toy Park
112 East 86th Street

OKLAHOMA
Tulsa
FAO Schwarz
Utica Square

OREGON
Portland
Child's Play
715 NW 23rd Avenue

PENNSYLVANIA
Monroeville
Enchanted Village
Monroeville Mall
Pittsburgh
South Hills Village Mall
Pittsburgh, PA 15241
Wayne
Wayne Toy Town
163 East Lancaster
Avenue

TENNESSEE
Memphis
Goldsmith
123 Mid America Mall

TEXAS
Dallas
Constructive Play Things
11100 Harry Hines
Boulevard
Lubbock
Bear Fair
2610 Salem Avenue

VIRGINIA
McLean
FAO Schwarz
Tyson's Corner
Springfield
Enchanted Village
6672 Springfield Mall

VERMONT
Burlington
Casslers Toys
336 North Winouski
Avenue

WASHINGTON
Bellevue
Arthur Bird Toys
Loehmann Plaza
3610 128th Avenue SE
Seattle
Christopher House Toys
1800 Fourth Avenue

Magic Mouse Toys
217 First Avenue South

The Orphanage
Lower Level
Pike Place Public Market

The Wood Shop
321 First Avenue South
Tacoma
Backyard Big Toys
2601 South Hood

I. SELECTED TOY CATALOGS

All Night Media
All Night Media Inc
Box 2666
San Anselmo, CA 94960
Rubber stamps, alphabet blocks
(alphabeasts), bears, and cats

American Express—World of Toys
produced by Dr. Stevanne
Auerbach
American Express Plaza
New York City, NY 10004
Selections of fine baby, children
to adult toys

Childcraft Education Corporation
20 Kilmer Road
Edison, NJ 08817
Variety of toys for indoors and
outdoors

Community Playthings
Route 213
Rifton, NY 12471
Educational toys, materials, and
equipment for children with
special needs

Constructive Playthings
1227 East 119th Street
Grandview, MO 64030
Educational toys, catalog free.
Free list of Jewish early childhood materials. Main school catalog $2

Creative Art Activities
2024 Lee Road
Cleveland Heights, OH 44118
Unique craft and activity kits.
Includes dolls, sculpture kits,
fiber art and puppets

Discovery Toys
Suite 300
400 Ellinwood May
Pleasant Hill, CA 94523
Variety of toys and games sold at
home gatherings

Dollspart Supply Company
5-15 49th Avenue
Long Island City, NY 11101
Anything and everything for the
doll: bodies, clothes, tools, patterns, books, and doll carriages

Doll Repair Parts
9918 Loraine Avenue
Cleveland, OH 44102
Catalog of supplies for making
and repairing dolls

Growing Child
PO Box 620
Lafayette, IN 47902
Variety of toys, activities, and
books

Happiness Shop
PO Box 2150
San Francisco, CA 94126
Catalog of Snoopy and friends

Horchow Collection
PO Box 819066
Dallas, TX 75381-9066
Selected toys

Just for Kids
Winterbrook Way
Meredith, NH 03253
Variety of toys, books, and
supplies

Model Expo
PO Box 4000
23 Just Road
Fairfield, NJ 07007
Model and radio-controlled
cars, boats, tools, and books

My Child's Destiny
PO Box 7366
San Francisco, CA 94120-7366
Variety of toys, clothing, and
books

The Nature Company Catalog
PO Box 2310
Berkeley, CA 94702
Nature and science related toys
and books

Neiman-Marcus
PO Box 2968
Dallas, TX 75221-9950

Penny Whistle
1283 Madison Avenue
New York City, NY 10128
Toys for all ages

Play Fair Inc
1690 28th Street
Boulder, CO 80302
Good primary products

Playmill of Maine
Route 3 Box 89
Dover-Foxcroft, ME 04426
Personalized wooden toys

Playways for Learning
PO Box 210300
San Francisco, CA 94121-0300
Products for construction and
education

Publishers in Sound
Willow Street
S. Lee, MA 01260
Children's stores, classics, nur-
sery stories and more.

Sears
Sears Tower
Chicago, IL 60684
The classic wish book

B. Shackman and Company Inc
85 Fifth Avenue
New York City, NY 10003
Antique reproductions of all
kinds

Signature Collection
5-15 49th Avenue
Long Island City, NY 11101
Catalog of dolls, bears, and
furniture

Smart Factory
65 Manor Drive
San Francisco, CA 94127
Range of educational toys

Smithsonian Catalogue
PO Box 2456
Washington, DC 20013
Toys, antique reproductions,
and science

Think Big
390 West Broadway
New York City, NY 10012
Everything in a big size, including crayola crayons

Toys to Grow On
PO Box 17
Long Beach, CA 90801
Variety of primary toys

Trifles
PO Box 819075
Dallas, TX 75381-9075
Selected special items

Uniquity
  PO Box 6
  Galt, CA 95632
  Educational products, toys, puzzles

Catalogs of Playground Equipment

Child Life
  55 Whitney Street
  PO Box 527
  Holliston, MA 01746
  Sandboxes, swings, and playground equipment

Playlearn
  5642 Natural Bridge
  Saint Louis, MO 63120
  Indoor and outdoor equipment, furniture, ride-ons, etc.

When you write for a catalog please tell them that you learned about their company in THE TOY CHEST.

J. SELECTED TOY MANUFACTURERS AND THEIR PRODUCTS

Most toy manufacturers sell their products to distributors through salespersons, to catalogs or stores. They cannot handle individual orders and will ask you to order the specific items desired from stores or catalogs. Some companies, particularly smaller ones, may be able to send catalogs and/or process individual orders. You can write to the companies listed to request more information, locate the location of a store nearest you that sells their products, or to ask questions that stores can't answer.

Contact Customer Service at any company. The department will handle the information or find out who can. If you have any problem with a product, please return to the place where you made your purchase. When you write, please let them know you found their company in THE TOY CHEST.

ABC School Supply
  Box 4750
  Norcross, VA 30091
  Cash register, spindle top, stubby paint brush, fife and drum, and balance board

Activision Inc
  PO Drawer 7286
  Mountain View, CA 94039
  Video Games

John Adams Toys
  Crazies Hill Wargrave
  Berkshire RG1-8LY
  England,
  Preschool toys

Adica-Pongo
  1111 Paulison Avenue
  Clifton, NJ 07011
  Clay, art, and craft materials

American Flyer
  See: Blazon-Flexible Flyer

American Print House for the Blind
  PO Box 6085
  Louisville, KY 40206
  Catalog of resource materials

American Publishing Company
  125 Walnut Street
  Watertown, MA 02172
  Puzzles

American Toy and Furniture
  Company
  5933 Lincoln Avenue
  Chicago, IL 60659
  Toychest, furniture, preschool toys, easels

Amloid Company
  One Amloid Drive
  Riverdale, NJ 02457
  Preschool vehicles, beach toys

AmToy Inc
  Suite 1260
  200 Fifth Avenue
  New York City, NY 10010
  Dolls, plush crib and playpen toys

An Da Company
  PO Box 43
  Amsterdam, NY 12010
  Wicker

Anderson-Swasey Inc
  51 Melcher Street
  Boston, MA 02210
  Represents Micki, original train system from Sweden, preschool toys, Stupsi dolls, Leismann America

Andras
  220 East 23rd Street
  New York City, NY 10011
  Replicas of toys and other objects in chocolate

Animal Fair Inc
  PO Box 1326
  Minneapolis, MN 55440
  Soft toys

Apple Computer Inc
  20525 Mariani Avenue
  Cupertino, CA 95014
  Computers and software

Aristo-Craft
  200 Fifth Avenue
  New York City, NY 10010
  Airplane model kits, radio controlled cars, gliders

Aristoplay Limited
  931 Oakdale
  PO Box 7645
  Ann Arbor, MI 48107

Ark Communications
  Suite 410
  5801 Christie Avenue
  Oakland, CA 94608
  Peace Trek, posters, puzzles

Artsana of America Inc
  Suite 910
  200 Fifth Avenue
  New York City, NY 10010
  Baby and preschool activities

Artwood
  PO Drawer A
  Woodland, GA 31836
  Barn and animals in solid hardwoods

Atari Inc
  1196 Borregas Avenue
  PO Box 61657
  Sunnyvale, CA 94088
  Computers and software

Atlanta
  108 Mason Street
  Woonsocket, RI 02895
  Stuffed toys, dolls

Avalon Industries Inc
  95 Lorimer Street
  Brooklyn, NY 11206
  Hobbies, crafts, crayons, art supplies

Aviva Hasbro
  1027 Newport Avenue
  Pawtucket, RI 02861
  Soft toys

Axlon Games
  1287 Lawrence Station Road
  Sunnyvale, CA 94088
  Talking bear and more

Badger Basket Company
  835 Sterling Avenue
  Palatine, IL 60067
  Doll carriages, baskets, strollers

Bandai America
  6 Pearl Court
  Allendale, NJ 07401
  Robots

Barday School Supplies
  29 Warren Street
  New York City, NY 10007
  Water color crayons

Barr Company Inc
1531 First Street
Sandusky, OH 44870
Balls, jump ropes

Battat Inc
PO Box 836
Champlain, NY 12919
Educational and scientific,
baby, preschool, simplex puzzles

Russ Berrie and Company Inc
111 Bauer Drive
Oakland, NJ 07436
Stuffed animals

Binney and Smith Inc
Crayola Products Art Materials
Division
1100 Church Lane
PO Box 431
Easton, PA 18042
Crayola, kits, water colors, ac-
tivity sets

Blazon-Flexible Flyer Inc
100 Tubb Avenue
PO Box 1296
West Point, MS 39773
Classic red wagon, furniture,
spring horses

Dick Blick
PO Box 1267
Galesburg, IL 61401
Number cubes, rich art tempera
maker, palette markers, art-tote
kit

Brimm-Shield
425 Fillmore Avenue
Tonawanda, NY 14150
Foam products

Brio Scanditoy Corporation
6531 North Sidney Place
Milwaukee, WI 53209
Trains, preschool wooden toys,
Carolle dolls

Britains Miniatures
See: Reeves International
Miniatures

Broderbund Software
17 Paul Drive
San Rafael, CA 94903
Computer software

Brothers Brothers
590 South 400 West
Provo, UT 84601
Unusual and creative toys,
trucks, and trains

Buddy L Corporation
200 Fifth Avenue
New York City, NY 10010
Steel trucks, typewriters, die-
cast cars

Cadaco Inc
4300 West 47th Street
Chicago, IL 60632
Games

California Stuffed Toys
611 South Anderson Street
Los Angeles, CA 90023
Stuffed animals

Cantelli
230 Fifth Avenue
New York City, NY 10001
Playful and unique clocks for a
child's room

Carola Creations
144 North Clinton Avenue
Elmhurst, IL 60126
Doll patterns

Charm Gem
1504 York Avenue
San Mateo, CA 94401
Soft toys

Cherry Tree Toys
PO Box 369
Belmont, OH 43718
Wooden toys, trucks, and trains
to assemble yourself

Chicco
See: Artsana of America Inc.

Childcraft Education Corporation
20 Kilmer Road
Edison, NJ 08817
Waterpump bucket and mop,
touch and match, water play,
dressing-undressing puzzle

Child Guidance (CBS Toys)
41 Madison Avenue
New York City, NY 10010
Baby and preschool activity
toys, Sesame Street products

Child Life Play Specialties Inc
55 Whitney Street
Holliston, MA 01746
Home exercise mat, doorway
gym

Children's Video Library
1011 High Ridge Road
PO Box 4995
Stamford, CT 06907
Video tapes

Coleco Industries Inc
999 Quaker Lane South
West Hartford, CT 06110
Variations of Cabbage Patch
dolls

Colman & Hirschmann Inc
Suite 1452
200 Fifth Avenue
New York City, NY 10010
Duncan yo yos, furniture, and
bikes

Colorforms
133 Williams Drive
Ramsey, NJ 07446
Classic reusable pictures, plas-
ticine, transfers and stickers

Combex Limited
117-123 Great Portland Street
London W1N-6AH England
Fingered teething ball

Combi Industries Inc
300 Broad Street
Stamford, CT 06901
Ride-on toys

Commonwealth Toy and Novelty Co
Suite 526
200 Fifth Avenue
New York City, NY 10010
Soft toys and lots of Lego

Community Playthings
Rifton, NY 12471
Toys for children with special
needs

Connor Toy Corporation
833 South 60th Avenue
Wausau, WI 54401
Wood puzzles, play furniture

Construction Playthings
1040 East 85th Street
Kansas City, MO 64131
Child-sized gardening tools

Constructive Playthings
2008 West 103rd Terrace
Leawood, KS 66206

Corgi
See: Reeves International
Miniatures

Country Critter Puppets
217 Neosho
Burlington, KS 66839
Puppets

Country Wood Shop Limited
14 Mill Street
PO Box 536
Delevan, NY 14042
Wooden horses and furniture

Craftmaker
26750 23 Mile Road
Mount Clemens, MI 48043
Puzzles, art crafts

Craft Master
26750 23 Mile Road
Mount Clemens, MI 48043
Puzzles, art crafts

Creative Art Activities
2024 Lee Road
Cleveland Heights, OH 44118
Art supplies

Creative Educational Distributor
(CED)
159-163 East Lancaster Avenue
Wayne, PA 19087
See-saw horse

Creative Playthings
41 Madison Avenue
New York City, NY 10010
Preschool line

Crusader Wood Products
PO Box 85
San Marcos, CA 92069
Hardwood toys

Cycle Products Company
PO Box 278
Commack, NY 11725
Cookie Monster baby seat

R Dakin and Company
PO Box 7746
San Francisco, CA 94120
Stuffed animals, Garfield and
friends

Davis-Grabowski Inc
6350 NE Fourth Avenue
PO Box 381594
Miami, FL 33138
Quadro, dolls, marbles

Determined Toy Limited
315 Pacific Avenue
San Francisco, CA 94126
Plush dolls, Snoopy and friends

Developmental Learning Materials
7440 Natchez Avenue
Niles, IL 60648
Animal puzzles

Walt Disney Productions
500 South Buena Vista
Burbank, CA 91500
Films. videos, music

DLM Teaching Resources
PO Box 4000
Allen, TX 75002
Educational materials, games,
and software

The Dolly Toy Company
320 North Fourth Street
Tipp City, OH 45371
Mobiles, accessories, soft blocks

Douglas Company Inc
Drawer D
Kriff Road
Keene, NH 03431
Musical instruments

Don Drumm Studios and Gallery
437 Crouse Street
Akron, OH 44311
Soft sculpture fantasies

Duncan Toys Company
801 Lynn Avenue
Baraboo, WI 53913
Yo Yos and trucks

Durham Industries
Suite 25-A
41 Madison Avenue
New York City, NY 10010
Play sets, typewriters, and erec-
tor sets

Eden Toys
112 West 34th Street
New York City, NY 10120
Soft toys, Paddington Bear,
Beatrix Potter Collection

Edmund Scientific Company
300 Edscorp Building
Barrington, NJ 08007
Compass, jumbo dial ther-
mometer, giant balloons

Educational Teaching Aids
159 West Kinzie Street
Chicago, IL 60610
Steering truck, infant wooden
stacking cubes, jumbo wooden
pounding bench, nature lotto

Edumate
PO Box 2467
Delmar, CA 92014
Anatomically accurate dolls, ed-
ucational puzzles

Effanbee Doll Corporation
200 Fifth Avenue
New York City, NY 10010
Dolls

Empire of Carolina
PO Box 427
Tarboro, NC 27886
Dolls

Entex Industries
See: Placo
Plastic Box

Estes Industries
PO Box 227
Penrose, CO 81240
HI-Flier kites, model rockets,
science kits

Eugene/World Doll Inc
4012 Second Avenue
Brooklyn, NY 11232
Dolls and accessories

Euro Imports
23 Just Road
Fairfield, NJ 07006
Unique cars, models

European Toy Collection
254 Midland Avenue
Montclair, NJ 07042
Miniature auto replicas

Ezytips Sales Corporation
1160 East Watson Center Road
Carson, CA 90745
The "Whizzer" ride-on

Fischer America Inc
175 Route 46 West
Fairfield, NJ 07006
Preschool and infant toys

Fisher-Price Toys
636 Girard Avenue
East Aurora, NY 14052
Baby and preschool, medical
kit, play family, doll house, music box, tape recorder, Activity
Centers

Frechette's Heirloom Toys
PO Box 4567
Spokane, WA 99202
Animal rockers, teeter totter,
wooden pony

Freemountain Toys
23 Main Street
Bristol, VT 05443
Soft sculpture toys, hats

Froebel Gifts
See: Korver Thorpe
Wooden blocks

Fun Farm
PO Box 7969
San Francisco, CA 94120
Soft toys

Fun-da-mentals
PO Box 263
South Pasadena, CA 91030
Robot, full-color plastic coated
cards depict careers in a nonsexist, multiracial way

Furry Folk Puppets
1219 Park Avenue
Emeryville, CA 94608
Puppets

Lewis Galoob Company
500 Forbes Boulevard
South San Francisco, CA 94080
Touch and Tell Me Math and
water jump rope

James Galt and Company Inc.
63 North Plains Highway
Wallingford, CT 06492
Art supplies, creative toys

Game Designers Workshop
PO Box 1646
Bloomington, IL 61701
Role playing and historical
games

Gerico
12520 Grant Drive
PO Box 33755
Denver, CO 80233
Baby stroller

Suzanne Gibson
See: Reeves International
Dolls

Globe United Toys
PO Box 98
Menomonee Falls, WI 53051
Roller skates and preschool activity toys

Go Fly A Kite Inc
PO Box AA
East Haddam, CT 06423
Kites

Goldberger Doll Manufacturing
Company
538 Johnson Avenue
Brooklyn, NY 11237
Dolls

Golden Ribbon Playthings
Suite 1016
200 Fifth Avenue
New York City, NY 10010
Huggy Bean (black character
doll)

Grandpa's Wooden Toys
Route 9, Box 453
Florence, AL 35630
Chair, block, wagons

The Great Game Company
450 North Park Road
Hollywood, FL 33021
Games

Greenleaf
Route 3 Box 100
Cooperstown, NY 13326
Designs for making doll houses

Greybridge Inc
542 High Street
Palo Alto, CA 94301
Preschool toys

Gund Inc
44 National Road
Edison, NJ 08817
Musical soft toys, Bialosky bear

H-G Toys Inc
750 Park Place
Long Beach, NY 11561
Dressing sets, batons, and doll
accessories

J L Hammet Company
2393 Vaux Hall Road
Union, NJ 07083
Rake, knitting frames, Unifix
cubes, loom cage

Handcraft Designs Inc
89 Commerce Drive
Telford, PA 18969
Wooden hand car

Burt Harrison
PO Box 730
Weston, MA 02193-0732
Educational materials and
games

Hasbro Inc
1027 Newport Avenue
Pawtucket, RI 02861
Preschool and older activities

Haviland Manufacturing Company
9 George Street
Fort Ann, NY 12827
Wooden toys, table tennis,
paddles

Hedstrom Company
PO Box 432
Bedford, PA 15522

Heirloom Designs
PO Box 12687
Dallas, TX 75225
Soft educational blocks, books

Holbrook-Patterson Inc
170 South Monroe Street
Coldwater, MI 49036
Dollhouse, balance boards,
wooden toys, climbing
equipment

J R Holcomb Company
3000 Quigley Road
Cleveland, OH 44113
Creative Wood Crafts, Hand
Puppets

Home Base Corporation
480 Potrero Avenue
San Francisco, CA 94110
Reusable Formica cutouts for
artwork

Horsman Dolls Inc
Suite 1440
200 Fifth Avenue
New York City, NY 10010
Dolls

House of Lloyderson
617 West Chestnut Street
Lancaster, PA 17603
Dolls

Huffy Bicycle
7701 Beyers Road
PO Box 1204
Dayton, OH 45401
Excellent bicycles from first bike to adult

IBM Corporation
PO Box 1328
Boca Raton, FL 33432
Computers and software

Innoland
11166 Downs Road
Pineville, NC 28134
Games for travel

Innovative Wooden Toys
2413 Parkview Avenue
Kalamazoo, MI 49008
Some games, rails of wood

Instant Products
PO Box 33068
Louisville, KY 40232
Imaginative small foam animals

International Games
One UNO Circle
Johet, IL 60435

International Playthings Inc
116 Washington Street
Bloomfield, NJ 07003
Sasha dolls, marbles, various preschool and educational toys

Jak-Pak Inc
236 North Water Street
PO Box 374
Milwaukee, WI 53201
Jump rope and vehicles

James Industries Inc
PO Box 407
Hollidaysburg, PA 16648
Slinky—walking spring toy

Jesco Inc
923 South Myrtle
Monrovia, CA 91016

Johnson and Johnson Baby Products Co.
Grandview Road
Skillman, NJ 08558
Baby to preschool activities

William G Johnston Company
PO Box 6759
Pittsburgh, PA 15212
Ladder exerciser

Judy Company
29 Warren Street
New York City, NY 10007
Assorted preschool and educational products, stringing beads

Just Wood
9 Coggswell Street
Pawcatuck, CT 02891
Wooden toys

Kadon Enterprises Inc
Suite 16
1227 Lorene Drive
Pasadena, MD 21122
Wooden and acrylic games and puzzles

Kamar International Inc
25550 Hawthorne Boulevard
Torrance, CA 90505
Stuffed animals

Kaplan School Supply Corporation
600 Jonestown Road
Winston-Salem, NC 27103
Assorted preschool and educational products

Keisha Dolls
524 West 175th Street
New York City, NY 10003
Black dolls in various costumes

Kenner Products
1014 Vine Street
Cincinnati, OH 45202
Playdoh

The Kids on the Block
822 North Fairfax Street
Alexandria, VA 22314
Puppets for handicapped children

Kindercastle
PO Box 272
Commerce, TX 27609
Wooden line of early learning toys

Koala Technologies Corportion
2065 Junction Avenue
San Jose, CA 95131
Add on alternatives for keyboard input devices, graphic touch tablets and light pens

Korver/Thorpe Limited
2244 15th Street
Boulder, CO 80302
Froebel gifts (blocks)

Kouvalias
See: Reeves International
Wooden toys

Kransco Manufacturing Inc
160 Pacific Avenue
San Francisco, CA 94111
Ride-ons, Hacky Sack, Frisbee

Tom Kuhn Custom Yo Yo's Limited
2383 California Street
San Francisco, CA 94115
High quality, modular design for beginners to advance players

L.G.B.-Railway Express Agency Inc
PO Box 1247
Milwaukee, WI 53201
Trains

Lakeshore Curriculum Materials
8888 Venice Boulevard
Los Angeles, CA 90034
Giant blocks, building sets

Lakeside Games
495 Post Road East
Westport, CT 06880
Games, playsets, puzzles

Larbar Corporation
PO Box 30024
Saint Paul, MN 55175
Alpha Bag

Lauri Inc
Box F
Phillips-Avon, ME 04966
Puzzles

The Learning Company
Suite 170
545 Middlefield Road
Menlo Park, CA 94025
Computer software

Learning Materials Workshop
58 Henry Street
Burlington, VT 05401
Unique educational toys

Lego Systems Inc
555 Taylor Road
Enfield, CT 06082
Construction sets, models

Leismann America Inc
Gardner Street
PO Box 95
Port Jervis, NY 12771
Construction toys

Leisure Learning Products Inc
16 Division Street West
PO Box 4869
Greenwich, CT 06830
Games and activity sets

Julius Levenson Inc
Suite 400
1107 Broadway
New York City, NY 10024
Toy chests, Madamme Alexander dolls, and carriages

Lionel
26750 23-Mile Road
Mount Clemens, MI 48043
Model trains, sets, and accessories

Little Peoples Workshop
PO Box 99608
Louisville, KY 40299
Wooden toys, puzzles, blocks

Little Tikes Inc
2180 Barlow Road
Hudson, OH 44236
Excellent play items, train, furniture

LJN Toys Limited
Suite 734
200 Fifth Avenue
New York City, NY 10010
Play sets

Lundby of Sweden
Two Gill Street
Woburn, MA 01801
Doll houses, furniture, children's matching doll clothes

Magnus Organ Company
120 Arlington Avenue
Bloomfield, NJ 07003
Musical instruments

Majorette
8820 NW 24th Terrace
Miami, FL 33172
Tool sets

Bill Maller Wooden Toys
Rockhill Industrial Park
87 Commerce Drive
Telford, PA 18969
Wooden car, rocking horse

Marchon Inc
3395 North Arlington Heights Road
Arlington Heights, IL 60004
Preschool toys

Marklin Inc
5960 North 60th Street
Milwaukee, WI 53218
Trains from beginner to advanced

Marlon Creations Inc
35-01 36th Avenue
Long Island City, NY 11106
Wooden toys, sand castles, puzzles, learning aids

Matchbox Toys (USA) Inc
141 West Commercial Avenue
Moonachie, NJ 07074
Die-cast cars, Pre-school activities

Mattel Toys
5150 Rosecrans Avenue
Hawthorne, CA 90250
Activity toys and games

Milton Bradley Company
443 Shaker Road
East Longmeadow, MA 01028
Board games, puzzles, and electronic games

Model Rectifier Corp
2500 Woodbridge Avenue
Edison, NJ 08817
Train accessories

Nasco
901 Janesville Avenue
Fort Atkinson, WI 53538
Wooden telephone, gyroscope, scientific materials

Nasta Industries
10075 Sandmeyer Lane
Philadelphia, PA 19116
Remote control cars, wireless mikes, walkie talkies

Natural Science Industries Limited
51-17 Rockaway Beach Boulevard
Far Rockaway, NY 11691
Educational and scientific toys

Nienhuis Montessori USA
320 Pioneer Way
Mountain View, CA 94041
Counting Lotto, Montessori products

House of Nisbet Limited
Dunster Park—Woodborough Road
Winscomb, Avon B525 England
Dolls and teddy bears

Nomadics Tipi
17671 Snow Creek Road
Bend, OR 97701
Play house in tipi form

Norok Toy Company
256 Neiffer Road
Schwenksville, PA 19473
Wooden toys, puzzles, educational products

North American Bear
Suite 400
155 East Ohio Street
Chicago, IL 60611
Soft toys

Nylint Corporation
1800 16th Avenue
Rockford, IL 61108
Scale model trucks and cars

Off Our Rocker
PO Box 1606
Wilkes Barre, PA 18705
Colorful rocking animals

The Ohio Art Company
PO Box 111
Bryan, OH 43506
Etch A Sketch, musical toys, typewriters, and activity toys

Original Appalachian Artworks
PO Box 714
Cleveland, GA 30528
Furskins

Palo Imports
184 Greenwood Avenue
Bethel, CT 06801
Unusual varied collection, many versions of the Nutcracker

Palo Imports
184 Greenwood Avenue
Bethel, CT 06801
Various collections and the Nutcracker

Panosh Place Inc
29 Olney Avenue
Cherry Hill, NJ 08003
Preschool toys

Papa Don's Toys
87805 Walker Creek Road
Walton, OR 97490
Wooden alphabet numbers,
baby toys

Parker Brothers
50 Dunham Road
Beverly, MA 01915
Family and children's board
games, children's books and
tapes

Patterns
Box 57
Route 1
Blue Hill, NB 68930
Learning patterns

Placo Products Company
PO Box 5505
Gardena, CA 90249

Plakie
4105 Simon Road
Youngstown, OH
44512
Teething rings, bathtub toys

Play-Jour Inc.
Suite 1024
200 Fifth Avenue
New York City, NY 10010
Capsela

Playmates
200 Fifth Avenue
New York City, NY 10010
Preschool dolls

Playmobil
4409 West Grove Drive
Dallas, TX 75248
Preschool construction

Playmore Inc
200 Fifth Avenue North
New York City, NY 10010
Activity sets, stickers (It's OK to
say No)

Playskool
4501 West Augusta Boulevard
Chicago, IL 60651
Ringed stack toy, baby and preschool activity toys

Playspaces International Inc
31-D Union Avenue
Sudbury, MA 01776
Paddington Bear, Ambi toys,
sand boxes

Poppets
1800 East Olive Way
Seattle, WA 98102
Puppets

Practical Drawing Company
PO Box 5388
Dallas, TX 75222
Felt figures

Pressman Toy Corporation
745 Joyce Kilmer Avenue
New Brunswick, NJ 08091
Safety House games, Checkers,
and Chess

Preston Manufacturing Limited
185 King Street
Cambridge, ON N3H-4S1
Swing horses, toy chests, and
balls

Princess Soft Toys
1101 North Fourth Street
Cannon Falls, MN 55009
Large soft toys

Proll Toys Inc
120 Arlington Avenue
Bloomfield, NJ 07003
Musical instruments and toys

Quadro America Inc
Suite 662
200 Fifth Avenue
New York City, NY 10010
Large construction sets

Radio Steel and Manufacturing
Company
6515 West Grand Avenue
Chicago, IL 60635
Wagons, scooters, tricycles

Reeves International Inc
1107 Broadway
New York City, NY 10010
Steiff animals, Britains miniatures, Suzanne Gibson Dolls,
Corgi die cast vehicles, LGB
trains, Kouvalius toys

Revell Inc
4223 Glencoe Avenue
Venice, CA 90292
Model kits, push/pull and construction toys

Rose Art Industries Inc
118 Ninth Street
Passaic, NJ 07055
Art suppliies, easels, weaving
looms

Rotadyne Inc
8705 Freeway Drive
Macedonia, Ohio 44056
Tike slide

S & S Arts and Crafts
Colchester, CT 06415
Wooden beads and more

Safety Now Company Inc
Box 567
202 York Road
Jenkintown, PA 19046
Scotchlite Rescue Marker,
Swing Set Anchor

Salver U.S.A. Inc
8631 South 187th Street
Kent, WA 98031
Play and sport balls

Sax Arts and Crafts
PO Box 2002
Milwaukee, WI 53201
Lapboard

Schaper Manufacturing Company
PO Box 1426
Minneapolis, MN 55440
Cooties, stomper vehicles

Scholastic Software
730 Broadway
New York City, NY 10003
Educational computer software

School Days Equipment Company
973 North Main Street
Los Angeles, CA 90012
Plastic scales and weights

School Zone Publishing Company
1918 Industrial Drive
Grand Haven, MI 49417
Publications

Seamer Products
1307 John Reed Court
Industry, CA 91745
Preschool toys

Selchow & Richter
2215 Union Boulevard
Bay Shore, NY 11706
Board games

Selective Educational Equipment
Inc
3 Bridge Street
Newton, MA 02195
Stopwatch, elementary micro-
scope, hands free magnifier

B Shackman and Company Inc
    85 Fifth Avenue
    New York City, NY 10003
    Antique reproductions of toys
    and books

Stephen Shanan company
    874 Yorkchester
    Houston, TX 77079
    Light switch extension for safety

Shield Manufacturing Inc
    425 Fillmore Avenue
    Tonawanda, NY 14150
    Foam products

Shinsei Corporation
    12951 East 166th Street
    Cerritos, CA 90701
    Radio controlled vehicles

Shmuzzles Inc
    2251 North Geneva Terrace
    Chicago, IL 60614
    Puzzles and soft construction
    toys

Sierra On-Line Inc
    Sierra On-Line Building
    Coarsegold, CA 93614

Skilcraft Corporation
    8601 Waukegan Road
    Morton Grove, IL 60053
    Tool sets

Small World Toys
    PO Box 5291
    Beverly Hills, CA 90210
    Infant and preschool toys

South Bend Toys Inc
    404 West Sample Street
    PO Box 3675
    South Bend, IN 46619

Spinnaker Software
    215 First Street
    Cambridge, MA 02142
    Computer software

Springboard Software
    7807 Creekridge Circle
    Minneapolis, MN 55435
    Computer Software

Stampos
    PO Box 2590
    Eugene, OR 97402
    Stamps and sets

Stargate Enterprises
    PO Box 1006
    Orinda, CA 94563
    Games for older children and
    teens

Steiff Stuffed Animals
    1107 Broadway
    New York City, NY 10010
    Stuffed animals

Sunburst Communications
    39 Washington Avenue
    Pleasantville, NY 10570
    Muppet Learning Keys

Sweet and Simple Toys and
    Sculpture
    2521 Sunrise
    Los Vegas, NV 89101
    Toy families, mobiles, and ani-
    mals in wood

Tandy Leather Company
    PO Box 791
    Fort Worth, TX 76101
    Catalog of leather working kits

Tasco Sales Inc
    7600 NW 26th Street
    Miami, FL 33122
    Binoculars, microscopes and
    sets, science kits, science toys,
    starfinders, telescopes

Texas Instruments
    PO Box 53
    Lubbock, TX 79408
    Computer software

Those Characters from Cleveland
    See: Kenner Products

Tide-Rider
    85 Corporate Drive
    PO Box 12427
    Hauppauge, NY 11788
    Kites, Nisbet teddy bears, Lenci
    dolls

T C Timber/Habermaass Corp
    PO Box 42
    Skaneateles, NY 13152
    Wooden toys, sets, blocks

Tomy Company Inc
    901 East 23rd Street
    PO Box 6252
    Carson, CA 90745
    Robots and preschool items

Tonka Toys
    6000 Clearwater Drive
    Minnetonka, MN 55343
    Construction Toys

Toys for Adults (TFA)
    Suite 9
    11568 Sorrento Valley Road
    San Diego, CA 92121
    Large soft stuffed sports cars

Toys for Special Children
    101 Lefurgy Avenue
    Hastings-on-Hudson, NY 10706
    Products for children to facilitate
    development

Tupperware Home Parties
    Orlando, FL 32802
    Tupperware containers

Tyco Industries
    540 Glen Avenue
    Moorestown, NJ 08057
    Model trains, sets, and
    accessories

U-Bild Enterprises
    15241 Stagg Street
    Box 2383
    Van Nuys, CA 91409
    Patterns and directions for mak-
    ing toys

Uneeda Doll Company
    200 Fifth Avenue
    New York City, NY 10010
    Dolls

Unitarian Universalist Association
    25 Beacon Street
    Boston, MA 02108
    One Big Family Dolls

Velvet Stable
    PO Box 148
    Glastonbury, CT 06033-6148
    Hobby horse, Puppets (Rabbit,
    Duck, Goose, Dog)

Vestron Video
    1011 High Ridge Road
    PO Box 4000
    Stamford, CT 06907
    Excellent video programs for
    children

View-Master International Group
    Inc.
    PO Box 490
    Portland, OR 97207-0490
    Classic viewer with many
    choices of pictures

Vogue Dolls
3 Edison Place
Fairfield, NJ 07006
Dolls and accessories

Helen Webber Designs Limited
410 Townsend Street
San Francisco, CA 94107
Original toys and furnishings

Welsh Company
1535 South Eighth Street
Saint Louis, MO 63104
Toychest (photo on cover), carriages, furniture, rockers

Western Publishing Company Inc
1220 Mound Avenue
Racine, WI 53404
Activity books

Wham-O Company
835 East El Monte Street
PO Box 4
San Gabriel, CA 91778-0004
Frisbee, Hacky Sack, Hula Hoop, water toys

Willis Toys Limited
Robin Hood Road Elsenham
Bishops Stortford
Herts CM22–6EF, England
Puzzles and games

Wolverine Toy Company
PO Box 207
Booneville, AR 72927
Doll furniture, sports equipment

Wood Decor
14750 East Lincoln Way
Dalton, OH 44618
Furniture, wooden horses

Woodkrafter Kits
42-A North Elan Street
Yarmoth, ME 04096
Model Boats, cars, plans, bird houses

Woods and Woods
725 Bryant Street
San Francisco, CA 94107
Handcrafted bears and friends

Worlds of Wonder
4245 Technology Drive
Fremont, CA 94538
Teddy Ruxpin and friends

Yamaha International Corporation
6600 Orangethrope Avenue
Buena Park, CA 90620
Musical instruments

Charles Zadeh Inc
225 Fifth Avenue
New York City, NY 10011
Dolls by Pauline, puppet workshop, Small World Toys

Zee Toys
4130 North Santa Fe
Long Beach, CA 90810
Plastic die-cast cars, planes, bikes, and trucks

K. Museums with Toy, Doll, or Special Collections

Collecting antique and unusual toys is a big interest among men and women around the world. The collections include dolls, doll houses, paper dolls, furniture, cast iron toys, folk-art toys, mechanical and still banks, Cracker Jack toys, teddy bears, boats, planes, cars, pull and motor toys, tin toys, etc.

If you know of any museums that are not on this list, we would appreciate receiving specific information to update our resources. Thank you!

ARKANSAS
Guenther's Doll Museum
188 North Main Street
Eureka Springs, AR 72632
2000 cross cultural dolls,
library

CALIFORNIA
Craft and Folk Art Museum
5814 Wilshire Boulevard
Los Angeles, CA 90036
Folk art from many cultures

Los Angeles Children's
Museum
310 North Main Street
Los Angeles, CA 90012
Activities, puppets, and lego
construction pieces

Model Collections Showcase
Museum
23295 Arnold Drive
Sonoma, CA 95467
Fine collection of models

Western Railway Museum
Rio Vista Junction, Highway 12
(between Rio Vista and
Fairfield)
Run by the Bay Area Electric
Railroad Association
PO Box 3694, San Francisco,
CA 94119
Extensive railway collection
California State Railroad
Museum
PO Box 111
111 I Street at Second
Sacramento, CA 95814
A collection of real and toy
trains. Open to the public
seven days a week. Regular
rides on antique trains.
Research library.

DISTRICT OF COLUMBIA
Smithsonian Institution
   Arts and Industries
   Building
   900 Jefferson Drive
   National Museum of
   American History
   Constitution Avenue
   between 12th and 14th
   The complex of 11
   museums, most of which
   also have retail shops, is
   an excellent source of
   scientific and educational
   toys and provides exhibits
   on toys and their history
Washington Doll's House and
Toy Museum
5236 44th Street NW
Washington, DC
Birthday parties and other
events held amidst wonderful
collection. Museum shop.

FLORIDA
Museum of Yesterday's Toys
52 Saint George Street
Saint Augustine, FL 32084
Toys—from 500 years ago to
the present displayed in a 255
year old building known as the
oldest in the United States.

GEORGIA
The Mary Miller Doll Museum
1523 Glynn Avenue
Brunswick, GA 31520
More than 3000 dolls spanning
three centuries and
representing 90 countries.

Museum and Antique Dolls
505 President Street
Savannah, GA 31401
Dolls, doll houses, furniture,
toys, and books. Dolls
appraised.

ILLINOIS
Peace Museum
364 West Erie Street
Chicago, IL 60612
Exhibition of peace toys and
games

INDIANA
Indianapolis Children's
Museum
3000 North Meridian Street
PO Box 300
Indianapolis, IN 46206
Selected dolls, doll houses,
teddy bears and fully operating
indoor carousel

MASSACHUSETTS
Fairbanks Doll Museum
Old Sturbridge Village
Sturbridge, MA 01566
Life as depicted in a colonial
settlement with children's
playthings

Boston Children's Museum
Museum Wharf
300 Congress Street
Boston, MA 02210
Play spaces where touching of
objects encouraged

Yesteryears Museum
Main Street
Sandwich, MA 02563
Antique and rare dolls,
miniatures, toy collection,
library and shop

MISSOURI
Eugene Field House and Toy
Museum
634 South Broadway
Saint Louis, MO 63102
Historic house museum with
period rooms and collection of
antique and collectible dolls
from 1750 to the present.

MONTANA
House of a Thousand Dolls
PO Box 136
Loma, MT 59460
Dolls and toys from 1830 to
present

NEBRASKA

Old Brown House Doll
Museum
1421 Avenue F
Gothenberg, NE 69138
Collection dates back to the
1800's

NEVADA

Way It Was Museum
PO Box 158
Virginia City, NV 89440
Mining museum and collection
of dolls with authentic dress
from 1860 thru 1900's

NEW MEXICO

Museum of International Folk
Art
Unit of Museum of New
Mexico
706 Camino Lejo
Santa Fe, NM
An impressive collection by
Alexander Girard containing
over 100,000 pieces from all
over the world

NEW JERSEY

The Good Fairy Doll Museum
and Hospital
205 Walnut Avenue
Cranford, NJ 07016
Dolls from Black American
history, Shaker meeting house
complete in detail and
occupants, and many dolls by
famous doll makers of
yesteryear.

NEW YORK

Brooklyn Children's Museum
145 Brooklyn Avenue
Brooklyn, NY 11213
Collection from early settlers
and play areas

Margaret Woodbury Strong
Museum
One Manhattan Square
Rochester, NY 14607
Extensive collection of dolls,
toys, books and more, brought
together by an avid collector

Museum of the City of New
York
Fifth Avenue at 103rd Street
New York City, NY 10029
Collection of antique toys,
dolls, doll houses in settings

Aunt Len's
Doll and Toy House
6 Hamilton Terrace
New York City, NY 10031
Antique and rare dolls, doll
houses and miniatures

Native American Center for
the Living Arts
25 Rainbow Mall
Niagara Falls, NY 14303
Artifacts of family life

OKLAHOMA

Elizabeth and Hall Doll
Museum
Grand at E Northwest
Aidmore, OK 73401
Original dolls back to 1700's

OREGON

Dolly Wares Doll Museum and
Repairing
3620 Highway 101 North
Florence, OR 97439
Has everything from 17th
century wooden dolls to
present day varieties.

PENNSYLVANIA

Perelman Antique Toy Museum
270 South Second Street
Philadelphia, PA 19106
Three floors of memorabilia
opened since 1969. He has
written a book about the
collection.

Please Touch Museum
210 North 21st Street
Philadelphia, PA
Hands on experiences for play

SOUTH DAKOTA

Enchanted World Doll
Museum
615 North Main
Mitchell, SD 57301
Collection of dolls and toys

UTAH

McCurdy Historical Doll
Museum
246 North 100 East
Provo, UT 84601

McCurdy Museum of
Childhood
36 West Center Street
Provo, UT 84601

VIRGINIA

Robert McDowell Museum
Route 1, Box 15-A
Aldie, VA 22001
Museum and professional
restoration of antique dolls

L. Organizations Related to Toys

BICYCLES

Bicycle Manufacturers
Association
1055 Thomas Jefferson Street
NW
Washington, DC 25007

DOLLS

National Association of Doll
Manufacturers
605 Third Avenue
New York City, NY 10022

United Federation of Doll
Clubs Inc
8 East Street
Parkville, MO 64152

There are many organizations
specializing in making and
collecting dolls. To locate an
organization in your area write
to the above address.

ELECTRONICS

Electronic Industries
Association
2001 I Street NW
Washington, DC 20006

HOBBIES

Hobby Industries of America
319 East 54th Street
PO Box 348
Elmwood Park, NJ 07407

LICENSING

Licensing Industries
Association
75 Rockefeller Plaza
New York City, NY 10019

MARBLES

Marble Collectors Society of
America
PO Box 222
Trumbull, CT 06611
$10 annual membership

MINIATURES

Miniatures Industry of America
1113 15th Street NW
Washington, DC 20005

Miniatures Industry
Association of America
319 East 54th Street
Elmwood Park, NJ 00707

National Association of
Miniature Enthusiasts
PO Box 1178
Brea, CA 92622

NAME is a non-profit,
educational association
dedicated to creating,
stimulating, and maintaining
national interest in all matters
pertaining to miniatures.

Society of American Miniatures
Suite 413
13534 Preston Road
Dallas, Texas 75240

MODEL CARS

Scale Model Enthusiast
PO Box 10167
Milwaukee, WI 53210

Model Car Collectors
Association
5113 Sugar Loaf Drive SW
Roanoke, VA 24018

PUPPETS

Puppeteers of America
5 Cucklewood Path
Pasadena, CA 91107

TOYS

British Toy and Hobby
Manufacturers Association
80 Camberwell Road
London SE5-OEG England

Toy Manufacturers of America
200 Fifth Ave.
New York, NY 10010

TRAINS

National Model Railroad
Association
4121 Cromwell Road
Chattanooga TN 37421

$20 annual membership
includes monthly NMRA
Bulletin. Started in 1935 it has
over 24,000 members world
wide and sponsors a
convention each year.

Toy Train Operating Society
24672 Paige Circle
Laguna Hills, CA 92653

Membership newsletter and
information on the collection
and operation of trains with
regional and local meetings.

Train Collectors Association
PO Box 248
Strasburg, PA 17579

The Association is made up of
approximately 17,000 members
dedicated to the preservation
of tinplate trains. Informative
publications and an annual
convention at the end of June.
$41 to join, $16/annual dues.

Dr. Stevanne Auerbach has written ten books about children, child care, and administration of children's services. Her most recent books have been *The Whole Child: A Sourcebook*, an extensive review of all books written for parents and information on raising the child from infancy to age twelve, and *Choosing Child Care: A Guide for Parents*, a practical guide to selecting baby sitters and child care centers and homes. She is a consultant, spokesperson, and lecturer as well as mother. Dr. Auerbach was born and educated in New York City, attending Queens College for her B.A. Later she obtained an M.A. from George Washington University in Washington, D.C., and a Ph.D. from Union Graduate School, Cincinnati, Ohio. She has been a teacher, administrator in the federal government in education and child care, researcher, and specialist in media for parents. She is a frequent guest on radio and television due to her remarkable ability to make the complex amount of information on her subject easy to understand and utilize. She resides in San Francisco, where she created the largest and most complete library on parenting and toys at the Institute for Childhood Resources.